W9-CMB-715

CELESTIAL NAVIGATION

A programmed learning course

Gerry Smith 1931-

WITHDRAWN
FROM THE RODMAN PUBLIC LIBRARY

A & C Black · London

RODMAN PUBLIC LIBRARY

38212002325808
Main Adult   JUL 97
623.89 S648
Smith, Gerry, 1931-
Celestial navigation : a
programmed learning
course

BEFORE BEGINNING THIS PROGRAMME YOU SHOULD HAVE A WORKING KNOWLEDGE OF COASTAL NAVIGATION.

IN PARTICULAR YOU SHOULD KNOW WHAT IS MEANT BY THE FOLLOWING:

Latitude and longitude

Line of position

Bearing

Dead reckoning

A sextant

Please read the Introduction on page iv

Published by Adlard Coles Nautical 1996
an imprint of A & C Black (Publishers) Ltd
35 Bedford Row, London WC1R 4JH

Copyright © Gerry Smith 1996

ISBN 0–7136–4415–X

All rights reserved. No part of this publication may be reproduced in any form or by any means – graphic, electronic or mechanical, including photocopying, recording, taping or information storage and retrieval systems – without the prior permission in writing of the publishers.

A CIP catalogue record for this book is available from the British Library.

Typeset in 11/13.5 Memphis by Penny Mills.

Printed and bound in Great Britain by Hillman Printers Ltd, Frome, Somerset.

ACKNOWLEDGEMENTS

Sight Reduction Tables For Navigation data reproduced with the permission of the United States Defense Mapping Agency. This book is not approved, endorsed, or authorised by the Department of Defense.

Nautical Almanac extracts are a duplication of the Nautical Almanac published by the United States Naval Observatory at Washington DC.

Contents

Throughout the programme you will be directed to study certain pages. Resist the temptation to 'skip' pages unless you are advised to do so.

Begin the programme at page 1.

Introduction

It's a wonderful world right now for small boat sailors. A touch of a button will give you an illuminated, updated position. Flick a switch and the freezer activates to cool the beer. Gadgets all hum in sympathy with the navigator's needs and the crew can concentrate on the task in hand; especially useful when threatening seas are building.

And make no mistake about it, technology will improve beyond our wildest imaginations. Perhaps soon a solar panel set in the top of the mast will power all the vessel's electronics. In an historically short time mere thought processes will activate equipment. You want a position? Just think about it and up will glitter the ubiquitous digital display; it will happen.

So why bother to read yet another book on celestial navigation? In one word, 'curiosity'. You've heard so much about it. You've been scared off from the subject through high-powered talk of mathematics, trigonometry and tanker navigation. So now if there's a chance to get on top of it you're game for a try. Right?

Want another reason? What about the confidence in knowing that you can still navigate safely, confidently, if the unlikely happens and the energy source breaks down? It does happen.

This programme has been put together to allow you the time and the insight to enjoy celestial navigation. It gives you the basic skills necessary to take sun sights and use them to find a position; back-up skills in fact. There are no gimmicks, no pretensions, certainly no claims that childish simplicity alone will suffice to grasp the basics. You are required to think, answer questions and work things out. Definitely nothing more than very basic arithmetic is asked for.

If you're quick on the uptake you'll get through very quickly; it's designed that way. You may not have to read every page. On the other hand if you founder a bit, we'll do a bit of side-stepping, bide our time, patiently grasp the problem, and you'll get there in the end. That's indeed what most do who have followed this programme; all kinds of sailing folk who desire to put to sea and reach out for their dreams.

Make sure you glance through the Contents (page vi) which gives an overview of the programme.

Back to Basics

It's only those who do nothing that make no mistakes, I suppose.

Joseph Conrad *Outcast of the Islands* (1896)

If you're skilled in the use of a sextant **go immediately to page 5**. If not, **read on.**

A sextant measures angles. Because you have to sight the sun through a telescope it has shades to protect your eyes from the glare. There are two mirrors, index and horizon (half of which is plain glass). It also has a movable index bar which you can swing over a graduated arc. Study Fig 1:1 below.

Fig 1:1 The sextant (drum type).

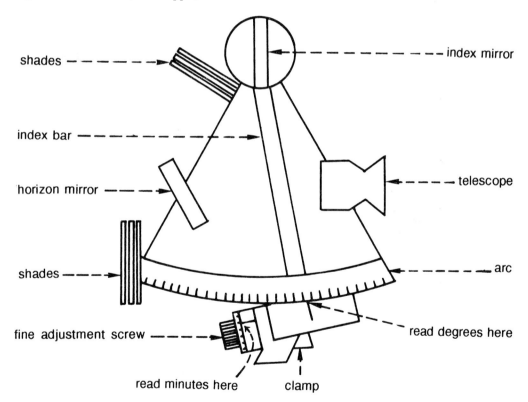

Now turn to page 3.

1

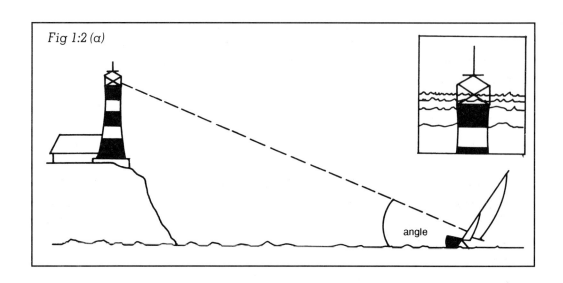

Fig 1:2 (α)

angle

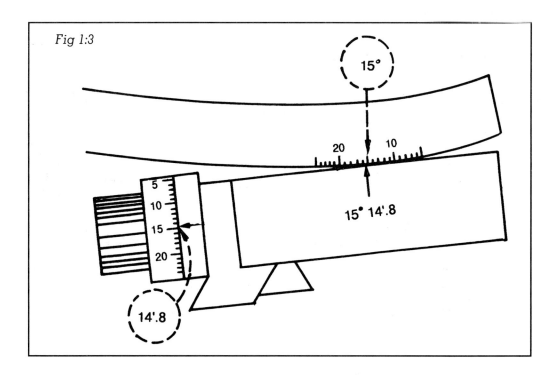

Fig 1:3

15°

20   10

15° 14'.8

5
10
15
20

14'.8

You can use a sextant to measure an angle between all kinds of objects; between the top and bottom of a building, or the sun and horizon.

Refer to Fig 1:2(a), opposite, where an angle between a beacon and sea level is measured. In this case you would:

- Set the index arm to zero (0°).
- Grasp the sextant by the handle and hold vertical with the index mirror uppermost and telescope close to the eye.
- View the beacon through the telescope (use the shades for any glare).
- Release the clamp so that you can move the index bar across the arc. Then 'drop' the image of the beacon to the sea level, seen through the clear portion of the horizon mirror. Fig 1:2(b).
- Fine-tune with the fine adjustment screw.
- After this is done, read the angle.

In Fig 1:3, opposite, the angle is 15°14'.8.

Solve the following problem:

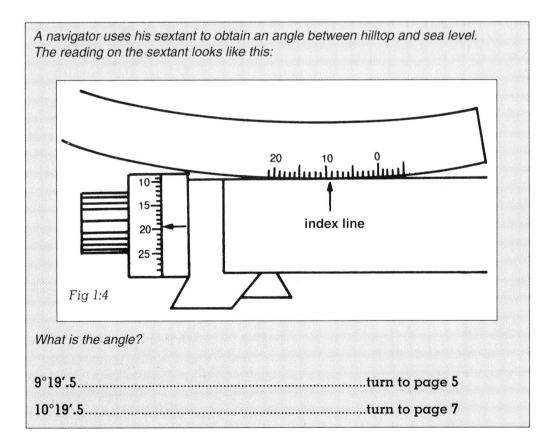

A navigator uses his sextant to obtain an angle between hilltop and sea level. The reading on the sextant looks like this:

index line

Fig 1:4

What is the angle?

9°19'.5..turn to page 5

10°19'.5..turn to page 7

Fig 1:5(a) Distance off by vertical sextant angle.

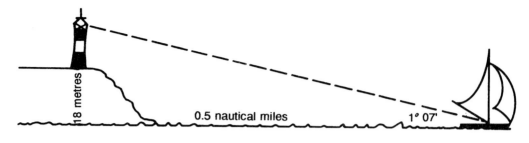

0.5 nautical miles   1° 07'

Fig 1:5(b) Example of table: Distance Off by Vertical Sextant Angle.

Height of object		Distances of object (nautical miles)									
ft	m	0.1	0.2	0.3	0.4	0.5	0.6	0.7	0.8	0.9	1.0
		o '	o '	o '	o '	o '	o '	o '	o '	o '	o '
33	10	3 05	1 33	1 02	0 46	0 37	0 31	0 27	0 23	0 21	0 19
39	12	3 42	1 51	1 14	0 56	0 45	0 37	0 32	0 28	0 25	0 22
46	14	4 19	2 10	1 27	1 05	0 52	0 43	0 37	0 32	0 29	0 26
53	16	4 56	2 28	1 39	1 14	0 59	0 49	0 42	0 37	0 33	0 30
59	18	5 33	2 47	1 51	1 24	1 07	0 56	0 48	0 42	0 37	0 33

height   angle   distance

Fig 1:6 Bearing and distance off

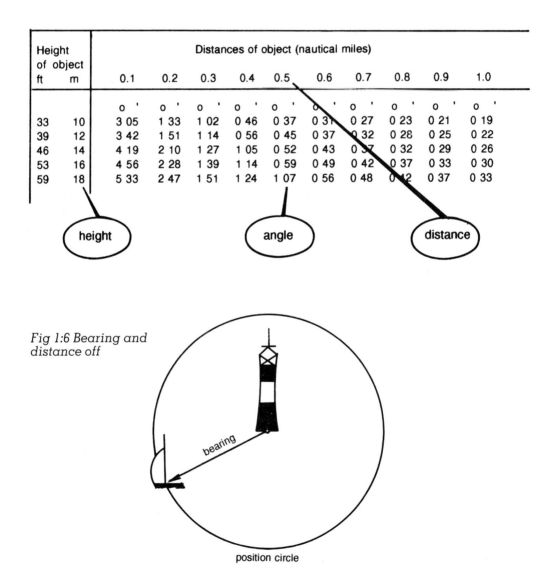

bearing

position circle

✔ Correct first time!

With an angle and the height of an object we can find the 'distance off'. Here's an example:

A skipper obtains a vertical sextant angle 1° 07′ of a lighthouse with a charted height of 18 metres above sea level. What is the distance off the light?

This can be found by calculation or by using a set of tables. We'll use 'Distance Off' tables; it's easier*. Fig 1:5(a) and (b) (opposite) shows the procedure. Select the angle and height and you get the distance off, in this instance 0.5 nautical miles.

With the lighthouse as the centre and radius 0.5 nautical miles, draw a circle. This is a line of position which means that you must be cruising *somewhere* along that line. To determine your exact position you must get at least one other line to intersect. A bearing will do fine as a second line of position. Where the two lines intersect will be your observed position (fix). See Fig 1:6 (opposite).

Solve the following problem:

Sloop Sea Raven *is on passage bound for Vancouver in DR position lat 49°19′.8N, long 123°14′.8W. The skipper obtained a vertical sextant angle of a lighthouse which stands 16 metres above sea level. The angle of 1°14′ established that the boat was 0.4 nautical miles off the mark. At the same time the bearing of the light was due west.*

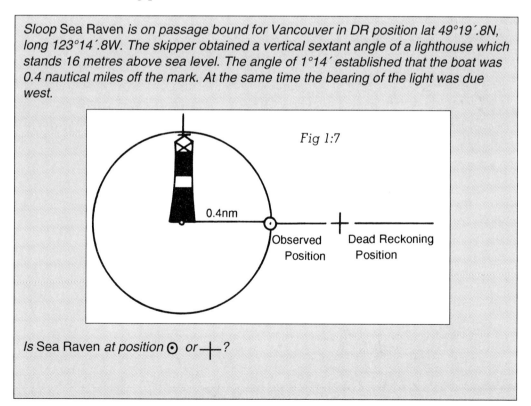

Fig 1:7

0.4nm

Observed Position

Dead Reckoning Position

Is Sea Raven *at position ⊙ or ┼ ?*

---

* Obtainable in some nautical almanacs.

See what it says on page 8.

Fig 1:8

Fig 1:9

Fig 1:10

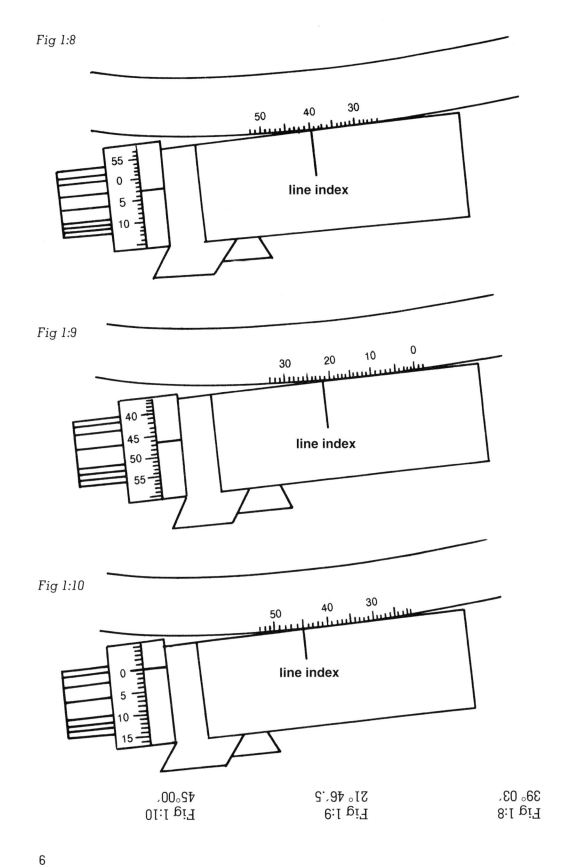

Fig 1:10
45°00′.

Fig 1:9
21° 46′.5

Fig 1:8
39° 03′.

☒ **Wrong answer.**

The line index (for reading full degrees) points between 9° and 10° in the scale range 0–10°. You mis-read this as being over the 10° mark. Better to make a mistake now than when it may be important at sea! Several students have got this one wrong. All you need is more practice.

Get hold of a sextant and practise with it ashore where you can rely on a stable platform. If you can't get to a beach and take a few sun sights using a natural horizon, use any available objects to practise on: tall buildings, trees, towers, chimneys. Drop the roof of a building down to ground level, or the sun down to a garden fence, and so on.

Best of all, however, is for you to find someone who can teach you the technique. There's nothing like 'hands-on' experience.

Opposite are three more examples (Figs 1:8, 1:9 and 1:10) on which to practise. The answers are upside-down at the foot of the page.

Return to page 3; look again at the problem, and make sure you understand where you went wrong.

Observed position ☉ is the correct answer.

The Dead reckoning (DR) position is obtained through course and speed (distance). The DR and observed positions rarely coincide. There is a discrepancy, due to such factors as leeway or tidal streams.

The DR position is fundamental to all navigation, coastal and celestial. Always keep the DR position updated even if highly sophisticated electronic navigation aids are available. Incidentally, the DR position may be shown as ╋ or ⌂ .

SUMMARY

a) A sextant is used to measure angles.
b) The intersection of lines of position provide a fix.
c) A bearing is a line of position.
d) The Dead reckoning (DR) position is fundamental to both coastal and celestial navigation.

The basic skills of coastal navigation, finding angles and lines of position, apply also to celestial navigation; the main difference being that we use celestial marks instead of land marks.

This was a simple enough unit, wasn't it? You have already mastered the few basic skills necessary to complete the programme; namely the use of tables and a little common sense.

Start the main programme on the next page. Good luck!

Celestial Marks

> Alone, alone, all, all alone,
> Alone on a wide wide sea!
> Samuel Taylor Coleridge
> *The Rime of the Ancient Mariner*

In coastal navigation we use landmarks such as lighthouses, chimneys, hills, towers: known points of fixed position. But when sailing offshore, with nothing visible except sea and sky, we use the heavenly bodies. So instead of landmarks we use celestial marks.

Close your eyes and indulge yourself! Imagine all these celestial marks, stars, sun, moon, planets, in their unique positions, neatly beamed on to the surface of an enormous, galactic, transparent sphere surrounding the Earth. This is called the *celestial sphere* and it shares the same centre point as the Earth (see Fig 2:1).

As we view the heavens from our spinning Earth we appear to see a lot of motion on the celestial sphere. The sun rises and sets, seasons come and go, the silent stars go by as grouped constellations.

Incidentally, for the remainder of the programme we'll refer to all heavenly bodies generally as 'stars', unless of course we want to refer to them individually as sun, moon, or planet.

Fig 2:1 The celestial sphere.

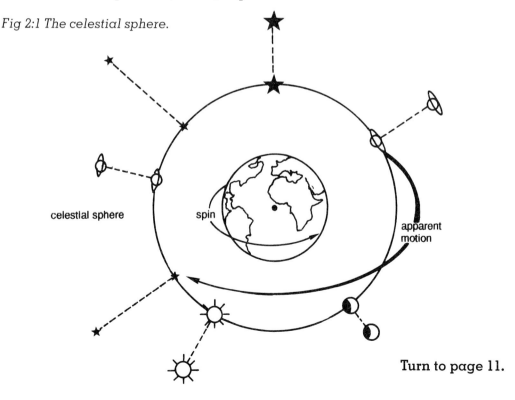

celestial sphere   spin   apparent motion

Turn to page 11.

Fig 2:2 Geographical position.

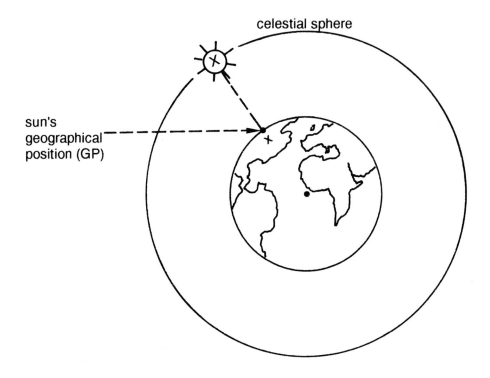

'Beam me up, Scotty', and Captain Kirk of SS *Enterprise* is vaporized, transported through space, only to materialize on another planet; adventures well known to generations of *Star Trek* fans.

As it happens, centuries before *Star Trek* ever came into being, when it was a mere twinkle in the galaxy in fact, navigators have long indulged in similar fantasies and used their imaginations to 'beam' anything on to, or from, the celestial sphere.

Let's beam the sun down from the celestial sphere along a line to the centre of the Earth. Where it touches the Earth's surface is called the *geographical position* (in future we'll call that the GP).

Refer to Fig 2:2 (opposite) and, after doing so, answer the following question:

Does the GP of a star remain in a fixed position on Earth?

Yes..turn to page 13

No ....turn to page 15

Fig 2:3 Star trails (the Plough).

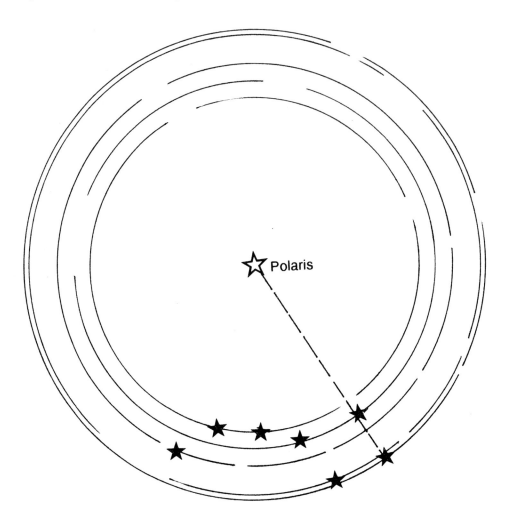

☒ **Wrong.**

Because of the Earth's spin, the stars on the celestial sphere appear to move while we, the observers, remain stationary. Therefore, because a star on the celestial sphere moves so does its geographical position (GP).

There's a lot of movement 'out there'. Some bodies which are closer to the Earth – sun, moon, planets – appear to move quickly. Others, such as the way out stars, are so distant from us that they appear to move as groups, or constellations.

To get a sense of this movement point a camera at the night sky on a starry night and leave the shutter open for a time exposure. The result will be traces of starlight which, over a duration, develop as star trails tracking across the firmament.

And if you go a step further and point the camera at the Pole star (Polaris), which is almost on the north/south axis of the Earth, you end up with arcs of star trails.

Fig 2:3 (opposite) illustrates a diagrammatic view of the constellation of the Plough as it circles the Pole star.

Return to page 11 and carry on.

Fig 2:4 The observer's zenith.

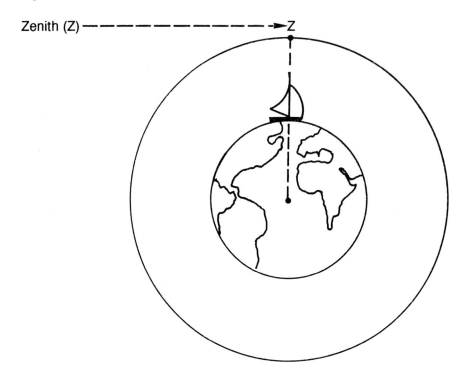

✔ Well done!

Our 'beaming' operations are not just one-way; they're not all down to Earth. We can, with a further stretch of the imagination, transport anything from Earth, upward, on to the celestial sphere.

Start from the Earth's centre and from there trace a line through the top of your mast and extend it right out to the celestial sphere. This is the celestial equivalent of the observer's position, called the *zenith* (Z) (see Fig 2:4, opposite).

Here's a problem. See what you make of it.

A yacht is on passage and the skipper observes that the sun is directly overhead.

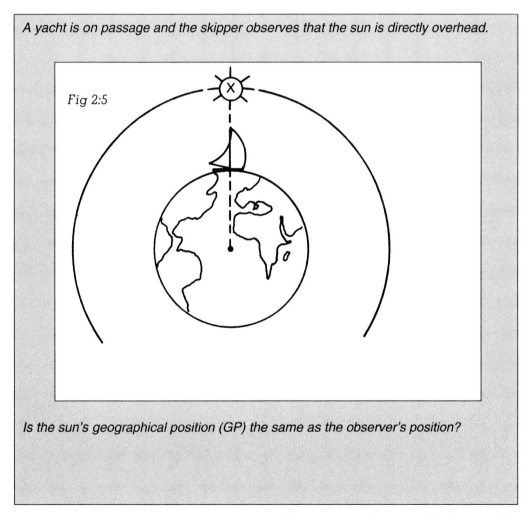

Fig 2:5

Is the sun's geographical position (GP) the same as the observer's position?

Carry on reading overleaf, page 16.

The answer is 'yes'.

The sun's GP is the same as the position of the vessel because both are on the same meridian and it is exactly overhead. If you beamed the sun down to Earth it would drop on the vessel!

SUMMARY

a) We imagine that celestial bodies are located on a huge celestial sphere surrounding the Earth.

b) Because the Earth spins, the celestial sphere *appears* to rotate.

c) The geographical position (GP) is a point on the Earth's surface directly beneath a heavenly body.

d) The zenith is a point on the celestial sphere directly overhead an observer.

Do the exercise on the next page.

EXERCISE FOR UNIT 2 (Before starting, cover up the previous page, 16)

This is the first complete exercise you have been given. Some students feel that drawing diagrams often helps their progress when answering questions. It works! Try it!

Also, because of several unfamiliar, but essential words appearing, you may want to copy the Glossary which is on pages 121–2 and have it readily to hand. You can then refer to helpful, instant information at any time.

1 What is the celestial sphere?
2 Define apparent motion.
3 Refer to the following diagram (Fig 2:6).

Name the following:

Fig 2:6

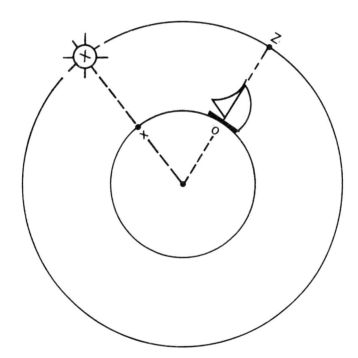

a) X
b) x
c) Z
d) o

Answers are overleaf, on page 18.

17

ANSWERS TO EXERCISE FOR UNIT 2

1 The celestial sphere is a huge imaginary sphere upon which the stars are assumed to be situated.

2 Apparent motion is the motion of the stars as they appear to an observer on Earth.

3 a) X is the sun's location on the celestial sphere.

   b) x is the geographical position (GP), which is the position on the Earth's surface directly beneath the sun, on a line between the sun and the Earth's centre.

   c) Z is the observer's zenith. This is a point on the celestial sphere directly above an observer on Earth, on a line between the Earth's centre and the observer extended to the celestial sphere.

   d) o is the observer's location on the Earth.

If you managed to get 100 per cent correct you did very well; you're sailing 'full and bye'. If, however, you got more than one incorrect answer work through this unit again before continuing.

Down to Earth

> In all my travels I have not managed to fall off the edge of the world.
>
> Stephen Hawking

Let's stay on the celestial sphere for a while and trace a line between the sun's position (X) and the zenith (Z). This line ZX is called the *zenith distance*, Fig 3:1 below. There are two things of interest to us:

- The first is that zenith distance (ZX) is measured as angular distance (which means that it is measured in degrees, minutes and seconds).
- And second, ZX is an arc of a great circle.

Can you remember what a great circle is? It's a circle on a sphere, the plane of which passes through the centre. Or to put it in simpler terms, if you were to cut a sphere through any great circle the 'cut' would always pass through the centre of the sphere. The equator is one of the Earth's great circles, and a meridian of longitude is a semi-great circle.

Fig 3:1 Zenith distance.

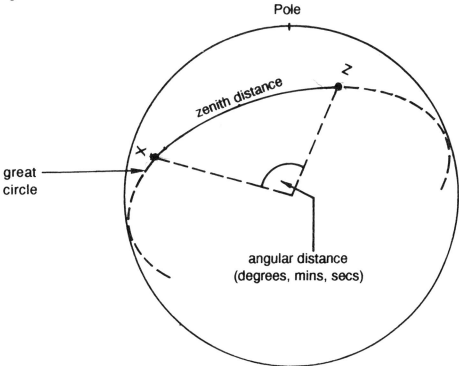

Please read on (page 21).

Fig 3:2 Zenith distance and geographical distance.

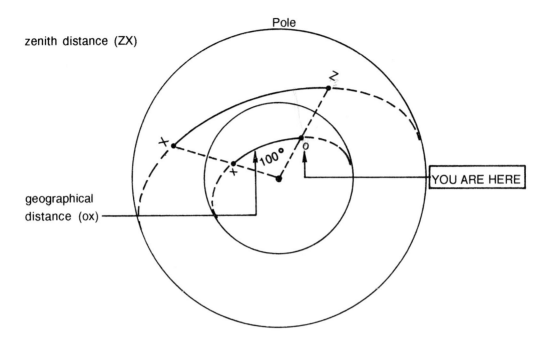

Z = zenith (observer's)

X = sun's position on the celestial sphere

x = geographical position (GP)

o = observer's position

Now let's get back down to Earth and see the link-up between celestial and earthly matters.

Refer to Fig 3:2 (opposite) and notice that on Earth there is a great circle arc (ox) from the observer (that's you) and the GP(x).

It's called the *geographical distance* and it is the earthly equivalent of the zenith distance (ZX), measured as angular distance.

In Fig 3:2 the angular distance of zenith distance (ZX) is 100°.

What is the angular distance of the geographical distance (ox)?

The answer is on page 23.

Fig 3:3 Celestial and terrestrial position circles.

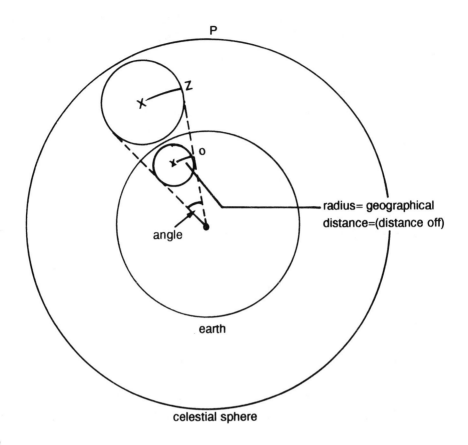

P

Z

X

o

radius= geographical
distance=(distance off)

angle

earth

celestial sphere

Fig 3:4

Position Circle

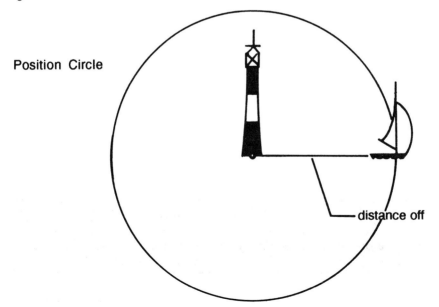

distance off

ox is 100°.

Both ZX and ox measure the same angular distance because *they stem from the same angle at the centre of the Earth.* Clearly, finding the zenith distance is our means of obtaining the geographical distance.

How do we find the zenith distance?
With the sextant. After measuring the angle (altitude) between the sun and horizon, and applying some *very* simple arithmetic, we emerge finally with the zenith distance (we'll do that very soon).

What use is the geographical distance?
By using it as radius (distance off, in fact), and the GP(x) as centre, we can plot a position circle (see Fig 3:3). This is a similar procedure to our lighthouse and distance off exercise illustrated in Fig 3:4.
    But angular distance has to be converted into nautical miles before we can make practical use of it. The conversion is simple; you're doing it all the time when you measure distances on a chart:

> There are 60 minutes in 1 degree;
> there are 60 seconds in 1 minute
> and 1 minute of arc equals 1 nautical mile.

Therefore a zenith distance (zx) of 100° gives us a related geographical distance of a 100° which equals 6000 nautical miles (100° × 60′).

What is 34° 30´ expressed as a geographical distance (nautical miles)?

Remember; there are 60 minutes of arc in 1°, and 1 minute equals 1 nautical mile.

Turn to page 25.

Fig 3:5 Discover the errors!

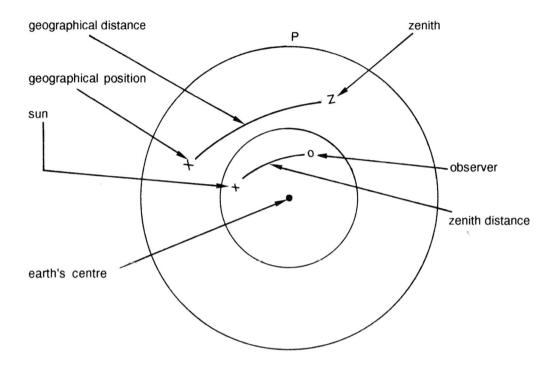

geographical distance

geographical position

sun

zenith

P

Z

o

observer

zenith distance

earth's centre

2070 nm is correct.

Here's the working:

```
34°× 60     = 2040 nm
              + 30
34° 30′     = 2070 nm
```

Clearly the geographical distances we are getting are very large, thousands of miles in fact. For example a position circle with a radius (geographical distance) of 3000 miles and with its centre (GP) at London, would track through places as far afield as Canada, Africa, the Middle East, and the Arctic. Such distances are too great to be considered for practical plotting.

You'll learn very soon how we overcome this problem.

Before we finish with this unit let's see whether we really do know our terms. It's important to understand the work we've covered here.

Solve the following problem:

In Fig 3:5 (opposite) four of the labels are incorrect.

Which are they?

The corrected diagram is given overleaf, page 26.

Here's the corrected version.

Fig 3:6

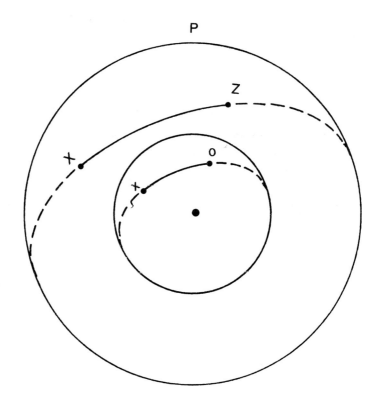

ZX = zenith distance ☑

ox = geographical distance ☑

X = sun ☀ ☑

x = geographical position (GP) ☑

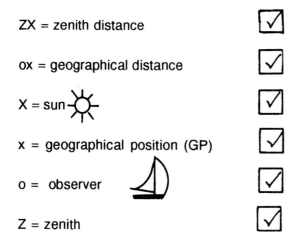

o = observer ☑

Z = zenith ☑

Read the summary on the next page.

SUMMARY

a) The zenith distance (ZX) is an arc of a great circle on the celestial sphere.

b) The zenith distance measures the same angular distance as the geographical distance (which is Earth distance) because they both stem from the same angle at the centre of the Earth. *(Understand this and you'll have few problems with the rest of the programme.)*

c) Angular distance can be converted into nautical miles.

d) The geographical distance can be seen as a radius of a position circle with the GP as its centre.

EXERCISE FOR UNIT 3

1 Define zenith distance.

2 Study Fig 3:7.
   What is the zenith distance (ZX) expressed as angular distance?

Fig 3:7

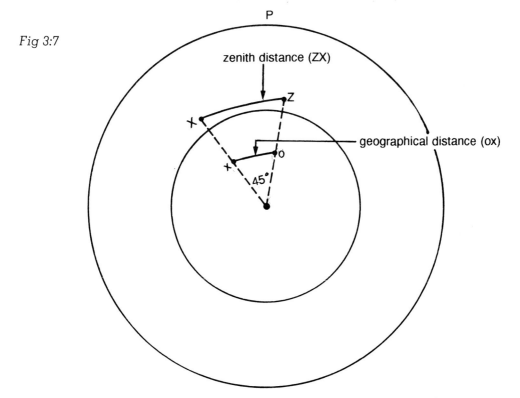

3 What is the geographical distance (ox) expressed as nautical miles?

Answers overleaf.

27

ANSWERS TO EXERCISE FOR UNIT 3

1 The zenith distance is the angular distance between the celestial body and the observer's zenith measured along an arc of a great circle on the celestial sphere.

2 The zenith distance (ZX) expressed as angular distance is 45°.

3 The geographical distance (ox) expressed in nautical miles is 2700 nm. The angular distance is 45°, the same as that of the zenith distance.

Here's the working:

45° × 60 minutes = 2700 nm.

(1 minute of arc on the Earth's circumference equals 1 nautical mile; there are 60 minutes in 1 degree).

Both the zenith distance (ZX) and geographical distance (ox) are the same angular distance because they stem from the same angle at the Earth's centre. Another way of expressing it is to say that both arcs subtend the same angle at the Earth's centre.

If you got *any* answers incorrect, work through this unit again.
It's a short unit which is important for complete understanding.

The Celestial Position

For a moment we have a glimpse of ourselves and of our world is landed in its stream of stars ...

Henry Beeston *The Outermost House*

We need to be able to define the actual position of a heavenly body on the celestial sphere (see Fig 4:1). To do this we use co-ordinates which are much the same as latitude and longitude on Earth.

But in the case of a heavenly body the co-ordinates used are called *declination* and *hour angle*. Right now we'll sort out the declination; in the next unit we'll deal with the hour angle.

Fig 4:1 Celestial co-ordinates.

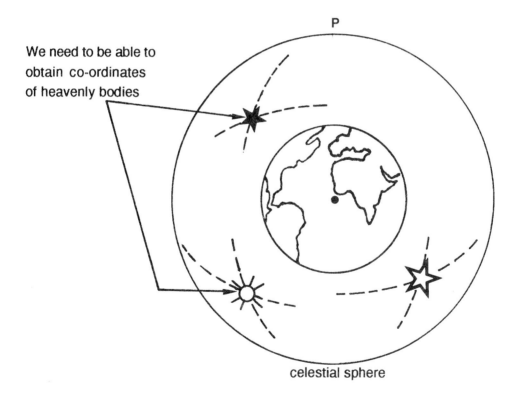

We need to be able to obtain co-ordinates of heavenly bodies

celestial sphere

Read on please (page 31).

29

Example: What is the declination of the sun on 4 May at the following times:

03h 00m 00s GMT and 04h 00m 00s GMT?

Look in the 'SUN' column under 'Dec' to find hourly values (Fig 4:3 below).
Alongside day 4 and 03h the Dec is N15° 47'.5
Alongside day 4 and 04h the Dec is N15° 48'.3
The declination can decrease or increase; here it increases by 0'.8

If there are minutes involved there's slightly more working-out to do.
Disregard seconds, they make no appreciable difference to the outcome.

Example: What is the declination of the sun on 4 May at 03h 32m 23s GMT? (use Figs 4:3 and 4:4)

At the foot of the Dec column is a quantity called the 'd' correction which accounts for minutes extra to the hour in question. On 4 May, this 'd' correction is 0'.7.

Next, to convert 'd' into a usable figure refer to the Increments and Corrections table, printed in the Almanac (Fig 4:4). On the 32 minutes page (32ᵐ) look in the column 'v' or 'd' correction (corrⁿ). The equivalent for 0'.7 is 0'.4. Apply this to the hourly declination, as follows:

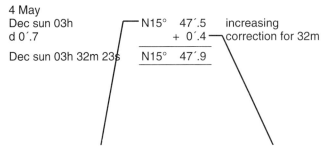

4 May
Dec sun 03h ——— N15° 47'.5 increasing
d 0'.7   + 0'.4 — correction for 32m
                      ─────────────
Dec sun 03h 32m 23s   N15° 47'.9

Fig 4:3 From the Almanac.

Fig 4:4 Increments and Corrections (from the Almanac).

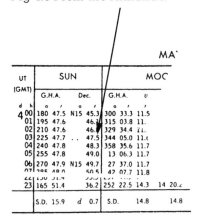

Return to page 31 and answer the question.

The celestial positions of the sun, moon, four planets and 57 stars can be found in the Nautical Almanac.

Declination is the celestial equivalent of latitude. It is measured from 0° – 90°, north or south of the equator. Fig 4:2 (below) illustrates the sun with a declination which is north, and a star which is south.

Fig 4:2 Declination.

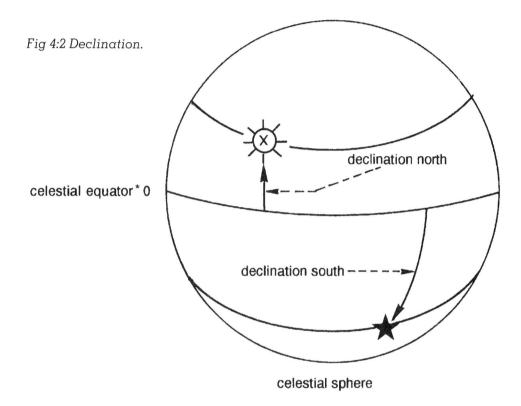

celestial sphere

HOW DO WE FIND THE DECLINATION?

From the Almanac. The procedure is explained on the opposite page. When you have studied the example, return here and answer the following question:

What is the declination of the sun on 4 May at 01h 32m 42s GMT? (use Figs 4:3, 4:4 opposite)

S 15° 45′.7 .... turn to page 33
N 15° 46′.5 .... turn to page 34

* The celestial equator is also known as the equinoctial

Do the following examples. (The answers are upside-down at the foot of the page.)

Example A: What is the declination of the sun on 9 Dec at 02h 29m 45s GMT? (use Fig 4:6 and Fig 4:7)

Fig 4:6. From the Almanac

Fig 4:7 Increments and Corrections (from the Almanac).

DECEMBER 9, 10, 11 (MON., TUES

UT (GMT)	SUN		MOON				Lat.	Twilight		Sur
	G.H.A.	Dec.	G.H.A.	v	Dec.	d	H.P.		Naut.	Civil
	° ′	° ′	° ′	′	° ′	′	′	°	h m	h m
d h								N 72	08 11	10 28
9 00	182 00.7	S22 44.7	148 22.3	12.4	S21 36.1	6.5	54.1	N 70	07 52	09 3ʳ
01	197 00.4	45.0	162 53.7	12.4	21 29.6	6.7	54.1	68	07 37	09 ;
02	212 00.1	45.3	177 25.1	12.5	21 22.9	6.7	54.1	66	07 25	0P
03	226 59.8 ..	45.5	191 56.6	12.5	21 16.2	6.8	54.1	64	07 15	˚
04	241 59.5	45.8	206 28.1	12.5	21 09.4	6.9	54.1	62	07 05	
05	256 59.3	46.0	220 59.6	12.7	21 02.5	7.0	54.1	60	06 57	
06	271 59.0	S22 46.3	235 31.3	12.6	S20 55.5	7.0	54.1	N 58	06 ᶜ	
07	286 58.7	46.5	250 02.9	12.8	20 48.5	7.2	54.1	56	06	
08	301 58.4	46.8	264 34.7	12.8	20 41.3	7.3	54.1	54	0	ᶜ
18	ʸₐ									
19	106 41.7				ₐₐ.ₐ 54.2					
20	121 41.4	00.4	5ⁱ ₓₐ.ₓ	.₋₋	11 14.3	11.3	54.2	Day	ᵗ	
21	136 41.2 ..	00.7	72 25.7	15.5	11 03.0	11.3	54.3		0ᶜ	
22	151 40.9	00.9	87 00.2	15.6	10 51.7	11.4	54.3		m ₃	
23	166 40.6	01.1	101 34.8	15.6	10 40.3	11.4	54.3	9	08 03	
								10	07 36	ᶜ
	S.D. 16.3	d 0.2	S.D.	14.7	14.7		14.8	11	07 09	06

29ᵐ

29	SUN PLANETS	ARIES	MOON	or Corrᵃ d —		or Corrᵃ d		v or Corrᵃ d	
	• ′	• ′	• ′	′	′	′	′	′	′
₁	• ′	• ′	• ′	′	′	′	′	′	′
00	7 15·0	7 16·2	6 55·2	0·0	0·0	6·0	3·0	12·0	5·9
01	7 15·3	7 16·4	6 55·4	0·1	0·0	6·1	3·0	12·1	5·9
02	7 15·5	7 16·7	6 55·7	0·2	0·1	6·2	3·0	12·2	6·0
03	7 15·8	7 16·9	6 55·9	0·3	0·1	6·3	3·1	12·3	6·0
04	7 16·0	7 17·2	6 56·1	0·4	0·2	6·4	3·1	12·4	6·1
05	7 16·3	7 17·4	6 56·4	0·5	0·2	6·5	3·2	12·5	6·1
06	7 16·5	7 17·7	6 56·6	0·6	0·3	6·6	3·2	12·6	6·2
07	7 16·8	7 17·9	6 56·9	0·7	0·3	6·7	3·3	12·7	6·2
08	7 17·0	7 18·2	6 57·1	0·8	0·4	6·8	3·3	12·8	6·3
09	7 17·3	7 18·4	6 57·3	0·9	0·4	6·9	3·4	12·9	6·3

Example B: What is the declination of the sun on 30 Nov at 07h 35m 01s GMT? (use Fig 4:8 and Fig 4:9)

Fig 4:8 From the Almanac.

Fig 4:9 Increments and Corrections (from the Almanac).

NOV. 30, DEC. 1, 2 (SAT

UT (GMT)	SUN		MOON				Lat.	Twil Naut
	G.H.A.	Dec.	G.H.A.	v	Dec.	d	H.P.	
	° ′	° ′	° ′	′	° ′	′	′	° ′
d h								N 72 07
30 00	182 54.8	S21 31.5	255 23.6	12.8	S 2 25.4	14.1	57.8	N 70 0ʳ
01	197 54.5	31.9	269 55.4	12.9	2 39.5	14.1	57.8	68 ᶜ
02	212 54.3	32.3	284 27.3	12.9	2 53.6	14.0	57.8	66
03	227 54.1 ..	32.7	298 59.2	12.9	3 07.6	14.1	57.7	64
04	242 53.9	33.1	313 31.1	12.9	3 21.7	13.9	57.7	67
05	257 53.7	33.6	328 03.0	13.0	3 35.6	14.0	57.7	ᶜ
06	272 53.4	S21 34.0	342 35.0	12.9	S 3 49.6	13.9	57.7	N 5
07	287 53.2	34.4	357 06.9	12.9	4 03.5	14.0	57.6	5ᶜ
S 08	302 53.0	34.8	11 38.8	13.0	4 17.5	13.8	57.6	54
A 09	317 52.8 ..	35.2	26 10.8	12.9	4 31.3	13.9	57.6	52
		₋₀ 42.8	11.8	16 29.2	1ₒ.₋			
20	122 ₃.₋₋	58.3	163 13.6	11.8	16 39.5	10.3	56.2	Dˢₒᵣ
21	137 38.8 ..	58.6	177 44.4	11.7	16 49.8	10.1	56.2	
22	152 38.6	59.0	192 15.1	11.7	16 59.9	10.1	56.2	m ₃
23	167 38.3	59.4	206 45.8	11.7	17 10.0	10.0	56.2	30 11 39	11 29ₗ
								1 11 18	11 07ₗ
	S.D. 16.2	d 0.4	S.D.	15.7	15.5		15.4	2 10 56	10 44

35ᵐ

35	SUN PLANETS	ARIES	MOON	v or Corrᵃ d		v or Corrᵃ d		v or Corrᵃ d	
	• ′	• ′	• ′	′	′	′	′	′	′
₁	• ′	• ′	• ′	′	′	′	′	′	′
00	8 45·0	8 46·4	8 21·1	0·0	0·0	6·0	3·6	12·0	7·1
01	8 45·3	8 46·7	8 21·3	0·1	0·1	6·1	3·6	12·1	7·2
02	8 45·5	8 46·9	8 21·6	0·2	0·1	6·2	3·7	12·2	7·2
03	8 45·8	8 47·2	8 21·8	0·3	0·2	6·3	3·7	12·3	7·3
04	8 46·0	8 47·4	8 22·0	0·4	0·2	6·4	3·8	12·4	7·3
05	8 46·3	8 47·7	8 22·3	0·5	0·3	6·5	3·8	12·5	7·4
06	8 46·5	8 47·9	8 22·5	0·6	0·4	6·6	3·9	12·6	7·5
07	8 46·8	·8 48·2	8 22·8	0·7	0·4	6·7	4·0	12·7	7·5
08	8 47·0	8 48·4	8 23·0	0·8	0·5	6·8	4·0	12·8	7·6
09	8 47·3	8 48·7	8 23·2	0·9	0·5	6·9	4·1	12·9	7·6
10	8 47·5	8 48·9	8 23·5	1·0	0·6	7·0	4·1	13·0	7·7
11	8 47·8	8 49·2	8 23·7	1·1	0·7	7·1	4·2	13·1	7·8
12	8 48·0	8 49·4	8 23·9	1·2	0·7	7·2	4·3	13·2	7·8
13	8 48·3	8 49·7	8 24·2	1·3	0·8	7·3	4·3	13·3	7·9
14	8 48·5	8 49·9	8 24·4			7·4	4·4	13·4	7·9

Turn to the summary on page 34.

Turn to the summary on page 34.

Example A 9 Dec
Dec sun 02h · · · S22° 45′.3
P 0′.1 +
S22° 45′.4 · · · Dec sun 02h 29m 45s

Example B 30 Nov
Dec sun 07h · · · S21° 34′.4
P 0′.2 +
S21° 34′.6 · · · Dec sun 07h 35m 01s

32

☒ You got two things wrong.

The declination was north (N) and not south (S) and it was increasing, not decreasing. You subtracted the d (0′.7 value) which, when corrected, came to 0′.4. It should have been added. Study Fig 4:5 (following).

Fig 4:5 Declination (north and south).

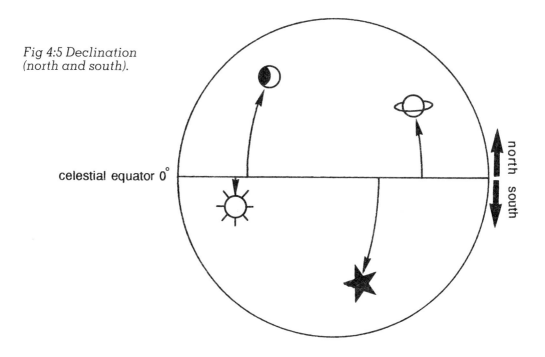

celestial equator 0°

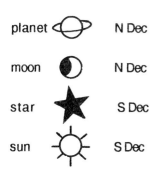

planet	⬭	N Dec
moon	☽	N Dec
star	★	S Dec
sun	☀	S Dec

And opposite are more examples for you to practise. Take care to label them correctly, north (N) or south (S). Do them before moving on through the programme.

Read the summary on page 34.

✔ Correct. You're doing well.

SUMMARY

a) The co-ordinates of a celestial body are called declination and hour angle.
b) These are listed in the Nautical Almanac.
c) The celestial equivalent of latitude is called the declination.
d) Declination is measured from 0° to 90° north or south of the celestial equator.

Now try an exercise (page 35).

EXERCISE FOR UNIT 4

1 Define declination.

2 In the following example is the declination increasing or decreasing?
S 23° 00′.0
S 23° 00′.2

3 At the foot of the sun column there is something called 'd'. What does this refer to?

4 In Fig 4:10, what is the corrected minute value for d 0′.2?

Fig 4:10 Increments and Corrections
(from the Almanac).

29ᵐ

29	SUN PLANETS	ARIES	MOON	v or Corr⁎ d	v or Corr⁎ d	v or Corr⁎ d
00	7 15·0	7 16·2	6 55·2	0·0 0·0	6·0 3·0	12·0 5·9
01	7 15·3	7 16·4	6 55·4	0·1 0·0	6·1 3·0	12·1 5·9
02	7 15·5	7 16·7	6 55·7	0·2 0·1	6·2 3·0	12·2 6·0

5 What is the declination of the sun on 9 Dec at 06h 32m 02s GMT? (use Figs 4:11 and 4:12)

Fig 4:11 From the Almanac.

Fig 4:12 Increments and Corrections (from the Almanac).

DECEM

UT (GMT)	SUN		MOC
	G.H.A.	Dec.	G.H.A. v [
d h	° ′	° ′	° ′ ′ ′
9 00	182 00.7	S22 44.7	148 22.3 12.4 S21
01	197 00.4	45.0	162 53.7 12.4 2
02	212 00.1	45.3	177 25.1 12.5 2
03	226 59.8 ..	45.5	191 56.6 12.5 2
04	241 59.5	45.8	206 28.1 12.5 2
05	256 59.3	46.0	220 59.6 12.7 2
06	271 59.0	S22 46.3	235 31.3 12.6 S2(
07	286 58.7	46.5	250 02.9 12.8 2(
21	136 41.2 ..	00.7	72 25.7 15.5 11
22	151 40.9	00.9	87 00.2 15.6 1(
23	166 40.6	01.1	101 34.8 15.6 1(
	S.D. 16.3	d 0.2	S.D. 14.7

32ᵐ

32	SUN PLANETS	ARIES	MOON	v or Corr⁎ d	v or Corr⁎ d	v or Corr⁎ d
00	8 00·0	8 01·3	7 38·1	0·0 0·0	6·0 2·9	12·0 5·7
01	8 00·3	8 01·6	7 38·4	0·1 0·1	6·1 2·9	12·1 5·7
02	8 00·5	8 01·8	7 38·6	0·2 0·1	6·2 2·9	12·2 5·8
03	8 00·8	8 02·1	7 38·8	0·3 0·2	6·3 3·0	

Answers follow on page 36.

35

ANSWERS TO EXERCISE FOR UNIT 4

1 Declination is the angular distance of a heavenly body measured from 0° to 90° north or south of the celestial equator. It can be considered the celestial equivalent of latitude.

2 The declination is increasing.

3 'd' refers to the correction which has to be applied for minutes in excess of the hourly value of declination.

- Obtain a value for 'd' from the respective column in the daily pages (eg at the foot of the Sun column).

- Then enter the Increments and Corrections tables with the 'd' value and alongside it you will find the actual number of excess minutes.

- Add these excess minutes to the hourly value if the declination is increasing, or subtract if decreasing.

All this seems a little tedious, doesn't it? No problem; a little practice will soon make permanent. *Incidentally, if you missed out the 'd' value altogether the outcome would be close to accuracy – no more than a mile in error!*

4 In the example the corrected value for d 0′.2 is 0′.1.

5 9 Dec
Dec sun 06h	S 22° 46′.3	increasing
d 0′.2	+ 0′.1	correction for 32m
Dec sun 06h 32m 02s GMT	S 22° 46′.4	

All answers correct? Excellent! If you failed to get answers 4 and 5, re-work this unit.

On the next page a surprise, more self-testing!

TEST PIECE A

To see whether you have grasped the fundamentals of the first four units here's a test piece to try.

1 What's the angle registered on this sextant?

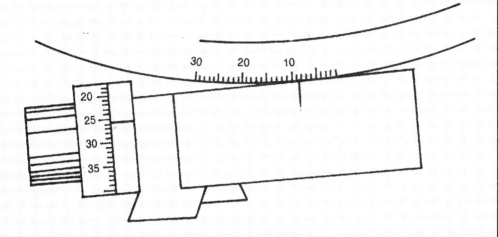

2 Refer to Fig 4:14 below. Name Z, X, o, x, ZX and ox.

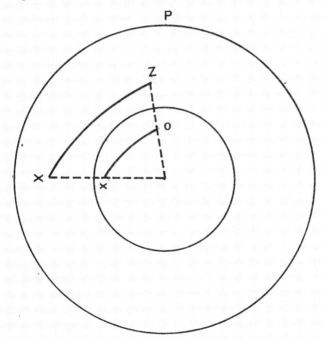

3 What's the relationship between arcs ZX and ox?

Answers overleaf.

ANSWERS TO TEST PIECE A

1 The sextant reading is 8° 25′.6.

2 Z = observer's zenith
   X = celestial position of the star
   o = observer's position (YOU ARE HERE)
   x = geographical position
   ZX = zenith distance
   ox = geographical distance

3 Both ZX and ox are the same angular distance; they both stem from the same angle. Study Fig 4:15, below.

Fig 4:15

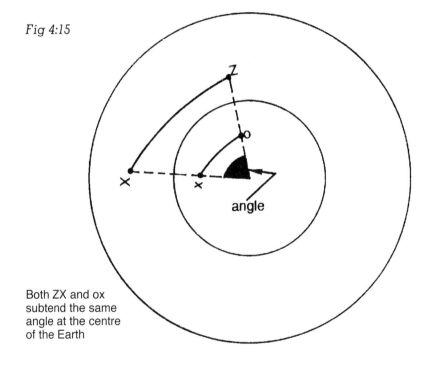

Both ZX and ox
subtend the same
angle at the centre
of the Earth

In the next unit we learn about the hour angle, the remaining co-ordinate for defining a celestial position.

The Hour Angle

> But the old men seemed to get there just as safely as today
> With their prehistoric methods, in their prehistoric way,
> And the records left behind them most indubitably tell
> That the modern navigator may be proud to do as well!
>
> H M Atkinson *Navigation*

Declination (dec) is one co-ordinate for getting the position of a heavenly body on the celestial sphere. The other is the Greenwich Hour Angle (GHA) which is:

* angular distance measured from the celestial Greenwich meridian (imagine the Greenwich meridian beamed on to the celestial sphere);
* measured along a parallel of declination *westwards* through 360° from Greenwich to the meridian of the body (see Fig 5:1).

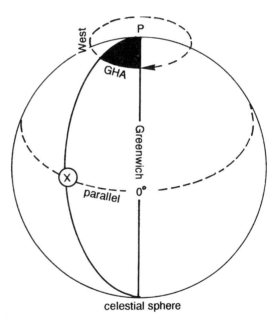

Fig 5:1 Greenwich Hour Angle (GHA).

How does the GHA differ from longitude? Well, longitude is measured through 180° east or west of the Greenwich meridian, not through 360° westwards, as is the GHA (Fig 5:2).

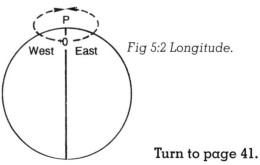

Fig 5:2 Longitude.

Turn to page 41.

Fig 5:3 Nautical Almanac (from the daily pages).

UT (GMT)	SUN		MOON				Lat.	Naut.
	G.H.A.	Dec.	G.H.A.	v	Dec. d	H.P.		h m
d h	° '	° '	° '	'	° '	'	N 72	////
4 00	180 47.5	N15 45.3	300 33.3	11.5	S24 04.3	4.8 54.1	N 70	////
01	195 47.6	46.1	315 03.8	11.6	23 59.5	5.0 54.2	68	////
02	210 47.6	46.8	329 34.4	11.6	23 54.5	5.0 54.2	66	////
03	225 47.7	.. 47.5	344 05.0	11.6	23 49.5	5.1 54.2	64	////
04	240 47.8	48.3	358 35.6	11.7	23 44.4	5.3 54.2	62	////
05	255 47.8	49.0	13 06.3	11.7	23 39.1	5.4 54.2	60	01 22
06	270 47.9	N15 49.7	27 37.0	11.7	S23 33.7	5.4 54.2	N 58	01 5
07	285 48.0	50.5	42 07.7	11.8	23 28.3	5.6 54.2	56	02
S 08	300 48.0	51.2	56 38.5	11.9	23 22.7	5.7 54.2	54	02
A 09	315 48.1	.. 51.9	71 09.4	11.8	23 17.0	5.8 54.2	52	02
T 10	330 48.1	52.6	85 40.2	12.0	23 11.2	5.9 54.2	50	03 0
U 11	345 48.2	53.4	100 11.2	11.9	23 05.3	6.0 54.2	45	03 31
R 12	0 48.3	N15 54.1	114 42.1	12.0	S22 59.3	6.1 54.2	N 40	03
D 13	15 48.3	54.8	129 13.1	12.1	22 53.2	6.2 54.2	35	0
A 14	30 48.4	55.5	143 44.2	12.1	22 47.0	6.3 54.2	30	
Y 15	45 48.4	.. 56.3	158 15.3	12.1	22 40.7	6.5 54.2	2	
16	60 48.5		172 46.4	12.2	6.5 54.2			
17	75 4		17.6		54.2			
18								

Fig 5:4 Nautical Almanac (from Increments and Corrections).

34ᵐ

INCREMENTS AND CORRECTIONS

34	SUN PLANETS	ARIES	MOON	v or Corrⁿ d	v or Corrⁿ d	v or Corrⁿ d	35	SUN PLANETS	ARIES	MOON
s	° '	° '	° '	' '	' '	' '	s	° '	° '	° '
00	8 30.0	8 31.4	8 06.8	0.0 0.0	6.0 3.5	12.0 6.9	00	8 45.0	8 46.4	8 2
01	8 30.3	8 31.6	8 07.0	0.1 0.1	6.1 3.5	12.1 7.0	01	8 45.3	8 46.7	8 2.
02	8 30.5	8 31.9	8 07.2	0.2 0.1	6.2 3.6	12.2 7.0	02	8 45.5	8 46.9	8 21
03	8 30.8	8 32.1	8 07.5	0.3 0.2	6.3 3.6	12.3 7.1	03	8 45.8	8 47.2	8 21
04	8 31.0	8 32.4	8 07.7	0.4 0.2	6.4 3.7	12.4 7.1	04	8 46.0	8 47.4	8 22.0
05	8 31.3	8 32.6	8 08.0	0.5 0.3	6.5 3.7	12.5 7.2	05	8 46.3	8 47.7	8 22
06	8 31.5	8 32.9	8 08.2	0.6 0.3	6.6 3.8	12.6 7.2	06	8 46.5	8 47.9	8 2
07	8 31.8	8 33.2	8 08.4	0.7 0.4	6.7 3.9	12.7 7.3	07	8 46.8	8 48.2	8 '
08	8 32.0	8 33.4	8 08.7	0.8 0.5	6.8 3.9	12.8 7.4	08	8 47.0	8 48.4	8
09	8 32.3	8 33.7	8 08.9	0.9 0.5	6.9 4.0	12.9 7.4	09	8 47.3	8 48.7	'
10	8 32.5	8 33.9	8 09.2	1.0 0.6	7.0 4.0	13.0 7.5	10	8 47.5	8 48.9	
11	8 32.8	8 34.2	8 09.4	1.1 0.6	7.1 4.1	13.1 7.5	11	8 47.8	8 49.2	8
12	8 33.0	8 34.4	8 09.6	1.2 0.7	7.2 4.1	13.2 7.6	12	8 48.0	8 49.4	8 2
13	8 33.3	8 34.7	8 09.9	1.3 0.7	7.3 4.2	13.3 7.6	13	8 48.3	8 49.7	8 2
14	8 33.5	8 34.9	8 10.1	1.4 0.8	7.4 4.3	13.4 7.7	14	8 48.5	8 49.9	8 24
15	8 33.8	8 35.2	8 10.3	1.5 0.9	7.5 4.3	13.5 7.8	15	8 48.8	8 50.2	8 24.7
16	8 34.0	8 35.4	8 10.6	1.6 0.9	7.6 4.4	13.6 7.8	16	8 49.0	8 50.4	8 24
17	8 3			1.7 1.0	7.7 4.4	7.9	17	8 49.3	8 50.7	8
				1.0			18	8 49.5	8	
								8 49.8		

The GHA is printed alongside the declination in the daily pages of the Almanac. The method of finding the GHA is similar to getting the declination, with a couple of small differences:

- first find the hourly value;
- then apply the increment for any extra minutes and seconds. (GHA seconds must be accounted for because they make quite a difference to the outcome. You will recall that this is not so in the case of the declination).

Example: What is the GHA of the sun on 4 May at 03h 34m 03s GMT? Refer to Figs 5:3 and 5:4 opposite.

```
4 May
GHA sun 03h                    225°    47'.7
Increment 34m 03s   +            8°    30'.8  (from the SUN column)
GHA sun 03h 34m 03s GMT  234°    18'.5
```

What is the GHA of the sun on 4 May at 06h 34m 05s GMT? (use Figs 5:3 and 5:4 opposite)

279° 19'.2 .... turn to page 43

262° 16'.6 .... turn to page 43

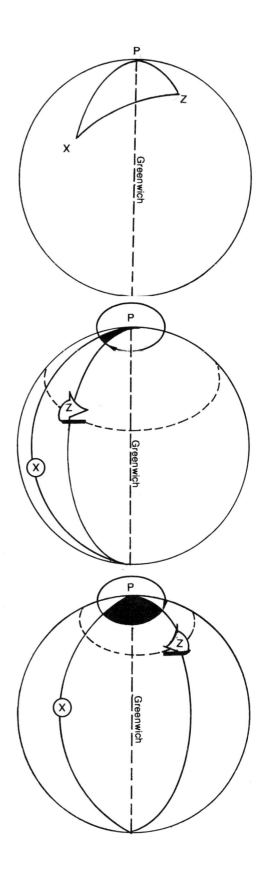

Fig 5:5 The PZX Triangle.

P is the Pole
Z is the zenith
X is the heavenly body

Fig 5:6 Local Hour Angle (LHA).
LHA=GHA – longitude west

Fig 5:7 Local Hour Angle.
LHA=GHA + longitude east

279° 19′.2 is the correct answer. Here's the working:

4 May
GHA sun 06h		270°	47′.9
Increment 34m 05s	+	8°	31′.3
GHA sun 06h 34m 05s GMT		279°	19′.2

If you got the incorrect answer, 262° 16′.6, it's because you *subtracted* the increment for 34m 05s which should be *added* since it denotes an increase.

Look at Fig 5:5 opposite. The triangle PZX has Z (zenith) and X (celestial position) as two of its angles – the third is at P (the celestial Pole). The PZX triangle is important. We'll refer to it throughout the programme because its solution – the size of its angles and length of its sides – can provide answers to many queries. Among other things we'll be able to calculate a zenith distance and obtain a bearing.

But at the moment we are more concerned with the angle at P, between PZ (observer's meridian) and PX (sun's meridian). It's called the *Local Hour Angle* (LHA). As with the GHA, it's measured westward through 360°.

The LHA is related to two other angles, the GHA and longitude, as follows:

LHA = GHA – longitude west (Fig 5:6)
LHA = GHA + longitude east.(Fig 5:7)

Example: What is the LHA of the sun on 4 May at 02h 32m 01s GMT in longitude 56° 45′.5W? Refer to Fig 5:8 and Fig 5:9 (below).

4 May
GHA sun 02h	210°	47′.6
Increment 32m 01s	+ 8°	00′.3
GHA sun 02h 32m 01s GMT	218°	47′.9
Longitude W	− 56°	45′.5
LHA sun 02h 35m 01s GMT	162°	02′.4

MAY 4,

UT (GMT)	SUN		MOON			
	G.H.A.	Dec.	G.H.A.	v	Dec.	d
d h	° ′	° ′	° ′	′	° ′	′
4 00	180 47.5	N15 45.3	300 33.3	11.5	S24 04.3	4.8
01	195 47.6	46.1	315 03.8	11.6	23 59.5	5.0
02	210 47.6	46.8	329 34.4	11.6	23 54.5	5.0
03	225 47.7	.. 47.5	344 05.0	11.6	23 49.5	5.1

Fig 5:8 From the Almanac (daily pages).

32ᵐ

32	SUN PLANETS	ARIES	MOON	v or Corrⁿ d		v or Corrⁿ d		v or Corrⁿ d	
s	° ′	° ′	° ′	′	′	′	′	′	′
00	8 00·0	8 01·3	7 38·1	0·0	0·0	6·0	2·9	12·0	5·7
01	8 00·3	8 01·6	7 38·4	0·1	0·1	6·1	2·9	12·1	5·7
02	8 00·5	8 01·8	7 38·6	0·2	0·1	6·2	2·9	12·2	5·8
03	8 00·8	8 02·1	7 38·9	0·3	0·2	6·3	3·0	12·3	5·8

Fig 5:9 Increments and Corrections (from the Almanac).

> *What is the LHA of the sun on 4 May at 01h 32m 02s GMT in longitude 32° 45′.8 east? (use Figs 5:8 and 5:9, above)*

The answer is overleaf.

The answer is LHA sun 01h 32m 02s GMT is 236° 33′.9. Here is the working:
8

GHA sun 01h	195°	47′.6
Increment 32m 02s	+ 8°	00′.5
GHA sun 01h 32m 02s	203°	48′.1
Long east +	32°	45′.8
LHA sun 01h 32m 02s GMT	236°	33′.9

It is customary to find the two co-ordinates, hour angle and declination, in the same operation and not separately.

Example 1: Use Figs 5:10 and 5:11 below. This example involves the GHA and dec. There are no longitude considerations.

What is the GHA and dec of the sun on 4 May at 10h 34m 06s GMT?

GHA sun 10h	330°	48′.1	Dec	N15° 52′.6	d + 0′.7 (increasing)
Increment 34m 06s	+ 8°	31′.5	d corrⁿ	+0′.4	
GHA sun 10h 34m 06s	339°	19′.6	Dec	N15° 53′.0	

Example 2: Here we must find the LHA, so do account for longitude. Use Figs 5:10 and 5:11.

4 May at 08h 34m 03s GMT. MV Sirius is on passage in the Atlantic bound for the Cape Verde Islands lat 20° 30′.4 N, long 27° 04′.0 W. What is the LHA and dec of the sun?

GHA sun 08h	300°	48′.0	Dec	N15° 51′.2	d + 0′.7
Increment 32m 03s	+8°	30′.8	d corrⁿ	+0′.4	
GHA sun 08h 32m 03s GMT	309°	18′.8	Dec	N15° 51′.6	
Longitude west	−27°	04′.0			
LHA sun 08h 32m 03s GMT	282°	14′.8			

MAY 4, 5

UT (GMT)	SUN		MOON			
	G.H.A.	Dec.	G.H.A.	v	Dec.	d
4 00	180 47.5	N15 45.3	300 33.3	11.5	S24 0.	
01	195 47.6	46.1	315 03.8	11.6	2.	
02	210 47.6	46.8	329 34.4	11.6		
03	225 47.7 ..	47.5	344 05.0	11.6		
04	240 47.7	48.3	358 35.6	11.7		
05	255 47.8	49.0	13 06.3	11.7		
06	270 47.9	N15 49.7	27 37.0	11.7	S.	
07	285 48.0	50.5	42 07.7	11.8	.	
IS 08	300 48.0 .	51.2	56 38.5	11.9	2	
IA 09	315 48.1 . . .	51.9	71 09.4	11.8	2	
IT 10	330 48.1	52.6	85 40.2	12.0	2.	
IU 11	345 48.2	53.4	100 11.2	11.9	2:	
22	150 51.4	35.5	23.		14 31.4 11.2 55.0	
23	165 51.4	36.2	252 22.5	14.3	14 20.2 11.2 55.0	
	S.D. 15.9	d 0.7	S.D.	14.8	14.8	14.9

Fig 5:10 From the Almanac (daily pages).

34ᵐ INCREMENTS

34	SUN PLANETS	ARIES	MOON	v or Corrⁿ d	v or Corrⁿ d	v or Corrⁿ d
00	8 30·0	8 31·4	8 06·8	0·0 0·0	6·0 3·5	12·0 6·9
01	8 30·3	8 31·6	8 07·0	0·1 0·1	6·1 3·5	12·1 7·0
02	8 30·5	8 31·9	8 07·2	0·2 0·1	6·2 3·6	12·2 7·0
03	8 30·8	8 32·1	8 07·5	0·3 0·2	6·3 3·6	12·3 7·1
04	8 31·0	8 32·4	8 07·7	0·4 0·2	6·4 3·7	12·4 7·1
05	8 31·3	8 32·6	8 08·0	0·5 0·3	6·5 3·7	12·5 7·2
06	8 31·5	8 32·9	8 08·2	0·6 0·3	6·6 3·8	12·6 7·2
07	8 31·8	8 33·2	8 08·4	0·7 0·4	6·7 3·9	12·7 7·3
08	8 32·0	8 33·4	8 08·7	0·8 0·5	6·8 3·9	12·8 7·4
09	8 32·3	8 33·7	8 08·9	0·9 0·5	6·9 4·0	12·9 7·4
10	8 32·5	8 33·9	8 09·2	1·0 0·6	7·0 4·0	13·0 7·5
11	8 32·8	8 34·2	8 09·4	1·1 0·6	7·1 4·1	13·1 7·5
12	8 33·0	8 34·4	8 09·6	1·2 0·7	7·2 4·1	13·2 7·6
13	8 33·3	8 34·7	8 09·9	1·3 0·7	7·3 4·2	13·3 7·6

Fig 5:11 Increments and Corrections (from the Almanac).

Turn to the next page.

SUMMARY

a) The Greenwich Hour Angle (GHA) and declination are co-ordinates that define the position of a heavenly body on the celestial sphere.

b) The angle at P in the PZX triangle is the Local Hour Angle (LHA).

c) The LHA is related to the GHA and longitude.
GHA – Longitude west = LHA
GHA + Longitude east = LHA

d) Hour angles are always measured along a parallel of declination from a selected meridian, westward through 360°. See Figs 5:12(a) and 5:12(b) (following).

Fig 5:12(a) GHA from Greenwich to star.   *Fig 5:12(b) LHA from Observer to star.*

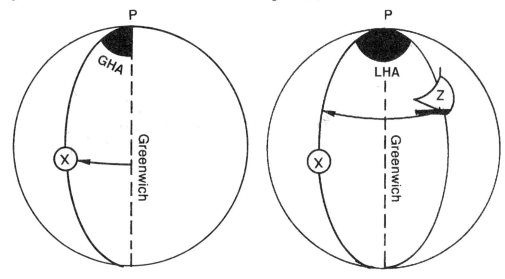

EXERCISE FOR UNIT 5 (Use tables in Figs 5:10 and 5:11 opposite)

1   What is the GHA and dec of the sun on 4 May at 09h 34m 05s GMT?

2   Find the GHA and dec of the sun on 4 May at 11h 34m 12s GMT.

3   4 May: the Sloop *Wendy Mary* is in position lat 45° 43′.2N, long 06° 23′.2W. What is the LHA and dec of the sun at 08h 34m 11s GMT?

4   4 May: the aux. yacht *Crombie* is on passage in the Pacific in position lat 30° 12′.4N, long 130° 04′.3E. What is the LHA and dec of the sun at 06h 34m 10s GMT?

The detailed answers are overleaf, page 46.

ANSWERS TO EXERCISE FOR UNIT 5

1 4 May

GHA sun 09h	315°	48′.1	Dec	N15°	51′.9	d + 0′.7
Increment 34m 05s	+ 8°	31′.3	d corrⁿ +		0′.4	
GHA sun 09h 34m 05s GMT	324°	19′.4	Dec	N15°	52′.3	

2 4 May

GHA sun 11h	345°	48′.2	Dec	N15°	53′.4	d + 0′.7
Increment 34m 12s	+ 8°	33′.0	d corrⁿ +		0′.4	
GHA sun 11h 34m 12s GMT	354°	21′.2	Dec	N15°	53′.8	

3 4 May

GHA sun 08h	300°	48′.0	Dec	N15°	51′.2	d + 0′.7
Increment 34m 11s	+ 8°	32′.8	d corrⁿ +		0′.4	
GHA sun 08h 34m 11s	309°	20′.8	Dec	N15°	51′.6	

Long W (−)	− 6°	23′.2
LHA sun 08h 34m 11s GMT	302°	57′.6

4 4 May

GHA sun 06h	270°	47′.9	Dec	N15°	49′.7	d + 0′.7
Increment 34m 10s	+ 8°	32′.5	d corrⁿ +		0′.4	
GHA sun 06h 34m 10s GMT	279°	20′.4	Dec	N15°	50′.1	

Long E (+)	130°	04′.3
LHA sun 06h 34m 10s GMT	409°	24′.7
	− 360°	00′.0
LHA sun 06h 34m 10s GMT	49°	24′.7

Note: An hour angle can never exceed 360° and it must be of positive value. Therefore if you get an angle over 360° then subtract 360° (as above). If the hour angle is negative, add 360°.

This is probably one of the more tedious units. If you managed it all correctly that's an excellent performance. Carry on if you managed at least one GHA and one LHA answer. If you didn't you should do this unit again.

Time

And that lucky old sun's got nothing to do,
Except roll around heaven all day!
Song. Sam Lewis and George Meyer

In this unit we probe deeper into 'time' and its implications for the navigator.

Time begins with the sun which follows an apparent path on the celestial sphere called the ecliptic. Because the Earth's axis slopes 23° 27′ away from the perpendicular the ecliptic makes a similar angle to the celestial equator (see Fig 6:1).

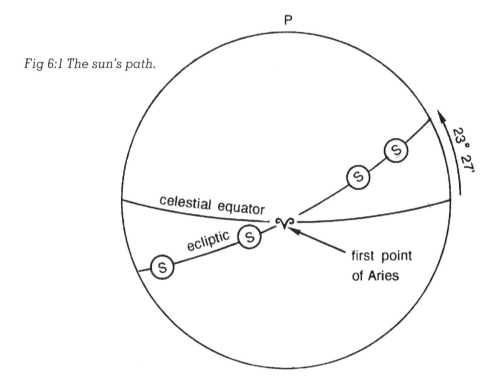

Fig 6:1 *The sun's path.*

The sun rises in the east and sets in the west. Twilight occurs when the sun is just below the horizon, before sunrise and after sunset.

Turn to page 49 next.

Fig 6:2 The true sun is an unreliable timekeeper.

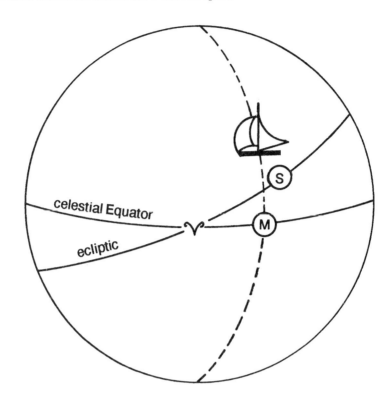

Here the constant mean sun (M) is crossing the boat's meridian but the irregular true sun (S) doesn't coincide.

The time difference between the two suns is called the 'Equation of Time' and it is printed in the Almanac (alongside the meridian passage of the sun; bottom right on the sun's daily pages).

Fig 6:3 Equation of Time, from the Almanac. In this example the equation of time for 12h on day 4 is 3m 13s.

Day	SUN Eqn. of Time 00 ʰ	12 ʰ	Mer. Pass.
	m s	m s	h m
4	03 10	03 13	11 57
5	03 16	03 18	11 57
6	03 21	03 23	11 57

Accurate time is needed for succesful navigation. The sun is an unreliable timekeeper; its path along the ecliptic is irregular. So an imaginary 'mean sun' has been devised which moves on the celestial equator averaging out the real sun's irregularities. It observes the basic yearly and daily solar durations but it keeps regular, perfect time. Study Fig 6:2 opposite and the accompanying notes.

When mean time is referred to the Prime Meridian at Greenwich it is called Greenwich Mean Time (GMT)*. It's the principal time reference used by navigators throughout the world and *all navigational data printed in the Nautical Almanac are based on GMT.*

At the start of a voyage set your chronometer to GMT. The modern wrist watch is excellent for this purpose and you should make sure a spare is carried on board. Some navigators do not carry the chronometer around with them when taking sights. For this purpose they use a subsidary timepiece called a deck watch which is compared with the chronometer and any necessary corrections made.

Radio time signals are used for time checks, but sometimes reception is poor; get to know the chronometer error so that you can, if necessary, manage without radio signals.

Example: On 4 May a chronometer which gains 1 second a day was 11 seconds fast. On 10 May, the time shown was 14h 24m 05s GMT. What was the correct GMT on 10 May?

Here's the working:

Daily gain	1	second
Total gain over 6 days	6	seconds
Error 4 May	11	seconds
Error 10 May	17	seconds fast (subtract this)

	h	m	s
Chronometer time 10 May	14	24	05
Error 10 May	–		17
Correct GMT 10 May	14	23	48

Try the following exercise:

*On 12 February a chronometer which loses 2 seconds a day was 15 seconds **slow**. On 19 February the time was 12h 36m 03s GMT. What was the correct GMT on 19 February?*

Go to page 51.

*Also referred to as Universal Time (UT) or Zulu Time (ZT)

Fig 6:4 Longitude and time.

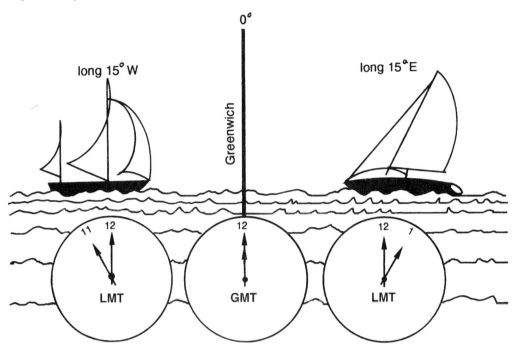

Fig 6:5 Extract from Conversion of Arc to Time tables (from the Almanac).

0° – 59°		
°	h	m
43	2	52
44	2	56
45	3	00
46	3	04
47	3	08

The correct GMT was 12h 36m 32s.

Here's the working:

Daily loss   2   seconds
Total loss 12/19 Feb (7 days)   14   seconds
Error 12 Feb   15   seconds slow
Error 19 Feb   29   seconds slow (add this)

		h	m	s
Chronometer time 19 Feb		12	36	03
Error 19 Feb	+			29
Correct GMT 19 Feb		12	36	32

When mean time is referred to a meridian other than Greenwich it is called Local Mean Time (LMT).

To find GMT from LMT, longitude has to be taken into account because there is a link between longitude and time; the Earth rotates 360° in 24 hours, 15° in 1 hour, 1° in 4 minutes. Clearly we can convert longitude (as an arc of angular distance) into time.

Look at the three clocks in Fig 6:4 opposite. The central clock, at Greenwich, is at 12 noon GMT. If, at that time, you were on the ketch, cruising at 15° W, LMT would be 11 am. However, on the sloop, at longitude 15° E, LMT would be 1 pm. We can sum up the rule for converting LMT to GMT as follows:

Longitude west, Greenwich time *best* (greater than LMT)
Longitude east, Greenwich time *least* (less than LMT)

An easy way of converting longitude into time is by using the Conversion of Arc to Time tables which are printed in the Nautical Almanac*.

Example: A ship is in longitude 44° 00´ W. The LMT is 1025. What is the GMT?
Remember, because the longitude is west the GMT is 'best' (greater than the LMT).

		h	m	
LMT		10	25	
Long 44°00´W	+	2	56	(using the excerpt from the Conversion of Arc to Time tables, Fig 6:5, opposite page).
GMT		13	21	

A ship is in longitude 47°00E at 0934 LMT. What is the GMT?
(Use the extract from 'Conversion of Arc to Time' tables in Fig 6:5 opposite)

The answer is on page 53.

* 'Conversion of Arc to Time' tables are also printed in Appendix A

Fig 6:6 Time zones.

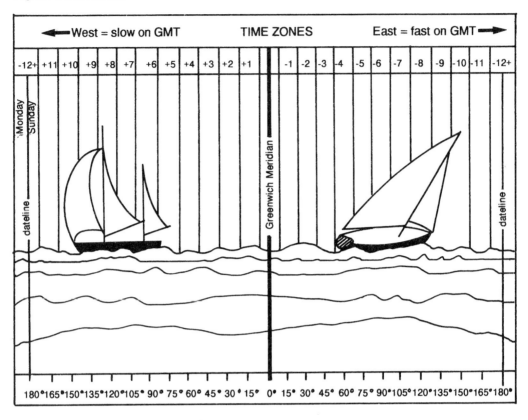

The answer is:

	h	m	
LMT	09	34	You are dealing with longitude east so
Long 47° 00′E	− 3	08	GMT will be *least* (less than) LMT
GMT	06	26	

Navigators use GMT constantly, but if we ran our clocks on it for standard daily routines throughout the world there would be utter confusion. The application would be too general; noon would coincide with night-time in Anchorage, 'happy' hour in Miami and early morning in Hong Kong.

Likewise LMT couldn't be used for standard routines because the 'correct' time would vary from location to location. We would have a different 'correct' time from our immediate neighbour's 'correct' time.

The solution is to divide the world into 24 time zones which observe the zone times of central meridians 15° (ie 1 hour) apart, which are all referred to Greenwich (see Fig 6:6 opposite).

In this way time is standardized into bands of operation for convenient community schedules. For this reason the ship's routine conforms to zone time. It is customary for the ship's clock *(not the chronometer)* to keep zone time.

To the west of Greenwich are the plus (+) zones which are *slow* on GMT. To the east they're minus (−) or *fast* on GMT. When you move from one zone to another you should alter the ship's clock by 1 hour to suit the current zone. When westbound retard the clock and when eastbound advance it.

Example: A boat is cruising through the Panama Canal (Zone +5 hours) and the ship's clock reads 1410 zone time. What is the GMT?

	h	m
Zone time	14	10
Zone	+ 5	00
GMT	19	10

Note that this problem involves a vessel cruising in longitude west and zone time is slow (+) on GMT. When in longitude east zone time is fast on GMT (−).

Why is it customary for the ship's clock and not the chronometer to keep zone time?

Go to page 54, overleaf.

It is customary for the ship's clock to keep zone time because day-to-day living schedules relate to zone time. The chronometer, which is specifically concerned with navigation, is *always* kept on GMT.

The 12 zones either side of the Greenwich meridian meet at the International Date Line. This is situated half way round the Earth from Greenwich (ie 180°) (see Fig 6:7 below).

Fig 6:7 The International Date Line.

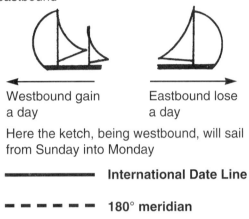

Whenever this line is crossed a day is gained or lost, depending on whether you are westbound or eastbound

Westbound gain a day

Eastbound lose a day

Here the ketch, being westbound, will sail from Sunday into Monday

━━━━━━━━ **International Date Line**

━ ━ ━ ━ ━ ━ **180° meridian**

SUMMARY

a) The true sun is an irregular timekeeper. An imaginary, mean sun is devised which keeps constant time.

b) GMT is mean time referred to the Prime Meridian at Greenwich.

c) GMT is kept on the ship's chronometer.

d) Chronometers have to be corrected. This is done through radio time signals.

e) LMT is mean time referred to a specific, local meridian.

f) Zone time is used for daily routines in everyday living. Zone time is kept on the ship's clock.

g) When westbound retard the ship's clock when crossing time zones; eastbound advance it.

h) When crossing the International Date Line westbound vessels gain a day, eastbound they lose a day.

Now do the exercise on the next page.

EXERCISE FOR UNIT 6

1 What is the ecliptic?

2 Why is the chronometer always kept on GMT?

3 Why isn't GMT used for daily (ie non-navigational) routines worldwide?

4 How can you check out the accuracy of your chronometer?

5 On 5 Jan a sailor obtains a sextant altitude of the sun and at the same time records GMT as 10h 32m 05s on his chronometer, which gains 1 second daily. If the chronometer error on 1 Jan was 1m 03s fast what was the correct GMT on 5 Jan?

6 Convert 28° 45′ into time (use Conversion of Arc to Time tables, Appendix A).

7 A ship is in longitude 54° 33′E at 1159 LMT. What is the GMT?

8 What are time zones? Why use them?

9 A ship is cruising in the Indian Ocean (Zone –6) and the ship's clock reads 1621 (Zone Time). What is the GMT?

10 On 15 Jan a boat on course 090° crosses the International Date Line. What would be the new Greenwich date on crossing the line?

Answers are overleaf.

ANSWERS TO EXERCISE FOR UNIT 6

1 The ecliptic is the apparent path of the sun on the celestial sphere.

2 The chronometer is always kept on accurate GMT because it is the universal time reference. All data listed in the Nautical Almanac refer to GMT.

3 GMT is not used for worldwide daily routines because it would be too confusing for regionalized order. We are creatures of habit and live by standard routines.

4 Chronometers can be checked by comparison with radio time signals. (Details of these are listed in such publications as the Admiralty List of Radio Signals Vol. 5.)

5 GMT on 5 Jan was 10h 30m 58s. Here's the working:

Daily gain	1 second
Total gain over 4 days	4 seconds
Error 1 Jan	1m 03 seconds FAST
Error 5 Jan	1m 07 seconds FAST

	h	m	s
Chronometer time 5 Jan	10	32	05
Error 5 Jan	−	1	07
Correct GMT 5 Jan	10	30	58

6 28° 45′ converted into time is 1h 55m (ie 28° = 1h 52m, 45′ = 3m).

7

	h	m	s	
LMT	11	59	00	
Long 54° 33′E	− 3	38	12	(east = GMT *least*)
GMT	8	20	48	

8 There are 24 time zones which are bands of time, each referred to its central meridian. These meridians are 15° apart. Zones were devised for regionalized convenience so that communities (eg countries, states) could organize daily routines and services such as business hours, or sea, land and air transportation schedules.

9

	h	m
Zone time	16	21
Zone	− 6	00
GMT	10	21

10 The new Greenwich date would be 14 Jan. An eastbound (090°) vessel loses a day when crossing the International Date Line.

Get an Angle on it

Wait till the sun shines, Nellie,

when the clouds go drifting by.

1905 song A B Sterling, music by H von Tilzer

You will recall that we have already stressed, in Unit 3, the importance of finding the zenith distance, ZX of the triangle PZX. Zenith distance can be translated into geographical distance as nautical miles and used as the radius of a position circle.

To jog your memory, look at Fig 7:1.

Fig 7:1 Position circles.

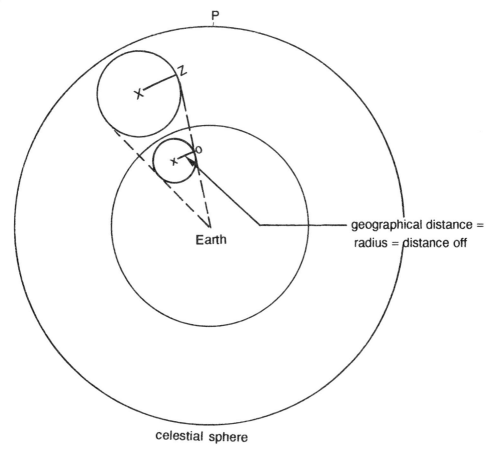

geographical distance =
radius = distance off

celestial sphere

Turn to page 59.

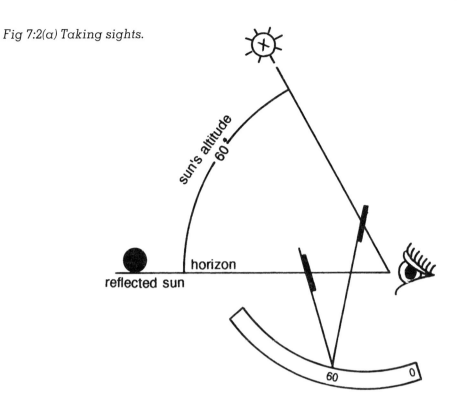

Fig 7:2(a) Taking sights.

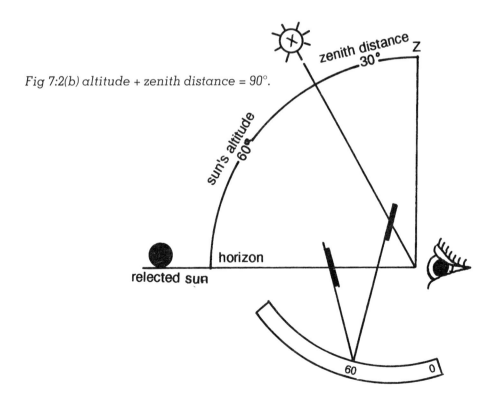

Fig 7:2(b) altitude + zenith distance = 90°.

HOW DO WE FIND THE ZENITH DISTANCE?

By using a sextant. What you have to do is wait until you get a good view of the sun (when the clouds have drifted by!) and then get the altitude: the vertical angle between the sun and the horizon (see Fig 7:2(a) opposite).

Our zenith, directly overhead, makes an angle of 90° to the horizon. This angle is made up of altitude and zenith distance, both complementary because they add up to 90° (see Fig 7:2(b) opposite).

Clearly, having found the altitude we can find the zenith distance (zenith distance = 90° – altitude).

Example: A sight is taken of the sun's lower limb. The true altitude was 69° 45′.7. What is the zenith distance?

Zenith distance = 90° – 69° 45′.7 = **20°14′.3**

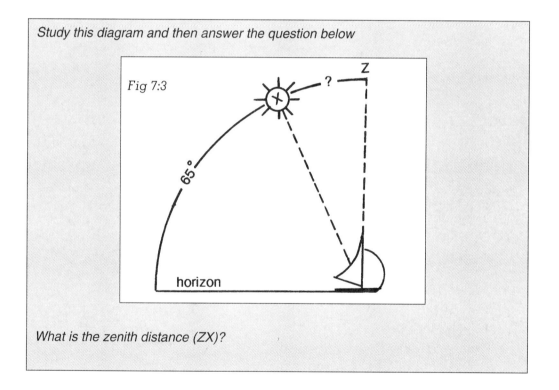

Study this diagram and then answer the question below

Fig 7:3

65°

horizon

Z

?

What is the zenith distance (ZX)?

Turn to page 61.

Fig 7:4 The altitude we get and the altitude we want.

What we get is the sextant altitude (SA), between the sun and the visible horizon, which is the horizon that we can see. But the measurement required for accuracy is the angle at the centre of the Earth, between the celestial horizon and the sun. This is the true altitude (TA), and this is what we want.

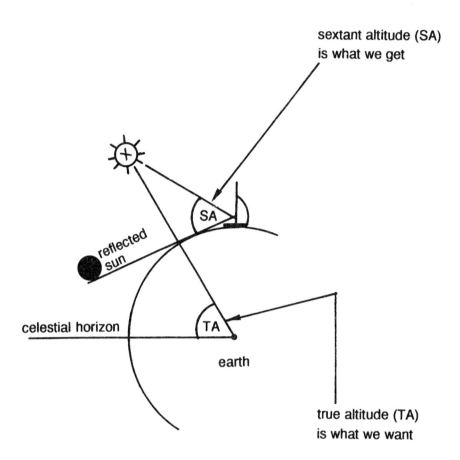

sextant altitude (SA)
is what we get

reflected sun

SA

celestial horizon

TA

earth

true altitude (TA)
is what we want

The answer is 25°00′.0 (90°− 65°)

We have a clear idea of the procedure for getting the zenith distance but at this point we must fine-tune our sextant work to ensure accuracy.

The sextant altitude has to be corrected by adjusting and taking out any instrumental errors.* Other, non-instrumental, corrections to be taken care of are due to natural features such as our height of eye, the effect of the atmosphere on the sun's rays, or the diameter of the sun. Study Fig 7:4 (opposite) and read the notes.

There are three main corrections to make: index error, height of eye and total correction.

INDEX ERROR

After taking out as many instrumental errors as you can there will be one remaining, the index error (IE) which is tested regularly just prior to taking each sight. To find it set the index at 0°, hold the sextant vertically and view the distant horizon. If there is a 'step' on the horizon there is error (see Fig 7:5(a)). If there is no index error (highly improbable), the two images will coincide and the horizon will appear as a continuous line (Fig 7:5(b)).

Fig 7:5   *(a)*   *(b)*

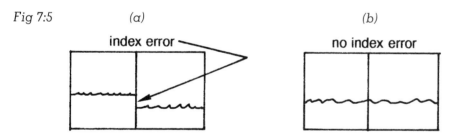

By fine-tuning the micrometer head you can get the step effect to diminish until you get a continuous horizon. Read the error. If it is on the plus side of the arc from 0° ('ON the arc') the sextant altitude will over-read. In this case subtract the index error from the altitude. If it's OFF the arc, on the negative side of 0°, add it.

Example: A sextant altitude (SA) of the sun was 46° 34′.6. The index error (IE) was 2′.0 on the arc. What is the corrected SA? (note: 'on the arc', therefore subtract IE)

Sextant altitude	46°	34′.6
Index error	−	2′.0
Corrected sextant altitude	46°	32′.6

Now turn to page 63.

*Detailed information about sextant adjustments is given in Appendix G. You've no need to look at them now. Refer to them after you have completed this unit.

Fig 7:6 Height of eye (DIP).

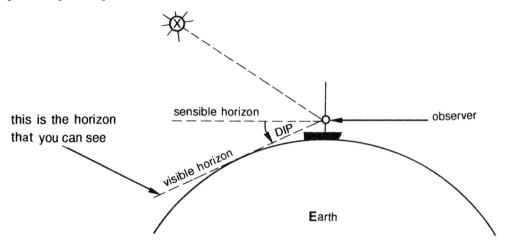

Fig 7:7 Altitude Correction Tables (from the Almanac).

Check that you choose the appropriate column for the sun's total correction; Oct–Mar, or Apr–Sept. Also check which column is required;Lower Limb (LL) or Upper Limb (UL)

ALTITUDE CORRECTION TABLES 10°–90° – SUN, STARS, PLANETS
(from the Almanac).

OCT.–MAR. SUN APR.–SEPT.						STARS AND PLANETS				DIP				
App. Alt.	Lower Limb	Upper Limb	App. Alt.	Lower Limb	Upper Limb	App. Alt.	Corr^n	App. Alt.	Additional Corr^n	Ht. of Eye	Corr^n	Ht. of Eye	Ht. of Eye	Corr^n
										m		ft.	m	
9 34	+10.8	−21.5	9 39	+10.6	−21.2	9 56	−5.3		1991	2.4	−2.8	8.0	1.0 −	1.8
9 45	+10.9	−21.4	9 51	+10.7	−21.1	10 08	−5.2		VENUS	2.6	−2.9	8.6	1.5 −	2.2
9 56	+11.0	−21.3	10 03	+10.8	−21.0	10 20	−5.1			2.8	−3.0	9.2	2.0 −	2.5
10 08	+11.1	−21.2	10 15	+10.9	−20.9	10 33	−5.1	Jan. 1–May 10	3.0	−3.1	9.8	2.5 −	2.8
10 21	+11.2	−21.1	10 27	+11.0	−20.9	10 46	−5.0	Dec. 12–Dec. 31	3.2	−3.2	10.5	3.0 −	3.0
10 34	+11.3	−21.0	10 40	+11.1	−20.7	11 00	−4.9	•	3.4	−3.3	11.2	See table	
10 47	+11.4	−20.9	10 54			11 14	−4.8	60 + 0.1	3.6	−3.4	11.9		
							−4.7			3.8	−3.5	12.6	m	
	+14.6	−17.7	30 00	+14.3	−17.5	32 00	−1.5	Jan. 1–Feb. 4		−6.6			
30 46	+14.7	−17.6		+14.4	−17.4	33 45	−1.4	•	14.2	−6.7	46.9	90 −	9.2
32 26	+14.8	−17.5	31 35	+14.5	−17.3	35 40	−1.3	0 + 0.2	14.7	−6.8	48.4	95 −	9.5
34 17	+14.9	−17.4	33 20	+14.6	−17.2	37 48	−1.2	41 + 0.1	15.1	−6.9	49.8		
36 20	+15.0	−17.3	35 17	+14.7	−17.1	40 08	−1.1	76	15.5	−7.0	51.3	100 −	9.7
38 36	+15.1	−17.2	37 26	+14.8	−17.0	42 44	−1.0	Feb. 5–Dec. 31	16.0	−7.1	52.8	105 −	9.9
41 08	+15.2	−17.1	39 50	+14.9	−16.9	45 36	−0.9	•	16.5	−7.2	54.3	110 −	10.2
43 59	+15.3	−17.0	42 31	+15.0	−16.8	48 47	−0.8	0 + 0.1	16.9	−7.3	55.8	115 −	10.4
47 10	+15.4	−16.9	45 31	+15.1	−16.7	52 18	−0.7	60	17.4	−7.4	57.4	120 −	10.6
50 46	+15.5	−16.8	48 55	+15.2	−16.6	56 11	−0.6		17.9	−7.5	58.9	125 −	10.8
54 49	+15.6	−16.7	52 44	+15.3	−16.5	60 28	−0.5		18.4	−7.6	60.5		
59 23	+15.7	−16.6	57 02	+15.4	−16.4	65 08	−0.4		18.8	−7.7	62.1	130 −	11.1
64 30	+15.8	−16.5	61 51	+15.5	−16.3	70 11	−0.3		19.3	−7.8	63.8	135 −	11.3
70 12	+15.9	−16.4	67 17	+15.6	−16.2	75 34	−0.2		19.8	−7.9	65.4	140 −	11.5
76 26	+16.0	−16.3	73 16	+15.7	−16.1	81 13	−0.1		20.4	−8.0	67.1	145 −	11.7
83 05	+16.1	−16.2	79 43	+15.8	−16.0	87 03	0.0		20.9	−8.1	68.8	150 −	11.9
90 00			86 32	+15.9	−15.9	90 00			21.4		70.5	155 −	12.1
			90 00											

App. Alt. = Apparent altitude = Sextant altitude corrected for index error and dip.

There are two further corrections to make.

One is our *height of eye*. If this were at sea level no correction would be necessary. But because we are above sea level any sextant altitude we obtain will be excessive; therefore any correction for height of eye must be negative (see Fig 7:6).

To find the correction for height of eye refer to the table in the Almanac (also on a loose-leaf card, Altitude Correction Tables under the column 'DIP'). This correction is *always subtracted* from the sextant altitude. Look at Fig 7:7.

After correcting the sextant altitude for index error and dip we arrive at the *apparent altitude (AA)*.

Example: A sextant altitude of the sun's lower limb LL was 41° 43´.9. IE 2´.0 on the arc. Height of eye was 2.8m. What is the apparent altitude (AA)?

SA	41° 43´.9
IE	− 2´.0
dip	− 2´.9
AA	41° 39´.0

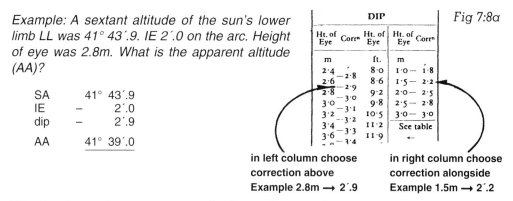

Fig 7:8a

in left column choose
correction above
Example 2.8m → 2´.9

in right column choose
correction alongside
Example 1.5m → 2´.2

The final, *total correction*, embodies others, refraction, semi- diameter and parallax. It is found on the same loose-leaf card as the dip (Altitude Correction Tables). The procedure for applying these corrections is:

Sextant altitude (SA) →   apparent altitude (AA) → true altitude (TA)
corrected for IE and dip   apply total correction

Example: On 12 Mar a sextant altitude of the sun's lower limb (LL) was 41° 25´.2. IE−1´.1. Height of eye was 3.2m. What was the true altitude (TA)?

SA	41° 25´.2	
IE	− 1´.1	
dip	− 3´.1	
AA	41° 21´.0	*find this in Oct–Mar (LL) column. (Fig 7:7 opposite.)*
corrⁿ +	15´.2	*add(+) LL subtract (−) UL*
TA	41° 36´.2	

On 26 Dec a sight of the sun's LL gave a sextant altitude of 38° 34´.1 IE 1´.9 off the arc. Height of eye 3.4m. What was the true altitude? (use Fig 7:7)

38° 47´.8? ....turn to page 65
38° 44´.0? ....turn to page 66

Fig 7:8

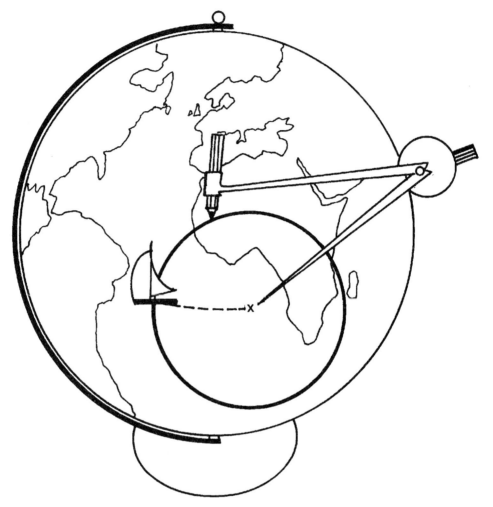

✔ **Very good.**

We now have an accurate true altitude and true zenith distance. From this we can find the geographical distance.

In theory we should be able to plot a position circle on a chart with the GP as the centre and the zenith distance the radius (converted into nautical miles). This idea is just not feasible, as the distances involved are too great (see Fig 7:8).

An alternative method is studied in the next unit.

SUMMARY

a) *Sextant altitude (SA)*
   Index error (on –) (off+)
   Dip (always subtract)

   Apparent altitude (AA)
   Total correction

   True altitude (TA)

b) Zenith distance = 90°– true altitude (TA).
c) Zenith distance (converted into nautical miles) = geographical distance.
d) Geographical distance = radius of a position circle with the geographical position (GP) as the centre.

Now do the exercise on page 67.

$\boxed{X}$ **Wrong answer.**

You subtracted the index error instead of adding it. Here's the working:

SA	38°	34´.1
IE		+1´.9
dip		−3´.2
AA	38°	32´.8
corrⁿ		+15´.0
TA	38°	47´.8

After you have fine-tuned the micrometer screw to take out the 'step' effect in the true and reflected horizons the error will read either 'on' or 'off' the scale. (See Fig 7:9 below.)

Fig 7:9

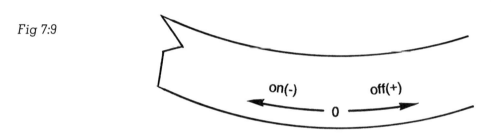

on(-)   off(+)

Look at another example: *In Fig 7.10 below a sextant arc shows the index error IE as 1´ on the arc. Clearly, any reading on this sextant will be in excess by 1´. Therefore 1´ must be subtracted to take out this IE. After studying Fig 7:10 complete the example below. (The answer is upside-down at the foot of the page.)*

Fig 7:10

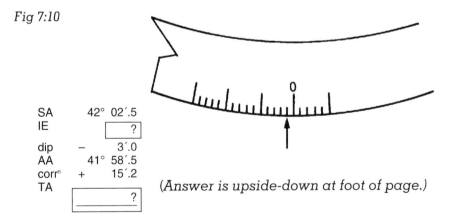

SA	42°	02´.5
IE		?
dip	−	3´.0
AA	41°	58´.5
corrⁿ	+	15´.2
TA		?

(Answer is upside-down at foot of page.)

Turn back to page 65 and carry on following the programme.

Answer: IE 1´.0 on the arc (therefore subtract) TA = 42° 13´.7

EXERCISE FOR UNIT 7 (Use the table in Fig 7:11 where appropriate.)

1   What is sextant altitude (SA)?

2   How can we check out the index error (IE)?

3   If the height of eye is 2.7m what is the angle of dip?

4   Define apparent altitude (AA).

5   On 14 Feb a sextant altitude (SA) of the sun's lower limb (LL) was 43° 24'.5. Index error (IE) was 1'.7 off the arc. Height of eye was 2.8m. What was the apparent altitude (AA)?

6   What is meant by true altitude (TA)?

7   On 12 Apr a skipper took a sight of the sun's lower limb (LL) and obtained a sextant altitude of 42° 43'.8. IE 1'.5 off the arc. Height of eye was 2.5m. What was the true altitude (TA)?

8   What is zenith distance? Explain in detail how you would find it.

9   On 24 Feb a sextant altitude of the sun's LL was 45° 55'.2. IE–1'.0 (on the arc). Height of eye 3.0m.

   a) What was the true altitude (TA)?

   b) What was the zenith distance?

10 What is an angular distance of 36° 44'.5 expressed as nautical miles?

Fig 7:11

ALTITUDE CORRECTION TABLES 10°–90° – SUN, STARS, PLANETS
(from the Almanac).

OCT.–MAR.	SUN	APR.–SEPT.		STARS AND PLANETS			DIP		
App. Alt.	Lower Limb	Upper Limb	App. Alt.	Lower Limb	Upper Limb	App. Alt.	Corrⁿ	App. Alt.	Additional Corrⁿ	Ht. of Eye	Corrⁿ	Ht. of Eye	Ht. of Eye	Corrⁿ

OCT.–MAR. SUN		APR.–SEPT.		STARS AND PLANETS		DIP		
App. Alt. / Lower Limb Upper Limb	App. Alt. / Lower Limb Upper Limb	App. Alt. / Corrⁿ	App. Additional Alt. Corrⁿ	Ht. of Eye / Corrⁿ	Ht. of Eye	Ht. of Eye / Corrⁿ		
9 34 +10·8 −21·5	9 39 +10·6 −21·2	9 56 −5·3	**1991**	m 2·4 −2·8	ft. 8·0	m 1·0− 1·8		
9 45 +10·9 −21·4	9 51 +10·7 −21·1	10 08 −5·2	**VENUS**	2·6 −2·9	8·6	1·5− 2·2		
9 56 +11·0 −21·3	10 03 +10·8 −21·0	10 20 −5·1		2·8 −3·0	9·2	2·0− 2·5		
10 08 +11·1 −21·2	10 15 +10·9 −20·9	10 33 −5·0	Jan. 1–May 10 Dec. 12–Dec. 31	3·0 −3·1	9·8	2·5− 2·8		
10 21	10 27	10 46		3·7	10·5	3·0− 3·0		
41 08 +15·1 −17·2	42 31 +14·9 −16·9	45 36 −1·0	Feb. 5–Dec. 31	16·5 −7·1	54·3	110 −10·2		
43 59 +15·2 −17·1	45 31 +15·0 −16·8	48 47 −0·9	°	16·9 −7·2	55·8	115 −10·4		
47 10 +15·3 17·0	45 31 +15·1 −16·7	52 18 −0·8	60 + 0·1	17·4 −7·3	57·4	120 −10·6		
50 46 +15·4 −16·9	48 55 +15·2 −16·6	56 11 −0·7		17·9 −7·4	58·9	125 −10·8		
54 49 +15·5 −16·8	52 44 +15·3 −16·5	60 28 −0·6		18·4 −7·5	60·5			
59 23 +15·6 −16·7	57 02 +15·4 −16·4	65 08 −0·5		18·8 −7·6	62·1	130 −11·1		
64 30 +15·7 −16·6	61 51 +15·5 −16·3	70 11 −0·4		19·3 −7·7	63·8	135 −11·3		
70 12 +15·8 16·5	67 17 +15·6 −16·2	75 34 −0·3		19·8 −7·8	65·4	140 −11·5		
76 26 +15·9 16·4	73 16 +15·7 −16·1	81 13 −0·2		20·4 −7·9	67·1	145 −11·7		
83 05 +16·0 −16·3	79 43 +15·8 −16·0	87 03 −0·1		20·9 −8·0	68·8	150 −11·9		
90 00 +16·1 −16·2	86 32 +15·9 −15·9	90 00 0·0		21·4 −8·1	70·5	155 −12·1		
	90 00							

App. Alt. = Apparent altitude = Sextant altitude corrected for index error and dip.

Answers on the next page.

ANSWERS TO EXERCISE FOR UNIT 7

1   Sextant altitude is the angular distance, measured vertically with a sextant, from a heavenly body to a horizon.

2   Index error can be checked by comparing true and reflected images of the horizon. A step between the images when the index is set at 0° indicates error, which can be found by adjusting out the step with the micrometer screw. The error will read either 'on' or 'off' the arc.

3   Dip is 2′.9.

4   Apparent altitude = sextant altitude corrected for index error and dip.

5 | | | | |
    |---|---|---|---|
    | SA sun's LL | 43° | 24′.5 | |
    | IE | + | 1′.7 | |
    | Dip | − | 2′.9 | |
    | AA | 43° | 23′.3 | |

6   True altitude is the actual altitude of a celestial body above the celestial horizon.

7 | | | | |
    |---|---|---|---|
    | SA sun's LL | 42° | 43′.8 | |
    | IE | + | 1′.5 | |
    | Dip | − | 2′.8 | |
    | AA | 42° | 42′.5 | |
    | Corrⁿ | + | 15′.0 | |
    | TA | 42° | 57′.5 | |

8   True zenith distance is the angular distance from the observer's zenith to a heavenly body. Having found true altitude the true zenith distance can be found by subtracting true altitude from 90° (ie true zenith distance = 90° − TA).

9 | | | | |
    |---|---|---|---|
    | SA | 45° | 55′.2 | |
    | IE | − | 1′.0 | |
    | Dip | − | 3′.0 | |
    | AA | 45° | 51′.2 | |
    | Corrⁿ | + | 15′.3 | |
    | TA | 46° | 06′.5 | |

Zenith distance = 90° − 46° 06′.5
Zenith distance = 43° 53′.5

10 1 minute = 1 nautical mile.

36° = 2160.0 nm (36° × 60′)

36° 44′.5 = 2204.5 nm (2160.0nm + 44.5nm)

TEST PIECE B

Time for another test piece. Now you can see how well you've understood the programme so far.

1 What is the distinction between declination and latitude?
2 Convert 49° 23′ into time (use Conversion of Arc to Time tables in Appendix A).
3 Compare GHA with longitude. How do they differ?
4 In this diagram, Fig 7:12, which hour angle is featured, GHA or LHA?

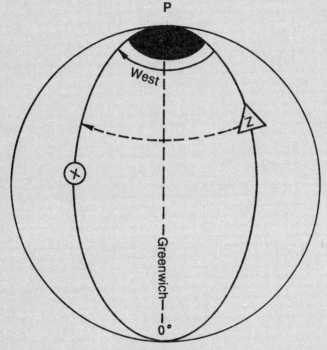

Fig 7:12

5 On 25 Dec a chronometer which loses 2 seconds daily was 2m 08s slow. On 31 Dec the time on the same chronometer was 12h 38m 04s. What was the correct GMT on 31 Dec?
6 Sloop *Sea Raven* is on passage from England to the Caribbean and sails from zone +5 into zone +6. Does the ship's clock have to be advanced or retarded one hour to keep zone time?
7 On 4 May yacht *Little Nell* is on passage in position lat 34° 32′.9N, long 07° 21′.5W. What is the LHA and dec of the sun at 11h 34m 47s GMT? (Use Appendix B (daily pages), and Appendix C (Increments and Corrections).

The answers are overleaf.

ANSWERS TO TEST PIECE B

1   Declination is one of the co-ordinates used in defining a celestial position. Latitude is one of the co-ordinates used in defining a position on Earth. Both are similar insofar as they are both measured as angular distance from an equator through 90° north or south.

2   49° 23′ converted into time is 3 hours 17 minutes 32 seconds.

3   Greenwich Hour Angle (GHA) is angular distance measured from the Prime Meridian at Greenwich, through *360° westwards* along a parallel of declination, between the celestial meridians of Greenwich and the heavenly body.

   Longitude is angular distance measured through *180° east or west* from Greenwich between the meridians of Greenwich and the observer.

4   LHA is featured in the diagram, and not GHA. LHA is angular distance measured from the observer's celestial meridian through 360° westwards along a parallel of declination between the celestial meridians of the observer's zenith (Z) and the heavenly body (X).

5
Daily loss	2 secs
Total loss over 6 days	12 secs
Error on 25 Dec	2m 08 secs *slow*
Error on 31 Dec	2m 20 secs *slow*

	h	m	s
Time on 31 Dec		12	38 04
Error 31 Dec	+		02 20
Correct time		12	40 24 GMT

6   When travelling west always *retard* the ship's clock by one hour when crossing zones.

7
GHA sun 11h		345° 48′.2	Dec	N15° 53′.4 d 0′.7 (increasing)
Increment 34m 47s	+	8° 41′.8	d corrⁿ +	0′.4
			Dec	N15° 53′.8

GHA sun 11h 34m 47s GMT	354° 30′.0
Long west	− 7° 21′.5
LHA sun 11h 34m 47s GMT	347° 08′.5

This test piece should have given you few problems. All answers correct is excellent. Less than 5 is less than average. In particular ensure that you understand the procedure for getting the final question, number 7, correct.

Distance and Bearing

Mathematicians go mad, and cashiers;
but creative artists very seldom.

G K Chesterton *Orthodoxy* (1908)

So how do you overcome the problem of not being able to plot these great earth distances directly on to a chart?

By using a smaller, usable distance which is called the *intercept*. You can find the intercept by calculating another zenith distance and then comparing it with the true zenith distance *(that's the one you find with the help of your sextant, remember?)*

By comparing the two zenith distances, true and calculated, you will find that they don't match; there is usually just a small difference. This is the intercept, simply the difference between two position circles, assumed and observed (see Fig 8:1).

Fig 8:1 Calculated and true zenith distances.

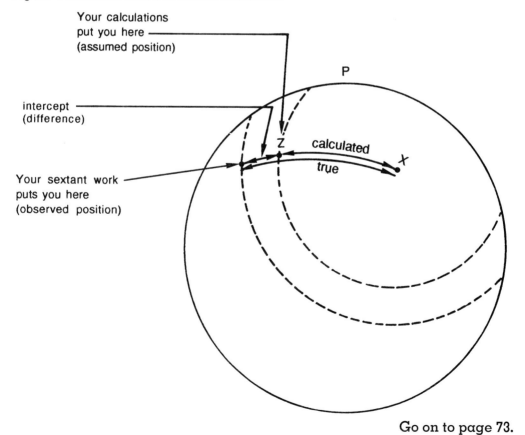

Go on to page 73.

Fig 8:2(a) Intercept TOWARDS.

True altitude (TA) greater than calculated altitude (Hc)

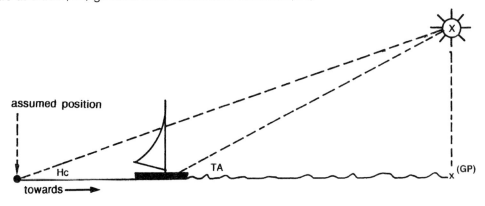

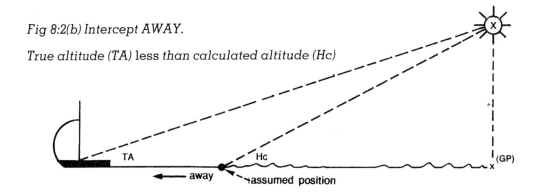

Fig 8:2(b) Intercept AWAY.

True altitude (TA) less than calculated altitude (Hc)

MEASURING THE INTERCEPT

To measure the intercept, merely compare the calculated and true zenith distances; subtract the smaller from the larger. The difference will be in angular measurement which, when converted, will give you the intercept in nautical miles.

Example:

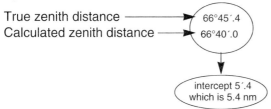

True zenith distance ⟶ 66°45′.4
Calculated zenith distance ⟶ 66°40′.0

intercept 5′.4 which is 5.4 nm

However, instead of using zenith distances there is an alternative way of finding the intercept, and that is by comparing altitudes. You compare the true altitude (TA) with the calculated altitude (Hc).

Example:

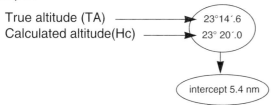

True altitude (TA) ⟶ 23°14′.6
Calculated altitude(Hc) ⟶ 23° 20′.0

intercept 5.4 nm

This is the method we shall use because it enables us to use sight reduction tables which are more user-friendly than complicated mathematics.

The intercept is named either *Towards* or *Away*.

Imagine that you are in your assumed position. If, to reach your observed position, you have to move towards the heavenly body the intercept is named 'towards'. The converse is true. We can sum it up thus:

True altitude (TA) > calculated altitude (Hc) = intercept *Towards*
True altitude (TA) < calculated altitude (Hc) = intercept *Away*

(Study Figs 8:2(a) and (b) opposite.)

> *The true altitude (TA) is 34° 04′.6 and the calculated altitude (Hc) is 33° 59′.4. What is the intercept? (Remember to state whether it is Towards or Away.)*

Next go on to page 75.

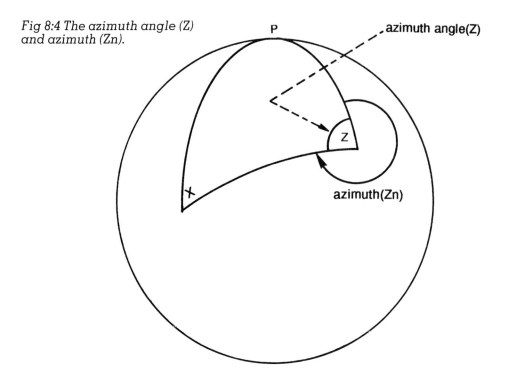

Fig 8:4 The azimuth angle (Z) and azimuth (Zn).

In this example the azimuth $(Zn) = 360° -$ azimuth angle (Z).

The azimuth (Zn) is calculated according to whether the LHA is less or more than $180°$ and whether you are in the northern or southern hemisphere. The rules governing this selection are given in the sight reduction tables; you'll use them in the next unit.

The intercept is 5′.2 Towards.

The intercept is a small usable distance which can be plotted on a chart from our assumed position. But we also need to know the direction in which to plot it; we need a bearing, in fact.

We could consider using a compass to get a bearing, as we do in coastal navigation. (See Fig 8:3 below.)

Fig 8:3 Bearing.

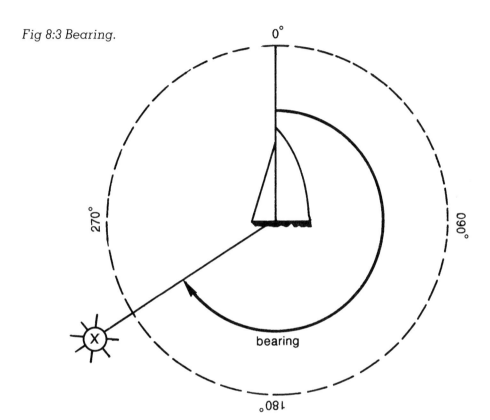

A compass bearing of celestial bodies is not considered sufficiently accurate so we have to find an alternative, more precise, method.

We use a celestial bearing called an *azimuth* and it is directly related to the angle at Z, called the *azimuth angle*, one of the three angles of the PZX triangle. (See Fig 8:4 opposite.)

However for plotting we require an azimuth which is measured, as in coastal navigation, eastwards through 360° from north. And the azimuth angle (Z), with a few rules applied, gives us the azimuth (Zn).

Unlike a compass bearing, an azimuth is free of all magnetic influences.

Read the next page, overleaf.

SUMMARY

a) The true altitude (TA) is compared with the calculated altitude (Hc) to find the intercept.

b) True altitude (TA) > calculated altitude (Hc) = intercept Toward.

c) True altitude (TA) < calculated altitude (Hc) = intercept Away.

d) Azimuth angle (Z) is the angle PZX of the spherical triangle.

e) An azimuth (Zn) is a bearing of a celestial body.

f) The azimuth angle (Z) is used to obtain the azimuth (Zn).

We know that we need an intercept and azimuth in order to begin our position plotting. In the next unit we shall learn how to obtain them.

Now do the exercise on the next page.

EXERCISE FOR UNIT 8 (Before starting this exercise cover up the previous page, 76)

1 What is the intercept?
2 In this diagram is the intercept Towards or Away?

Fig 8:5

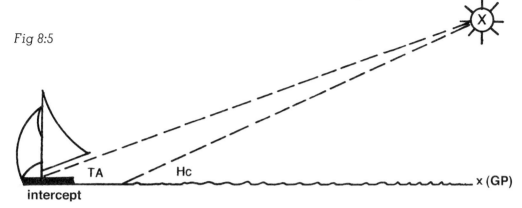

intercept

3

True altitude (TA)	Calculated altitude (Hc)	Intercept (T or A)
35° 36′.9	35° 38′.8	?
28° 59′.2	29° 01′.2	?
39° 03′.4	38° 58′.9	?
46° 12′.7	46° 06′.0	?
22° 56′.9	23° 00′.4	?

4 Define azimuth (Zn).
5 What is the azimuth angle (Z)?
6 Is Zn affected by magnetic influences?

Answers overleaf.

ANSWERS TO EXERCISE FOR UNIT 8

1 The intercept is the angular distance between the true and calculated altitudes. In simpler terms it is the difference in distance between our assumed and observed positions.

2 The intercept is *Away*.

3

True altitude (TA)	Calculated altitude (Hc)	Intercept (T or A)
35° 36′.9	35° 38′.8	1.9 nm away
28° 59′.2	29 01′.2	2 nm away
39° 03′.4	38° 58′.9	4.5 nm towards
46° 12′.7	46° 06′.0	6.7 nm towards
22° 56′.9	23° 00′.4	3.5 nm away

4 The azimuth is a bearing of a heavenly body.

5 The azimuth angle (Z) is the angle Z in the PZX triangle. From this the azimuth (Zn) can be found.

6 Unlike a compass bearing the azimuth (Zn) is a true bearing, and as such not affected by any magnetic influences.

You should have had no problems with these questions. If you got any incorrect read through this very short unit once more.

Get it Together

> Do we have all we need for navigation, and the ability to use it with
> confidence when, for weeks on end, our only trustworthy guides will be
> the sun, moon and stars?
>
> Eric Hiscock *Introduction, The Atlantic Crossing Guide*

Sight reduction tables, of varying length and accuracy, offer a quick, easy
method of solving the PZX triangle.

The particular tables we use are the Sight Reduction Tables For Air
Navigation, which were designed for aviation use but are excellent tables
for mariners. They are published in the USA as Pub no. 249 (usually
referred to as HO249) and in the UK as AP3270. There are three volumes
(See Fig 9:1). Volume 1 deals with certain stars and it is used for an epoch
of about 5 years and then has to be renewed. However,we are primarily
concerned with sun sights and will be dealing with volumes 2 and 3 which
are good for all time. The tables are accurate to the nearest mile.

Fig 9:1

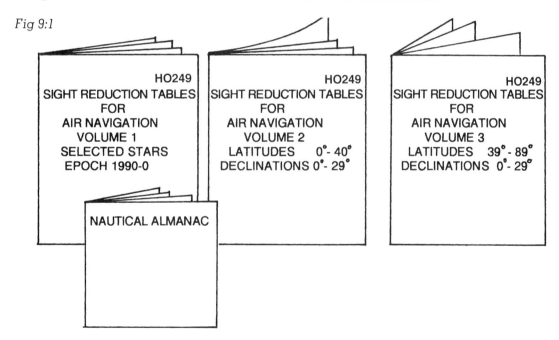

HO249 and the Nautical Almanac are our essential library for celestial
navigation. There are suitable alternatives to HO249. For example in the
USA, tables HO229 are available (these are published in Britain as NP401).

Go to page 81.

Complete the following (keep the assumed position close to the DR position). The answers are given at the foot of the page.

Example 1: DR pos lat 31° 28´.7N, long 131° 45´.2W   *GHA 189° 00´.0*

GHA	189° 00´.0
Assumed longitude (W) –	[?]
LHA	57° 00´.0

Assumed position.	lat	?	long	?

Example 2: DR pos lat 65° 14´.9S, long 25° 21´.8W   *GHA 159° 15´.8*

GHA	159° 15´.8
Assumed long (W) –	[?]
LHA	134° 00´.0

Assumed position.	lat	?	long	?

Example 3: DR pos lat 41° 39´.2N, long 128° 31´.9E   *GHA 301° 12´.2*

GHA	301° 12´.2
Assumed long (E) +	[?]
	−360° 00´.0
LHA	70° 00´.0

Assumed position.	lat	?	long	?

Answers. Ex 1   ass pos lat 31° 00´.0N   long 132° 00´.0W
Ex 2   ass pos lat 65° 00´.0S   long 25° 15´.8W
Ex 3   ass pos lat 42° 00´.0N   long 128° 47´.8E

HO249 are entered with Local Hour Angle (LHA), latitude (LAT) and declination (DEC).

In order to keep these tables reasonably small the LHA and the LAT are tabulated in *whole degrees*. Because of this we cannot use our DR position as it is. It has to be modified to an assumed position which should:

- be kept as close as possible to the DR;

- give the assumed latitude (LAT) in whole degrees;

- alter the assumed longitude so that the LHA is in whole degrees.

Example: Suppose we want an assumed position based on a DR position of lat 43° 14´.7 N, long 78° 34´.6W and the sun's GHA is 234° 43´.6.

The DR lat has to be rounded off to the nearest whole number to get the assumed latitude. And the longitude has to be altered to make the LHA a whole number as follows:

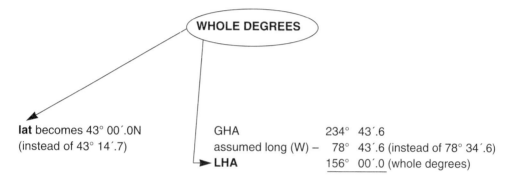

lat becomes 43° 00´.0N
(instead of 43° 14´.7)

GHA	234° 43´.6
assumed long (W) −	78° 43´.6 (instead of 78° 34´.6)
LHA	156° 00´.0 (whole degrees)

Assumed position: lat 43° 00´.0N long 78° 43´.6W

Opposite are three problems for you to solve. They are all concerned with the assumed position.

After you have worked through them turn to page 83.

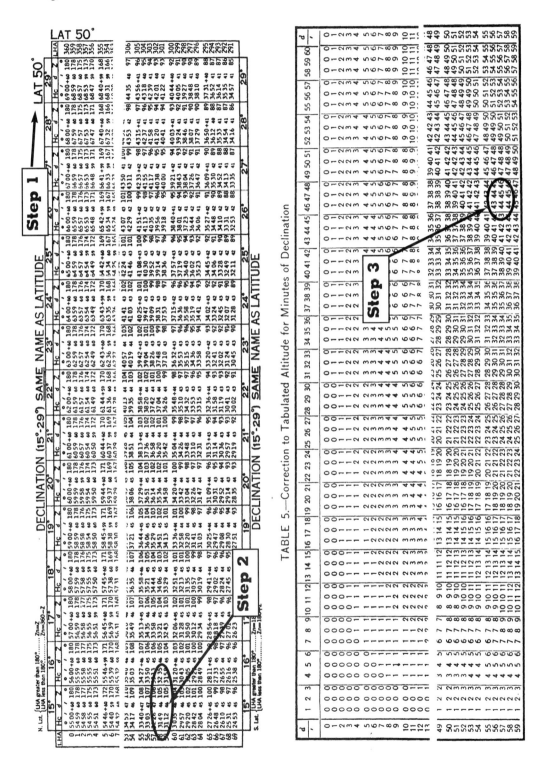

Fig 9:2 Sight Reduction Tables for Air Navigation. Vol 3 (from HO249)

Fig 9:3 Sight Reduction Tables for Air Navigation Vols 2 and 3 (from HO249).

TABLE 5.—Correction to Tabulated Altitude for Minutes of Declination

Here is an example of the use of the tables to find the intercept and azimuth. Follow the working carefully, step by step. Give yourself plenty of time.

4 May at 16h 33m 01s GMT ketch Solace *is in the North Atlantic bound for southern Ireland. DR position lat 49° 47´.3N, long 10° 30´. 2W. The true altitude of the sun's LL was 32° 01´.0. The GHA sun was 69° 03´.8. Dec N 15° 57´.4. What was the intercept and azimuth?*

As before, find the assumed position and LHA:

GHA	69° 03´.8	
Assumed long W –	10° 03´.8	
LHA	59° 00´.0	ass. pos. lat 50° 00´.0N long 10° 03´.8W

Select the volume of HO249 which accommodates our assumed LAT 50° and DEC 15°. Vol. 3 is what we want (latitudes 39°–89°; Decs 0°–29°). (Refer to Fig 9:2 opposite.)

Step 1 In the tables turn to page 'LAT 50', our assumed latitude. There's a choice of two pages, one headed '*SAME* NAME AS LATITUDE', the other '*CONTRARY* NAME TO LATITUDE'. If LAT and DEC are both north (or both south) refer to the '*SAME* NAME' page. Your LAT and DEC are both north therefore you want the *SAME* NAME page. (Ref Fig 9:2.)

Step 2 With Dec 15° and LHA 59° look at the tables, Fig 9:2, to get:

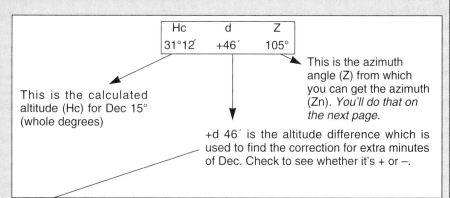

Hc	d	Z
31°12´	+46´	105°

This is the calculated altitude (Hc) for Dec 15° (whole degrees)

This is the azimuth angle (Z) from which you can get the azimuth (Zn). *You'll do that on the next page.*

+d 46´ is the altitude difference which is used to find the correction for extra minutes of Dec. Check to see whether it's + or –.

Step 3 With 'd' + 46´ and the nearest minute of Dec 57´ *(ignore seconds)* enter Table 5 Correction to Tabulated Altitude for Minutes of Declination (Fig 9:3). Read 'd' (+46´) along the top of the table and minutes of Dec (57´) vertically. Apply the correction (+44´) and find the calculated altitude (Hc) and the intercept as follows:

Calculated altitude (Hc)		31° 12´.0	
corrⁿ d +46´ (for Dec 57´)	+	44´.0	
Calc. altitude (Hc)		31° 56´.0	
True altitude (TA)		32° 01´.0	intercept 5 nm Towards

Read on at page 85.

Fig 9:5 Sight sheet. (You may want to make copies of this format or devise your own.)

	sight			sight			sight		
Date									
Course/speed	°			°			°		
DR lat	°	'		°	'		°	'	
DR long	°	'		°	'		°	'	
Ht of Eye									
Body									
Approx bearing	°			°			°		
Deck watch time	:	:		:	:		:	:	
corr^n +/−	:	:		:	:		:	:	
GMT	:	:		:	:		:	:	
Greenwich date									
GHA	°	'		°	'		°	'	
GHA incr	°	'		°	'		°	'	
360 +/−	°	'		°	'		°	'	
GHA	°	'		°	'		°	'	
Ass long W− E+	°	'		°	'		°	'	
LHA	°	'		°	'		°	'	
DEC	°	'	d	°	'	d	°	'	d
'd' corr^n +/−	°	'		°	'		°	'	
DEC	°	'		°	'		°	'	
Ass lat (same/contr)	°	'		°	'		°	'	
Hc (tabulated alt)	°	' d 'Z °		°	' d 'Z °		°	' d 'Z °	
corr for d +/−	°	'		°	'		°	'	
Hc (calc alt)	°	'		°	'		°	'	
SA (sextant alt)	°	'		°	'		°	'	
I E + /−	°	'		°	'		°	'	
DIP (always −)		'			'			'	
AA (app alt)	°	'		°	'		°	'	
corr^n	°	'		°	'		°	'	
TA (true alt)	°	'		°	'		°	'	
Hc (calc alt)	°	'		°	'		°	'	
Intercept (T or A)									
Zn (azimuth)	°			°			°		
Observed pos	Lat ° Long °								

84

The rules for changing the azimuth angle (Z) to the azimuth (Zn), printed at the top (N lat) and bottom (S lat) left of the tables, are clearly explained. (See Fig 9:4 below.)

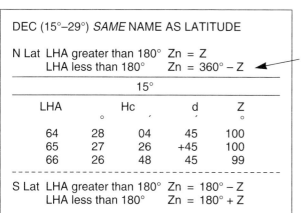

DEC (15°–29°) *SAME* NAME AS LATITUDE

| N Lat | LHA greater than 180° | Zn = Z |
| | LHA less than 180° | Zn = 360° – Z |

15°

LHA	Hc		d	Z
	°	′	′	°
64	28	04	45	100
65	27	26	+45	100
66	26	48	45	99

| S Lat | LHA greater than 180° | Zn = 180° – Z |
| | LHA less than 180° | Zn = 180° + Z |

Fig 9:4 From HO249 Vol. 3. LAT 50°.

Example: In N lat and with LHA 66° and Z 99° apply the rule LHA less than 180° Zn = 360°– Z (360° – 99° = 261°)

We're getting encumbered with increasing amounts of data; it's time to organize our information more efficiently. Opposite (Fig 9:5) is a sight sheet which keeps everything tidy and concise. It also helps to clarify the procedures, step by step. Make a copy of it and use it to solve the following problem.

On 4 May at 17h 34m 07s GMT (corrected time) the Schooner Valeda *was on passage bound for Portsmouth, England. DR pos lat 49° 38′N, long 19° 32′.2W. A sight was taken of the sun's LL and the sextant altitude (SA), when corrected, gave a true altitude (TA) of 28° 05′.6. The GHA of the sun was 84° 20′.4. The Dec was N15° 58′.1.*

What was the intercept and azimuth?

Intercept 5′.4 Towards.   Azimuth (Zn) 65° . . . . **turn to page 86**

Intercept 4′.4 Away   Azimuth (Zn) 260° . . . . **turn to page 87**

You already have the GHA, Dec and the TA. What you have to do is:

• find the assumed position

• find the LHA

• compare TA and Hc to get the intercept

• work out the azimuth (Zn) from the azimuth angle (Z). The rule for doing this is at the top and bottom left of HO249.
  (Use extracts from HO249, Figs 9:4 above and 9:6 below.)

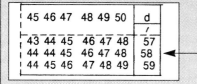

45	46	47	48	49	50	d
						′
43	44	45	46	47	48	57
44	44	45	46	47	48	58
44	45	46	47	48	49	59

Fig 9:6 From HO249 Correction to Tabulated Altitude for Minutes of Declination

enter with 'd' and nearest minute of Dec (ignore secs)

- a simple arithmetical error which amounted to one minute (mile)
- the wrong direction of the intercept; it was Away, not Towards (TA < Hc)
- and the third mistake was concerned with the azimuth (Zn). The azimuth angle (Z) should have been subtracted from 360° because the LHA of 65° was less than 180°. In this instance the rule is, N Lat [LHA less than 180° ... Zn = 360°–Z].

Remember that the rules governing Z in relation to Zn are conveniently printed at the top and bottom left of the tables so you don't need to memorize them.

Here is the detailed answer:

Fig 9:7 Sight sheet

	sight
Date	MAY 4
Course/speed	°
DR lat	49 ° 38 ' 0N
DR long	19 ° 32 ' 2 W
Ht of Eye	
Body	SUN'S LL
Approx bearing	°
Deck watch time	: :
corrⁿ +/-	: :
GMT	17 : 34 : 07
Greenwich date	
GHA	° '
GHA incr	° '
360 +/-	° '
GHA	84 ° 20 ' 4
Ass long (W-) E+	19 ° 20 ' 4
LHA	65 ° '
DEC	° '
'd' corrⁿ +/-	° '
DEC	N15 ° 58 ' 1
Ass lat (same) contr	50 ° N '
Hc (tabulated alt)	27 ° 26 ' · d₊45 ' Z100°
corrⁿ for d +/-	° 44 '
Hc (calc alt)	28 ° 10 '
SA (sextant alt)	° '
I E + /-	° '
DIP (always -)	'
AA (app alt)	° '
corrⁿ	° '
TA (true alt)	28 ° 05 ' 6
Hc (calc alt)	28 ° 10 '
Intercept T or A	4·4 A
Zn (azimuth)	260 ° T
Observed pos	Lat ° ' Long °

Read the summary on the next page.

 **Well done .**

Now read the summary and then do the Exercise for Unit 9.

SUMMARY

a) Sight Reduction Tables HO249 are a quick way of solving the PZX triangle.

b) The DR position has to be modified to an assumed position so that the tables can be entered with the LAT and LHA as whole degrees.

c) The tables are entered with LAT, LHA and DEC.

d) The purpose of using the tables is to find the calculated altitude (Hc) and azimuth.

e) The calculated altitude (Hc) is compared with the true altitude (TA) to get the intercept.

EXERCISE FOR UNIT 9 (use extracts from the Almanac and HO249 in the Appendices).

Cover the summary above.

1   Sight reduction tables are entered with $\boxed{\text{LAT}}$ $\boxed{\text{LHA}}$ and $\boxed{?}$

2   Referring to HO249, what is meant by 'DECLINATION <u>CONTRARY</u> NAME TO LATITUDE'?

3   Where do we look for the formula to translate azimuth angle (Z) to azimuth (Zn)?

4   *(This is a complete sight; all you are given is base data)*

On 4 May at 18h 34m 12s deck watch time, the aux. yacht *Maple Beaver* is on passage off Newfoundland in DR position lat 44° 25′.2N, long 47° 39′.5W. Course 090° T. Speed 6.5 knots. Log 110 nm. A sight is taken of the sun's lower limb (LL) and a sextant altitude of 37° 51′.4 is obtained. The chronometer error is 10s slow. Height of eye 2.8m. Index error (IE) 1′.5 on the arc (–). An approximate compass bearing of the sun is 260°.

What is the intercept and azimuth?

5   On 10 Dec at 12h 34m 19s deck watch time. on MV *Sunburst* is sailing in DR position lat 43° 49′.2N, long 30° 01′.9E. Course 112° T. Speed 5 knots. Log 097 nm. A sight is taken of the sun's LL and a sextant altitude of 12° 57′.9 is obtained. The chronometer error is 3 secs fast. Height of eye 3.4m and IE 2′ off the arc. An approximate compass bearing of the sun is 230°.

What is the intercept and azimuth?

Answers overleaf.

ANSWERS TO EXERCISE FOR UNIT 9

1 Sight reduction tables are entered with | LAT | | LHA | and | DEC |

2 'NAME' refers to north or south. Therefore 'DECLINATION <u>CONTRARY</u> NAME TO LATITUDE' means that the DEC is named differently from LAT (eg DEC north and LAT south; or DEC south and LAT north).

3 The formula for translating the azimuth angle (Z) to the azimuth (Zn) is printed at the top and bottom left of the HO249 pages.

4

	sight
Date	MAY 4
Course/speed	090° 6·5 KNOTS
DR lat	44 ° 25'·2 N
DR long	47 ° 39'·5W
Ht of Eye	2·8 metres
Body	Sun's LL
Approx bearing	260°
Deck watch time	18 :34:12
corrn ⊕-	: :10 (SLOW)
GMT	18 :34:22
Greenwich date	MAY4
GHA	90 ·48'·6
GHA incr +	8 · 35'·5
360° +-	° '
GHA	99 ·24'·1
Ass long Ⓦ E+	47 ·24'·1
LHA	52° '
DEC	N15 ·58'·4 d 0·7
'd' corrn ⊕-	° ·4
DEC	N15 ·58·8
Ass lat (same)contr	44 ·N ·
Hc (tabulated alt)	37 ·25· d+42'Z107°
corrn for d +-	·41·
Hc (calc alt)	38 ·06·
SA (sextant alt)	37 ·51'·4
I E +-	° 1'·5
DIP (always -)	2'·9
AA (app alt)	37 ·47·
corrn +	·14'·8
TA (true alt)	38 ·01'·8
Hc (calc alt)	38 ·06·
Intercept (T or A)	4'·2 A
Zn (azimuth)	253·T
Observed pos	Lat ° Long °

5

	sight
Date	DEC 10
Course/speed	112 ·T 5 KNOTS
DR lat	43 ·49'·2N
DR long	30 ·01·'9E
Ht of Eye	3·4 metres
Body	Sun's LL
Approx bearing	230·T
Deck watch time	12 :34:19
corrn +⊙	: :03 (FAST)
GMT	12 :34:16
Greenwich date	DEC 10
GHA	1·50'·6
GHA incr +	8·34·0
360° +-	° '
GHA	10 ·24'·6
Ass long W-(E+)	30 ·35'·4
LHA	41 ·00·
DEC	S22 ·53'·5 d 0'·2
'd' corrn ⊕-	° 0'·1
DEC	S22 ·53'·6
Ass lat (same contr)	44 ·N ·
Hc (tabulated alt)	14 ·04· d-52'Z141°
corrn for d +⊙	·47·
Hc (calc alt)	13 ·17·
SA (sextant alt)	12 ·57'9
I E +-	° 2·
DIP (always -)	3·2
AA (app alt)	12 ·56'·7
corrn +	·12·2
TA (true alt)	13 ·08'9
Hc (calc alt)	13 ·17·
Intercept (T or Ⓐ)	8'·1 A
Zn (azimuth)	219·T
Observed pos	Lat ° Long °

Do this unit again if you got questions 4 or 5 wrong.

Morning and noon sights had to be taken by the master and all the navigating officers separately, and the noon position was laid down on the chart by the second mate, who then passed the dividers to the master who checked that the position laid down was the correct one.

'The Silliest Thing You Ever Saw' Graham Sibly, Sea Breezes Oct 1994

(Despite all these precautions a position was plotted incorrectly and the ship in question, the Ping Suey of the Blue Funnel Fleet, later stranded on Dassen Island off Cape Town 24 June 1916.)

With an intercept and azimuth you can plot a line of position. Here's the procedure:

- Plot the assumed position (AP).
- Plot the azimuth and intercept (Towards or Away as the case may be).
- Finally plot the position circle; but earlier we discussed that this can't be done because the geographical distance is too great. Instead you draw an arc of the circle at right angles to the azimuth, at the end of the intercept, called the intercept terminal position (ITP). *In reality you draw a straight line, not an arc, and no accuracy is forfeited in so doing because of the immense distance involved. (See Fig 10:1.)*

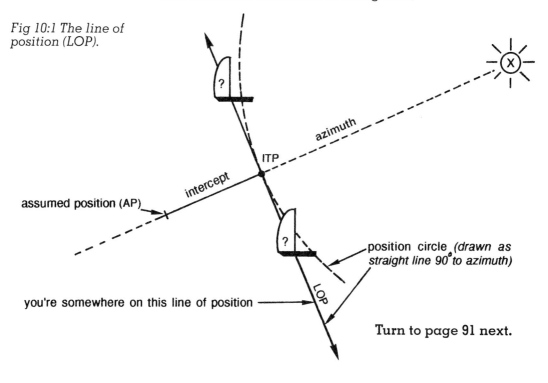

Fig 10:1 The line of position (LOP).

Turn to page 91 next.

Fig 10:2 Plotting the intercept and position line.

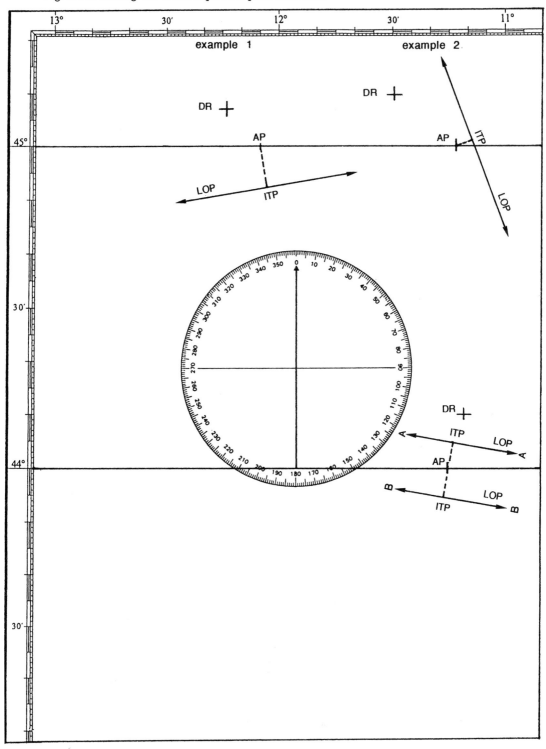

For practice only.

A standard chart, such as that used in Fig 10:2 (opposite), could be used for plotting providing it is of large enough, usable scale.

Example 1: Check this plot. You'll need dividers, parallel rule or protractor. Refer to Fig 10:2.

A vessel was in DR position lat 45° 07´.0N, long 12° 13´.8W. A sight of the sun's LL was taken and, using assumed position lat 45° 00´.0N, long 12° 05´.0W, an intercept of 7´.6 (Towards) and azimuth of 170°T was calculated.

Plot the line of position (LOP)

Example 2: A vessel was in DR position lat 45° 10´.0N, long 11° 30´.0W. A sight of the sun's LL was taken and, using assumed position lat 45° 00´.0N, long 11° 12´.5W, an intercept of 3´ (Away) and azimuth of 249°T was calculated.

Plot the line of position (LOP)

Try this exercise:

Ketch Serena *was on passage in the Atlantic bound for Northern Spain in DR position lat 44° 10´.0N, long 11° 10´.0W. Assumed position lat 44° 00´.0N, long 11° 15´.0W. A sight was taken of the sun's (LL) and an intercept of 5´(Away) and azimuth 190°T was calculated.*

Which is the correct LOP, 'A' or 'B' in Fig 10:2?

Remember the procedure:
• plot the assumed position
• along the line of azimuth plot the intercept (T or A) from the GP
• plot the line of position through the intercept terminal position (ITP) at right angles to the azimuth.

Answer on page 93.

Fig 10:3 running fix.

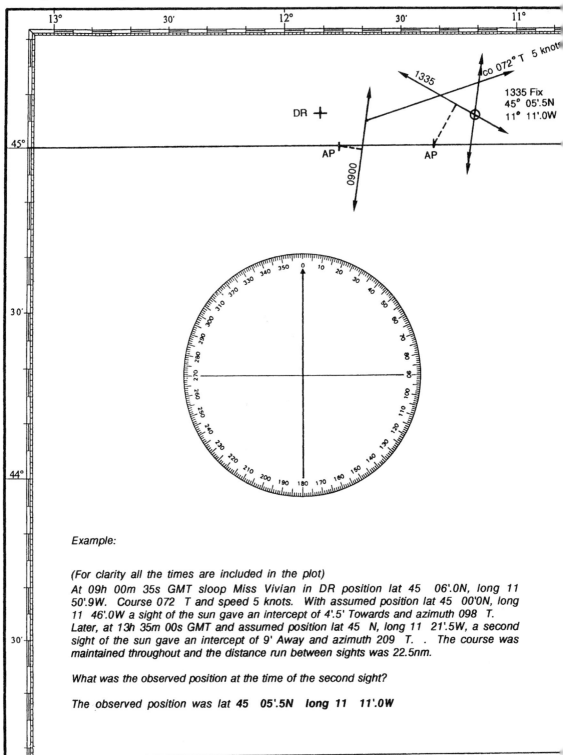

Example:

(For clarity all the times are included in the plot)

At 09h 00m 35s GMT sloop Miss Vivian in DR position lat 45 06'.0N, long 11 50'.9W. Course 072 T and speed 5 knots. With assumed position lat 45 00'0N, long 11 46'.0W a sight of the sun gave an intercept of 4'.5' Towards and azimuth 098 T. Later, at 13h 35m 00s GMT and assumed position lat 45 N, long 11 21'.5W, a second sight of the sun gave an intercept of 9' Away and azimuth 209 T. .   The course was maintained throughout and the distance run between sights was 22.5nm.

What was the observed position at the time of the second sight?

The observed position was lat 45 05'.5N long 11 11'.0W

For practice only.

Line of position 'A' is correct.

Unlike a bearing in coastal navigation where distances are quite small, an azimuth cannot be considered a line of position because the sun's GP is so far away. For this reason a single line of position is insufficient to give a precise fix; at least two are necessary.

For example, a line of position obtained from a sun sight coupled with another of a coastal feature would provide a fix.

However, since it is usual to be out of sight of land when cruising transocean a technique called the *running fix* (often used in coastal navigation) is employed during daylight hours when sun sightings are routine. This technique involves two sights of the sun with a time duration between, often referred to as 'sun-run-sun'.

Here's the procedure:

- A sight is taken and the first line of position is plotted.
- A second sight and line of position is plotted. The duration between the two lines should be sufficient to ensure an effective angle of cut; between 60° and 120° is deemed acceptable. Try to get as near to 90° as you can.
- From a point on the first line plot the course and distance run between sights, ensuring that any tidal streams, leeway, or compass and log precision is accounted for.
- Transfer the first line of position through the end of the distance
  run ◄◄─────►►
- The intersection of the transferred and second lines of position fixes the observed position.

Look carefully at the example of a running fix (opposite, Fig 10:3) and follow the procedure as outlined, step by step.

Why is an exact plot of the distance and course between sights crucial for the accuracy of the fix?

Follow on at page 95.

Fig 10:4 The plotting sheet.

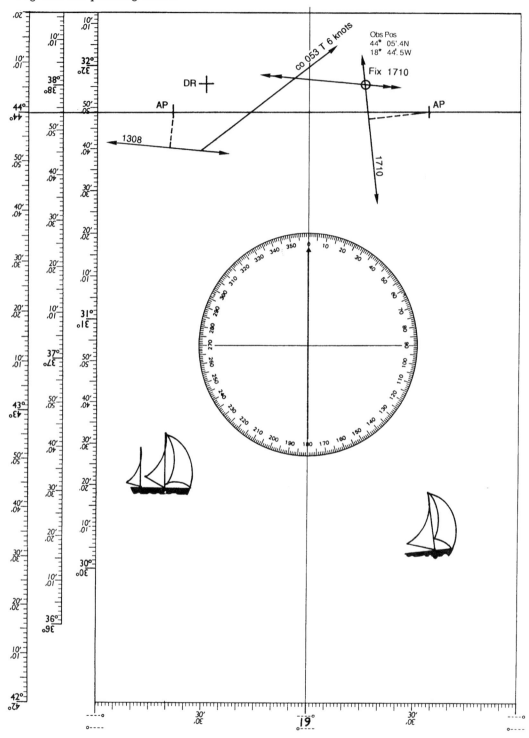

For practice only

If the course and distance is plotted inaccurately then, clearly, the final outcome, the observed position, will also be wrong. Take care to allow for such factors as tidal streams, leeway, and compass and log precision. You'll meet up with this problem in a short while, after you've been introduced to the plotting sheet.

THE PLOTTING SHEET

This is a versatile alternative to the standard chart which you can buy from a chart agent. It is a plain sheet with a selection of latitude scales and a longitude scale. Some sheets may have one or more compass roses. Being Mercator projection, it is essential to use *only the specific latitude appropriate to the area of operations*. The longitude scale is constant. The procedure is simple:

* Draw in the parallel of latitude appropriate to the area of operations (eg 44° —).

* Write in the required longitude in the space provided ($\frac{1}{o} \underline{\underline{}} \underline{\underline{}} \underline{o}$).

Then use as any standard chart. Here's another running fix example:

Example: The plot is opposite (Fig 10:4, top of chart).

At 13h 08m 10s GMT schooner Felicity *was on passage bound for the English Channel in DR position lat 44° 05´.5N, long 19° 29´.0W, course 053°T, speed 6 knots. A sight of the sun's LL is taken and, using an assumed position of lat 44° 00´.0N, long 19° 38´.4W, an intercept of 7´ Towards and azimuth of 185°T was calculated.*

Later in the day, at 17h 10m 20s GMT, assumed position lat 44° 00´.0N, long 18° 26´.1W, a second sight of the sun gave an intercept of 12´.5 Towards, and azimuth 264°T. There were no tidal streams or leeway to account for and the course and speed was maintained throughout. The distance run between sights was 24.1 nm.
What was the observed position at the time of the second sight?

The observed position at 1335 GMT was lat 44° 05´.4N, long 18° 44´.5W.

Now work this out:

> *What is the distance between the two yachts in positions lat 30° 18´.0N, long 19° 40´.0W and lat 30° 03´.0N long 18° 23´.5W?*
>
> **68 nm?** ....turn to page 96
>
> **58 nm?** ....turn to page 96

68 nm is the correct answer.

If you came up with 58 nm it is because the wrong latitude scale was chosen; latitude 42°N was used instead of 30°N.

SUMMARY

a) The intercept and azimuth are used for plotting a line of position.

b) The line of position is drawn as a straight line, representing an arc of the position circle.

c) The line of position is drawn through the intercept terminal position (ITP) at right angles to the azimuth (bearing).

d) At least two lines of position are needed for a fix. An angle of cut between 60° and 120° is acceptable. However, 90° is perfect.

e) A running fix is used in coastal and celestial navigation. It involves two sights of the same body and a transferred line of position at the end of a run.

f) Allowances must be made for factors such as tidal streams or leeway.

g) A standard chart may be used; it has to be of a large enough, usable scale.

h) An alternative is a plotting sheet.

i) On the plotting sheet draw in the parallel of latitude appropriate to the area of operation. Mark in the longitude required (⁝ ⁚ °); then use as any standard chart.

Now do the exercise on the next page.

EXERCISE FOR UNIT 10

1 What is the intercept terminal position (ITP)?

2 In the illustration below (Fig 10:5), which line of position, A or B, illustrates an intercept Towards the GP?

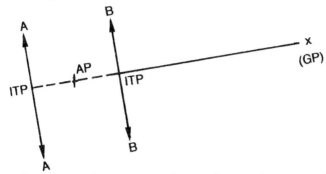

Fig 10:5

3 Why is the line of position drawn at right angles to the azimuth?

4 What is the difference between a chart and a plotting sheet?

5 Copy the blank plotting sheet in Appendix H (page 138) for the following plot.

(Note: In this question you will meet a tidal stream and this will have to be allowed for in the plot of distance run between sights.)

Plot the distance run from the first LOP and then plot the tidal factor on from that.

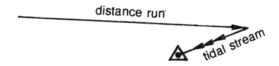

On 5 May at 10h 00m 12s GMT aux yacht Frederique *was on passage bound for Africa in DR position lat 30° 12′.8N, long 18° 56′.0W, course 103°T, speed 7.5 knots. The skipper took a morning sight of the sun's LL and, using an assumed position of lat 30° 00′.0N, long 18° 50′.0W, calculated an intercept of 5′.5 Towards and azimuth 098°T.*

At 13h 30m 02s GMT in DR position lat 30° 06′.0N, long 18° 26′.0W a second sight of the sun's LL was taken and, using assumed position lat 30° 00′.0N, long 18° 20′.0W, an intercept of 9.5′ Away and azimuth of 199°T was calculated. Between sights, a tidal stream of 1.5 knots, setting 218°T, was estimated. What was the observed position at 13h 30m 02s GMT?

Answers overleaf.

ANSWERS TO EXERCISE FOR UNIT 10

1   The intercept terminal position (ITP) is the end point of the intercept through which a line of position is plotted.

2   The line of position B illustrates an intercept Towards the GP.

3   The line of position is always drawn at right angles to the azimuth because it represents a very small portion of a very large position circle. No accuracy is lost in so doing.

4   Most charts have coastal features; a plotting sheet doesn't. Charts have a single, nominated latitude scale and a longitude scale.

Plotting sheets have a range of latitude scales (eg 30°–48°) which can be adapted to suit the area of operation. They also have a longitude scale which is marked in with the appropriate degree of longitude (eg $18°$).

5   The observed position was lat 30° 08′.3N, long 18° 14′.0W. Here's the plot. (See Fig 10:6).

From the end of the distance run which is 26.25 nm (3.5 hours × 7.5 knots) plot the tidal stream ➤➤➤ of 5.25 nm (3.5 hours × 1.5 knots). It's not necessary to draw three arrow heads; it's illustrated here for clarity only. The transferred line of position is plotted through the estimated position △

Fig 10:6 Plotting sheet.

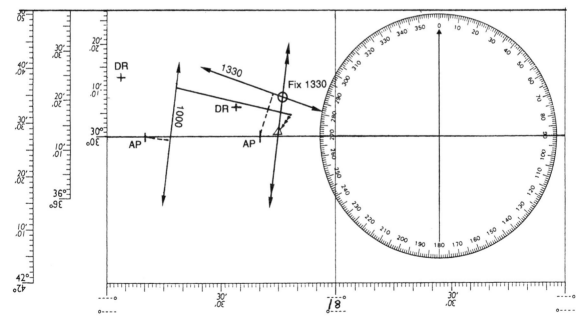

If you got question number 5 wrong, check it out again, and again, and again!

Noon Time

We have no fancy sounding gear,

No aids to navigation

A morning sight and one at noon

Give our precise location

Hugh J O'Donnell *Voyage of the 'Honorius'*, 1919–21

One of the lines of position frequently used in a running fix is when the latitude is found by meridian altitude; the traditional 'noon sight'. No precise chronometer reading is required and it's easily set up.

Wherever we are on Earth at about noon the sun climbs to its highest point in the sky as it transits (crosses) our meridian. This is called the meridian passage of the sun.

And since you, the observer, and the sun share the same meridian the LHA must be 0°.

Fig 11:1 The meridian passage of the sun.

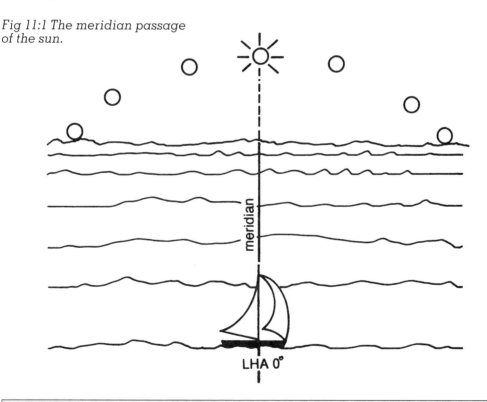

LHA 0°

How can you determine south without a compass?

Turn to page 101.

Fig 11:2 Latitude at noon.

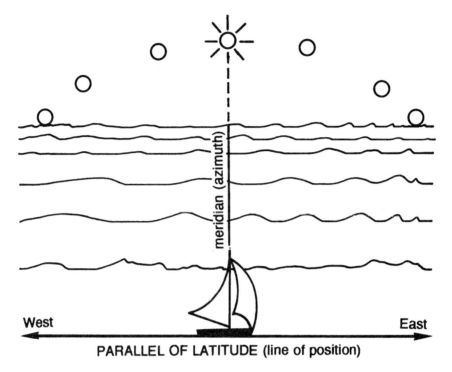

West

East

PARALLEL OF LATITUDE (line of position)

If you want to indicate south and you've no compass observe the sun crossing your meridian when it's at its highest, at noon, just before it starts its downward, westerly journey to sunset.

The bearing (azimuth) will then be exactly south or north. And if you follow your customary practice of plotting a line of position at right angles to the azimuth you will end up with a line which lies east/west.

And a line which is east/west must be a parallel of latitude. Right? (See Fig 11:2 opposite.)

The only new skill you will need to learn in order to find latitude by meridian altitude is how to find the time of the meridian passage (Mer Pass) of the sun. It's simplicity itself!

You can get this from the bottom right of the sun and moon daily pages of the Almanac, alongside the Equation of Time. (See Fig 11:3, below.)

Example: What is the time of the meridian passage of the sun on 3 June?

The answer is 11h 58m LMT.

Fig 11:3 Meridian passage (from the Almanac).

3 June

| Day | SUN | | | MOON | | | |
| | Eqn. of Time | | Mer. | Mer. Pass. | | Age | Phase |
	00 ʰ	12 ʰ	Pass.	Upper	Lower		
	ᵐ ˢ	ᵐ ˢ	ʰ ᵐ	ʰ ᵐ	ʰ ᵐ	ᵈ	
3	02 04	01 59	11 58	04 20	16 41	20	
4	01 54	01 49	11 58	05 03	17 24	21	
5	01 44	01 39	11 58	05 45	18 07	22	

> What is the time of the meridian passage of the sun on 5 June?

Refer to page 103.

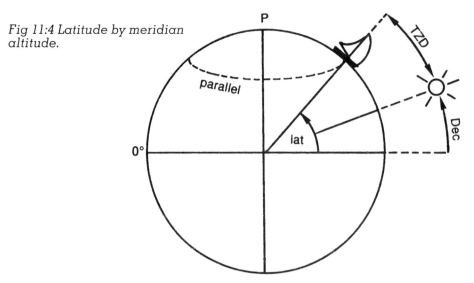

Fig 11:4 Latitude by meridian altitude.

P

parallel

0°

lat

TZD

Dec

Example: On 4 June the sloop Jem C *cruising off Vancouver Island in the Pacific North West in DR position lat 49° 10′.0N, long 129° 00′W, takes a sight of the sun's LL at the meridian passage and obtains a sextant altitude (SA) which, when corrected, gives a true altitude (TA) of 63° 27′. The declination of the sun at the time of taking the sight was N22° 27′.*

What was the latitude of the ship? The working is on the right sheet below, Fig 11:5. Use Fig 11:3 to find the sun's meridian passage. Use Appendix A to convert longitude into time.

Fig 11:5 Meridian passage sight sheet (make copies of the blank for future use).

Meridian Passage	Sun
Date	June 4
DR lat	49° 10′.0N
DR long	129° 00′.0W
LMT Mer Pass	11h 58m
long in time +W →E	8h 36m
GMT MerPass	20h 34m
Dec	°
'd' corrⁿ+ –	°
Dec	N22° 27′
SA	°
IE + / –	°
Dip (always -)	°
AA (app alt)	°
corrⁿ	°
TA (true alt)	63° 27′
ZD (90 – TA)	26° 33′
Dec (same/contr)N	22° 27
Lat	49° 00′.0N

Meridian Passage	
Date	
DR lat	°
DR long	°
LMT Mer Pass	
long in time +W –E	
GMT Mer Pass	
Dec	°
'd' corrⁿ + –	°
Dec	°
SA	°
IE + / –	°
Dip (always –)	°
AA (app alt)	°
corrⁿ	°
TA true alt)	°
ZD (90 – TA)	°
Dec (same/contr)	°
Lat	°

On 5 June the meridian passage of the sun is 1158 LMT.

Opposite is an example of a noon sight, (Fig 11:4). Please study and work through the opposite page carefully.

You can see that latitude is greater than declination and that latitude and declination both have the *same* names; in this case north. Therefore:

Latitude = true zenith distance + declination

This rule does not apply to all cases. In Fig 11:6 below it's different.

Fig 11:6 Contrary names.

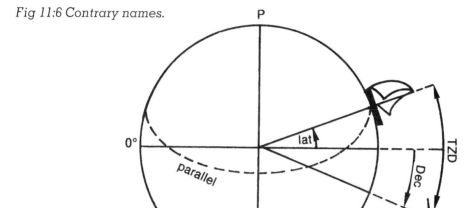

Study this illustration carefully before answering the following problem. Remember that the first thing to do is to work out the true zenith distance (90°–TA). And note that the declination and latitude are *contrary* names.

On 9 Dec, trawler yacht Pippa *on passage in the North Atlantic in DR position lat 20° 05′.6N, long 40° 15′.0W, obtained a sight of the sun's LL at the time of meridian passage. A sextant altitude (SA) was obtained which, when corrected, gave a true altitude (TA) of 47° 14′ and at the same time the declination of the body was S22° 48′.4.*

Was the latitude of the observer 65° 34′.4N?

On to page 104.

The correct answer is 19° 57′.6N.

If you came up with 65° 34′.4N, you must have added the TZD to the declination. Instead you should have found the difference between them, because latitude and declination were contrary names. Look at Fig 11:7 following where the individual angles, TZD, declination and latitude, have been illustrated.

Clearly, with latitude and declination contrary names:

Latitude = TZD – declination

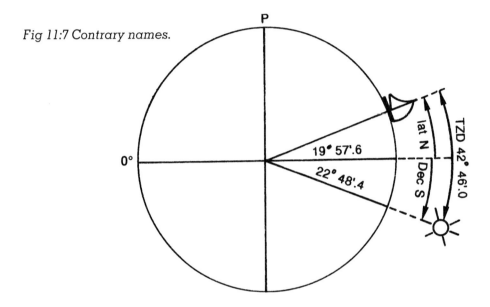

Fig 11:7 Contrary names.

SUMMARY

a) A line of position may be obtained by taking a meridian altitude sight of a heavenly body.

b) When the observer and the body is on the same meridian the LHA is 0°.

c) The azimuth of a body which is on the observer's meridian must be either north or south. The line of position, which is at right angles to the azimuth, is east/west. It is, therefore, a parallel of latitude.

d) A noon sight of the sun is a traditional way of finding latitude.

e) No precise chronometer work is required.

Do the exercise opposite.

EXERCISE FOR UNIT 11 (Use Appendices as necessary. Cover the opposite page before starting.)

1 What is meant by meridian passage?

2 What is the LMT of the sun's meridian passage on 6 May and on 11 Dec?

3 When a heavenly body is on the observer's meridian its azimuth must be either due [?] or due [?] .

4 Why is a line of position obtained from a noon sight of the sun a parallel of latitude?

5 DR position lat 45° 43′.9N, long 123° 30′.0E. What is the GMT of the meridian passage of the sun on 5 May?

6 Why is it necessary to find the GMT of the meridian passage?

In the following questions a sextant altitude (SA) only is given, which must be corrected to the true altitude (TA) before you can answer the question fully.

7 On 5 May ketch *Collie Dog* was in DR position lat 48° 59′.3N, long 129° 30′.0W. The skipper obtained a meridian altitude of the sun's LL which gave a sextant altitude of 57°17′. Index error 1′.0 off the arc (+). Height of eye 7.2m.

   What was the latitude?

8 On 11 Dec MV *Cowichan Belle* was in DR position lat 53° 05′.1N, long 04° 45′.0E. A meridian altitude of the sun's LL was obtained which gave a sextant altitude of 14° 00′.0. Index error 2′.5 on the arc. Height of eye 3.6m.

   What was the latitude?

Answers overleaf on page 106.

ANSWERS TO EXERCISE FOR UNIT 11

1 Meridian passage is when a heavenly body transits the same meridian as the observer. At that moment the LHÄ of the body is 0°.

2 6 May meridian passage of the sun is 1157 LMT.

11 Dec meridian passage of the sun is 1153 LMT.

3 When a heavenly body is on the observer's meridian its azimuth must be either due ⌐north⌐ or due ⌐south⌐.

4 A line of position is at right angles to the azimuth. If the azimuth is either 000° or 180° then a line of position must lie east/west and that is a parallel of latitude.

5 5 May

	h	m
LMT mer. pass. sun	11	57
long 123° 30′.0E in time	− 8	14
GMT mer. pass. sun	03	43

6 The GMT of the meridian passage is needed in order to find the declination.

7

Meridian Passage		
Date	MAY 5	
DR lat	48. 59′. 3N	
DR long	129. 30 ⋮ 0W	
LMT Mer Pass	11 : 57 : 00	
long in time (+W) -E	8 : 38 : 00	
GMT MerPass	20 : 35 : 00	
Dec	N16 ∘ 17 ⋮ 1	d0.7
'd' corrn (+) -	0.4	
Dec	N16 ∘ 17 ⋮ 5	
SA	57. 17 ⋮ 0	
IE (+) -	1′. 0	
Dip (always -)	4′. 7	
AA (app alt)	57. 13 ⋮ 3	
corrn +	15 .4	
TA (true alt)	57. 28′. 7	
ZD (90° - TA)	32 ∘ 31′. 3	
Dec (same) contr	N16 ∘ 17 ⋮ 5	
Lat	48. 48′. 8 N	

8

Meridian Passage		
Date	DEC 11	
DR lat	53. 05′. 1N	
DR long	4 . 45′. 0E	
LMT Mer Pass	11 : 53 : 00	
long in time +W (-E)	19 : 00	
GMT MerPass	11. 34 ⋮ 00	
Dec	S22. 58 ⋮ 6	d 0.2
'd' corrn (+) -	0. 1	
Dec	S22. 58 ⋮ 7	
SA	14. 00 ⋮ 0	
IE + (-)	2 ⋮ 5	
Dip (always -)	3 ⋮ 3	
AA (app alt)	13 . 54 ⋮ 2	
corrn +	12 ⋮ 4	
TA (true alt)	14. 06 ⋮ 6	
ZD (90° - TA)	75. 53 ⋮ 4	
Dec (same (contr)	S22. 58 ⋮ 7	
Lat	52. 54 ⋮ 7N	

Ensure that you understand the working of questions 7 and 8.

Polaris

The stars above us, govern our conditions
Shakespeare *King Lear*

This programme is concerned principally with the sun. But there is one star, which, since time immemorial, has provided sailors with a quick means of finding latitude and therefore a line of position. It's Polaris, the Pole star.

The Plough, an easily recognized constellation in the northern hemisphere, has two stars which are used as pointers to locate Polaris. (See Fig 12:1.)

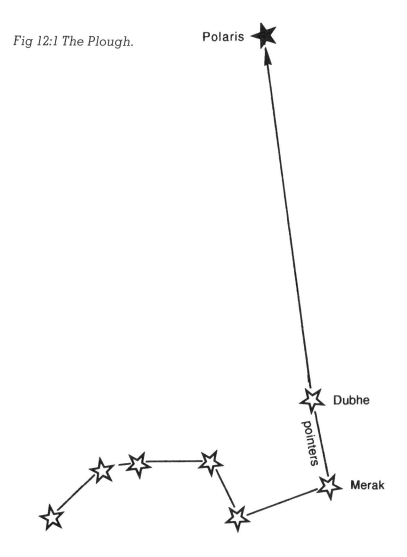

Fig 12:1 The Plough.

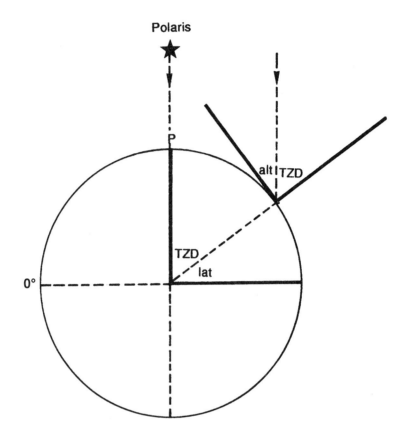

Polaris appears to lie directly over the North Pole. In reality it's extremely close, but not *exactly* in line with the Earth's axis. However, for the moment assume that it is precisely in line. (See Fig 12:2 opposite.)

In the illustration you can see two distinct right angles, with angles TZD similar.

TZD + *latitude* = 90°

TZD + *altitude* = 90°

Therefore:

Latitude = altitude.

But because Polaris is not exactly in line with the Earth's axis its declination is not 90°, it's about 89°. Polaris therefore tracks a small 1° circle around the axis. (See Fig 12:3, below.)

Fig 12:3 Polaris is circumpolar.

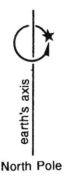

North Pole

This small difference has to be accounted for, as you will see shortly.

Try this exercise:

(Just for the moment assume that Polaris is directly over the North Pole with a declination of 90°)

A ship was cruising transatlantic in DR position lat 40° 02´.8N, long 20° 56´.9W and a sight of Polaris was obtained. The sextant altitude (SA), when corrected, gave a true altitude (TA) of 40°.

What was the latitude of the vessel?

Go on to page 111.

Fig 12:4. Polaris (Pole star) tables. From the Almanac.

POLARIS (POLE STAR) TABLES,
FOR DETERMINING LATITUDE FROM SEXTANT ALTITUDE AND FOR AZIMUTH

L.H.A. ARIES	120°–129°	130°–139°	140°–149°	150°–159°	160°–169°	170°–179°	180°–189°	190°–199°	200°–209°	210°–219°	220°–229°	230°–239°
	a_0	a_0	a_0	a_0	a_0	a_0	a_0	a_0	a_0	a_0	a_0	a_0
°	° ′	° ′	° ′	° ′	° ′	° ′	° ′	° ′	° ′	° ′	° ′	° ′
0	0 54·5	1 02·6	1 10·6	1 18·1	1 25·1	1 31·3	1 36·5	1 40·6	1 43·4	1 44·9	1 45·0	1 43·7
1	55·3	03·4	11·3	18·9	25·8	31·9	37·0	40·9	43·6	44·9	44·9	43·5
2	56·2	04·2	12·1	19·6	26·4	32·4	37·4	41·2	43·8	45·0	44·8	43·3
3	57·0	05·0	12·9	20·3	27·1	33·0	37·9	41·6	44·0	45·0	44·7	43·0
4	57·8	05·8	13·6	21·0	27·7	33·5	38·3	41·9	44·1	45·1	44·6	42·8
5	0 58·6	1 06·6	1 14·4	1 21·7	1 28·3	1 34·0	1 38·7	1 42·1	1 44·3	1 45·1	1 44·5	1 42·5
6	0 59·4	07·4	15·2	22·4	28·9	34·6	39·1	42·4	44·4	45·1	44·4	42·3
7	1 00·2	08·2	15·9	23·1	29·5	35·1	39·5	42·7	44·6	45·1	44·2	42·0
8	01·0	09·0	16·7	23·8	30·1	35·6	39·9	42·9	44·7	45·1	44·1	41·7
9	01·8	09·8	17·4	24·5	30·7	36·0	40·2	43·2	44·8	45·0	43·9	41·4
10	1 02·6	1 10·6	1 18·1	1 25·1	1 31·3	1 36·5	1 40·6	1 43·4	1 44·9	1 45·0	1 43·7	1 41·1

Lat.	a_1	a_1	a_1	a_1	a_1	a_1	a_1	a_1	a_1	a_1	a_1	a_1
°	′	′	′	′	′	′	′	′	′	′	′	′
0	0·2	0·2	0·3	0·3	0·4	0·4	0·5	0·6	0·6	0·6	0·6	0·6
10	·3	·3	·3	·4	·4	·5	·5	·6	·6	·6	·6	·6
20	·3	·3	·4	·4	·4	·5	·5	·6	·6	·6	·6	·6
30	·4	·4	·4	·5	·5	·5	·5	·6	·6	·6	·6	·6
40	0·5	0·5	0·5	0·5	0·5	0·6	0·6	0·6	0·6	0·6	0·6	0·6
45	·5	·5	·5	·6	·6	·6	·6	·6	·6	·6	·6	·6
50	·6	·6	·6	·6	·6	·6	·6	·6	·6	·6	·6	·6
55	·7	·7	·7	·7	·6	·6	·6	·6	·6	·6	·6	·6
60	·8	·8	·8	·7	·7	·7	·6	·6	·6	·6	·6	·6
62	0·8	0·8	0·8	0·8	0·7	0·7	0·7	0·6	0·6	0·6	0·6	0·6
64	·9	·9	·8	·8	·8	·7	·7	·6	·6	·6	·6	·6
66	0·9	0·9	0·9	·9	·8	·7	·7	·6	·6	·6	·6	·6
68	1·0	1·0	1·0	0·9	0·8	0·8	0·7	0·7	0·6	0·6	0·6	0·6

Month	a_2	a_2	a_2	a_2	a_2	a_2	a_2	a_2	a_2	a_2	a_2	a_2
	′	′	′	′	′	′	′	′	′	′	′	′
Jan.	0·7	0·6	0·6	0·5	0·5	0·5	0·5	0·4	0·4	0·4	0·4	0·4
Feb.	·8	·8	·7	·7	·6	·6	·5	·5	·4	·4	·4	·3
Mar.	0·9	0·9	0·9	·8	·8	·7	·7	·6	·5	·5	·4	·4·
Apr.	1·0	1·0	1·0	0·9	0·9	0·9	0·8	0·8	0·7	0·6	0·6	0·5
May	0·9	1·0	1·0	1·0	1·0	0·9	0·9	·9	·8	·8	·7	·6
June	·8	0·9	0·9	0·9	1·0	1·0	1·0	·9	·9	·9	·8	·8
July	0·7	0·7	0·8	0·8	0·9	0·9	0·9	0·9	0·9	0·9	0·9	0·9
Aug.	·5	·5	·6	·6	·7	·7	·8	·8	·8	·9	·9	·9
Sept.	·3	·4	·4	·5	·5	·6	·6	·7	·7	·8	·8	·8
Oct.	0·2	0·2	0·3	0·3	0·3	0·4	0·4	0·5	0·5	0·6	0·6	0·7
Nov.	·2	·2	·2	·2	·2	·2	·2	·3	·3	·4	·5	·5
Dec.	0·3	0·2	0·2	0·1	0·1	0·1	0·1	0·2	0·2	0·2	0·3	0·4

Lat.					AZIMUTH							
°	°	°	°	°	°	°	°	°	°	°	°	°
0	359·2	359·2	359·3	359·3	359·4	359·5	359·6	359·7	359·9	0·0	0·1	0·3
20	359·2	359·2	359·2	359·3	359·4	359·5	359·6	359·7	359·8	0·0	0·1	0·3
40	359·0	359·0	359·1	359·1	359·2	359·3	359·5	359·6	359·8	0·0	0·2	0·3
50	358·8	358·8	358·9	359·0	359·1	359·2	359·4	359·6	359·8	0·0	0·2	0·4
55	358·7	358·7	358·7	358·8	359·0	359·1	359·3	359·5	359·8	0·0	0·2	0·4
60	358·5	358·5	358·6	358·7	358·8	359·0	359·2	359·5	359·7	0·0	0·2	0·5
65	358·2	358·2	358·3	358·4	358·6	358·8	359·1	359·4	359·7	0·0	0·3	0·6

Latitude = Apparent altitude (corrected for refraction) − 1° + a_0 + a_1 + a_2

The table is entered with L.H.A. Aries to determine the column to be used; each column refers to a range of 10°. a_0 is taken, with mental interpolation, from the upper table with the units of L.H.A. Aries in degrees as argument; a_1, a_2 are taken, without interpolation, from the second and third tables with arguments latitude and month respectively. a_0, a_1, a_2 are always positive. The final table gives the azimuth of *Polaris*.

The answer is lat 40°N.

However, the small difference of 1° must be accounted for and there are special Polaris tables in the Almanac that do this. (See Fig 12:4, opposite.)

You have to take a sight of Polaris and get a sextant altitude (SA), correct it to a true altitude (TA) and then enter the tables with:

- LHA Aries ♈. (Aries because all stars' hour angles are related to a datum meridian which passes through the First Point of Aries ♈);
- the DR latitude;
- the month of operation.

Example: On 9 Dec at 07h 35m 00s GMT in DR position lat 45° 06´.8N, long 15° 45´.4W a sight was taken of Polaris. The sextant altitude (SA), when corrected, gave a true altitude (TA) of 44° 00´.0. What was the latitude?

To find LHA Aries for 07h 35m 00s GMT (Almanac daily pages; Aries, Venus etc. Appendix B).

GHA Aries 07h	182° 31´.7
Increment 35m	+ 8° 46´.4 (get this from Aries column)
GHA Aries 07h 35m 00s	191° 18´.1
DR long W(−)	−15° 45´.4
LHA Aries	175° 32´.7

Finally enter the Polaris tables.

Use formula: Latitude = TA−1° +a_0+a_1 +a_2 (This is also printed at foot of tables.)

	TA	44° 00´.0
Step 1 enter LHA Aries column 170°–179° (for 175° 32´.7 interpolate)	a_0	1° 34´.3
Step 2 enter Lat section in column 170°–179° (lat 45° approx)	a_1	0´.6
Step 3 enter Month section in column 170°–179° (December)	a_2	0´.1
Approximate altitude		45° 35´.0
Correction for 1°		− 1° 00´.0
Latitude		44° 35´.0

On 4 June at 21h 34m 33s GMT in DR position lat 41° 34´.8N, long 25° 12´.7W a sight was taken of Polaris. The sextant altitude (SA) when corrected gave a true altitude (TA) of 41° 03´.9. Use Polaris tables Fig 12:4 (opposite).

What was the latitude?

Go to page 112.

The answer is Lat 41° 46′.4N.

Here's the working:

GHA Aries 21h	207° 48′.1	from Appendix B
Increment 34m 33s (for Aries)	8° 39′.7	from Appendix C
GHA Aries 21h 34m 33s GMT	216° 27′.8	
DR long W(−)	25° 12′.7	
LHA Aries	191° 15′.1	

True altitude		TA 41° 03′.9
LHA Aries	column 190°−199° (for 191° 15′.1 interpolate)	a_0 1° 41′.0
Lat	column 190°−199° (for lat 40° approx)	a_1 0′.6
Month	column 190°−199° (June)	a_2 0′.9

Approximate altitude	42° 46′.4
Correction for 1°	−1° 00′.0
Latitude	41° 46′.4N

Finally, to round off this unit you must pay regard to the time of day when it is possible to obtain star sights.

Twilight is the time of the day when it is generally accepted that star sights are possible because then both stars and horizon are visible.

There are two twilights, civil and nautical. Civil is the one you want. How is the time of civil twilight obtained?

Refer to Almanac at the daily 'sun' page in the twilights column. Check the tables at the appropriate latitude (some interpolation will be needed) and find the time. Then apply longitude as time to find GMT.

Here's an example: On 5 May a vessel is on passage in DR position lat 35° 45′.3N, long 18° 00′.0W and the skipper decides to get an evening sight of Polaris. What is the approximate time to expect suitable conditions? Refer to Fig 12:5, below.

	h	m	
Dusk twilight for lat 35° 45′.3	19	18	LMT
Long W (arc to time)	+ 01	12	
Dusk twilight	20	30	GMT

SUMMARY

a) Polaris is nearly in transit with the two markers of the Plough.

b) It is close to the Earth's axis, almost directly over the North Pole.

c) Latitude can be found by taking a sextant angle of Polaris and making some small adjustments.

Do the exercise, opposite.

MAY 4, 5, 6

		Twilight	
Lat.	Sunset	Civil	Naut.
°	h m	h m	h m
N 72	22 44	▬	▬
N 70	21 49	▬	▬
68	21 16	▬	▬
66	20 52	22 27	▬
64	20 34	21 49	▬
62	20 19	21 22	▬
60	20 06	21 02	22 37
N 58	19 56	20 46	22 02
56	19 46	20 32	21 37
54	19 38	20 21	21 18
52	19 31	20 10	21 03
50	19 24	20 01	20 50
45	19 10	19 43	20 24
N 40	18 58	19 28	20 04
35	18 48	19 16	19 49
30	18 40	19 05	19 36
20	18 25	18 48	19 15

Fig 12:5 Sunset and dusk twilights. From the Almanac.

EXERCISE FOR UNIT 12 (Use any relevant Appendices and the Polaris tables, Fig 12:4).

Fig 12:4 Polaris sight sheets (make copies of them for future use).

Date	
Deck watch time	
corr[n] +/-	
GMT	
Greenwich date	
GHA ♈	
increment	
GHA ♈	
DR long – W +E	
LHA ♈	
SA (sextant alt)	
IE	
Dip	
AA (apparent alt)	
corr[n]	
TA (true alt)	
a^0	
a^1	
a^2	
approx alt	
corr[n] (for 1°)	
Latitude	

Date	
Deck watch time	
corr[n] +/-	
GMT	
Greenwich date	
GHA ♈	
increment	
GHA ♈	
DR long – W +E	
LHA ♈	
SA (sextant alt)	
IE	
Dip	
AA (apparent alt)	
corr[n]	
TA (true alt)	
a^0	
a^1	
a^2	
approx alt	
corr[n] (for 1°)	
Latitude	

1   Why isn't a true altitude (TA) of Polaris the exact equivalent of latitude?

2   What is the GMT of dawn twilight on 4 May in DR position lat 60° 43′.2N, long 20° 41′.2E?

3   On 4 May at 04h 35m 59s GMT in DR position lat 33° 39′.3N, long 53° 01′. 3W a vessel was on passage off America bound for Baltimore. A morning sight was taken of Polaris and a sextant altitude (SA) of 33° 14′.5 was obtained. IE 1′.5 on the arc (–). Height of eye 4m. What was the latitude?

Answers overleaf on page 114.

ANSWERS TO EXERCISE FOR UNIT 12

1   A true altitude (TA) of Polaris is not the exact equivalent of the latitude because Polaris is not directly over the North Pole; it's not precisely on the Earth's axis. In fact its declination is about 89°. To be directly over, it would have to be 90°.

2   (In this question the longitude was east and not west)

	h m
Dawn twilight at lat 60° 43′.2N	02 47 LMT
Long 20° 41′.2E (in time)	−1 23
Dawn twilight	01 24 GMT

3

Date	4 MAY
Deck watch time	
corr^n +/−	
GMT	04h 35m 59s
Greenwich date	
GHA ♈ 04h	281° 32′.9
increment 35m 59s	9° 01′.2
GHA ♈ 04h 35m 59s	290° 34·1
DR long (W)+E	−53° 01′.3
LHA ♈	237°32·8
SA (sextant alt)	33° 14′.5
IE −	1′.5
Dip −	3′.5
AA (apparent alt)	33° 09′.5
corr^n −	1′.5 ◄——— From Altitude Correction Tables in 'Stars and Planets' column
TA (true alt)	33° 08′.0
a^0	1° 41′.8
a^1	0′.6
a^2	0′.6
approx alt	34° 51′.0
corr^n (for 1°) −	1° 00′.0
Latitude	33° 51′.0

114

Sailing Across Oceans

We sail the ocean blue,

And our saucy ship's a beauty.

Sir William Schwenk Gilbert *HMS Pinafore*

Where are we now? Which course do we steer? How far to our next port of call? Prevailing questions, whether we are just starting our cruise or at every position fix.

A great circle track is the shortest distance between two locations on Earth. Sailing along such a line is called great circle sailing. (See Fig 13:1.)

Fig 13:1 Great circle track.

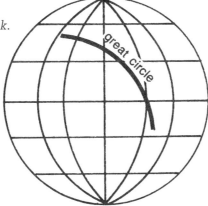

When you use the usual Mercator projection chart for coastal work you plot your course and then maintain it until you reach your destination or until you want to make a course alteration. In fact you sail along a rhumb line, a straight line which cuts the meridians at the same angle. Mercator charts are effective for distances of up to about 600 nautical miles. And directions and distances can be measured directly from the chart. (See Fig 13:2.)

Fig 13:2 Mercator projection.

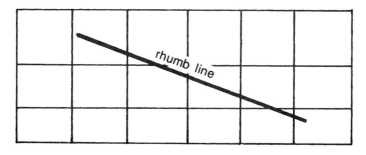

Go to page 117.

Fig 13:3 A great circle track on Mercator projection is curved.

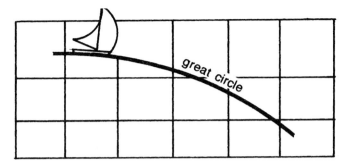

Fig 13:4 A great circle track on a gnomonic projection is straight.

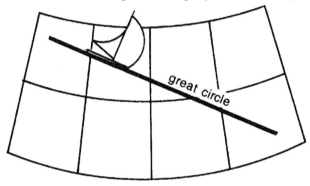

Fig13:5 A great circle track as a series of rhumb lines on a Mercator chart.

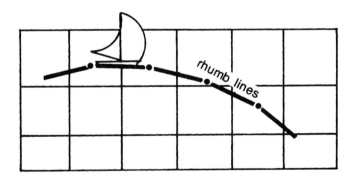

WHAT IS A GREAT CIRCLE?

A great circle is a circle on a sphere; its plane cuts through the sphere's centre. However, if you were to plot a great circle on a Mercator chart it would appear as a curve unless it was a meridian or the equator. (See Fig 13:3 opposite.)

Rhumb line tracks are considerably longer than great circle tracks over greater distances. In coastal work the excess is insignificant but in transocean sailings it can be excessive.

A chart of Gnomonic projection however, unlike Mercator, is used to plot a great circle track because it appears as a straight, not curved, line. (See Fig 13:4, opposite.) But you cannot measure directions and distances directly, as you can on a Mercator chart. So you use the best of both charts.

An easy, popular way of finding the initial course and distance is to use charts of Gnomonic and Mercator projections. The usual practice is to plot the overall great circle route on a Gnomonic chart. Then, take off the latitude and longitude route co-ordinates at about every 5° along the track and transfer them on to the Mercator chart directly, point for point. The result is a series of rhumb lines. (See Fig.13:5, opposite.)

What you are doing is ensuring that the great circle track is divided into sections which are easily plotted on a Mercator chart so that distances and courses can be measured as parts of a planned whole.

SUMMARY

a) Over long distances great circle tracks are considerably shorter than rhumb line tracks.

b) Plot the initial great circle track on a Gnomonic chart.

c) Transfer the latitude and longitude co-ordinates from Gnomonic to Mercator and section the route as a series of rhumb lines.

Now for the Final Test Piece, overleaf. Best of luck!

FINAL TEST PIECE

This tests whether you've really learned the work. Good luck! Before starting this exercise please cover the opposite answer page.

1 What is the GHA and declination of the sun on 4 May at 20h 35m 40s GMT?

2 A boat is in DR position lat 35° 47′.7N, long 26° 30′.0W at 14h 59m LMT. What is the GMT?

3 What is the relationship between the zenith distance and the geographical distance?

4 The intercept is the difference between the ? and ?

5 What is the true zenith distance if the true altitude is 44° 59′.3?

6 The azimuth angle (Z) has to be converted to azimuth (Zn). Where are the rules printed which govern this conversion?

7 On 10 Dec a boat in DR position lat 30°16′.5N, long 40°15′.0W, takes a meridian altitude of the sun's LL which gave a sextant altitude of 36° 41′.3. Index error −1′.5 (on the arc). Height of eye 4.5m. What was the latitude?

8 (*This is a running fix, sun-run-sun,1 involving a morning sight and then a run on to an afternoon sight.*) Use the plotting sheet, Appendix H.

On 6 May at 10h 35m 03s deck watch time the yacht *Pacific Star* is in DR position lat 44° 05′.N, long 6° 34′.5W (assumed position lat 44° 00′.0N, long 6° 39′.6W). Course 106° T. Speed 6.5 knots. Approximate bearing of the sun 138° T. A sight of the sun's LL gave a sextant altitude of 54°14′.5. Index error 2′ on the arc (−). Height of eye 6m. Chronometer error 12 secs slow.

a) What was the intercept and azimuth?

Later, at 13h 34m 11s deck watch time in DR position lat 43° 53′.0N, long 05° 58′.0W (assumed position lat 44° 00′.0N, long 05° 26′.7W) a second sight of the sun's LL was taken and the sextant altitude obtained was 58° 09′.5. IE 2′ on the arc (−). Height of eye 6m. Chronometer error was 12 seconds slow. The course and speed was maintained throughout. There were no tidal streams or leeway. The distance run between sights was 26 nm. Approximate bearing 210° T.

b) What was the intercept and azimuth and the observed position at the time of taking the second sight?

Answers opposite, on page 119.

ANSWERS TO FINAL TEST PIECE

1 4 May

GHA 20h	120° 48'.7	Dec	N15° 59'.9
Increment 35m 40s	+8° 55'.0	d	+0'.4
GHA 20h 35m 40s	129° 43'.7	Dec	16° 00'.3

2

	h	m	
	14	59	LMT
Long 26° 30'.0W in time	+ 1	46	
	16	45	GMT

3 The zenith distance and the geographical distance both stem from (subtend) the same angle. Therefore they measure equal angular distance.

4 The intercept is the difference between the true altitude (TA) and the calculated altitude (Hc).

5 The true zenith distance is 45° 00'.7 (90° – 44° 59'.3).

6 The rules which apply to the conversion from azimuth angle (Z) to azimuth (Zn) are printed at the top and bottom left of pages of HO249.

7

Meridian Passage	SUN	
Date	DEC 10	
DR lat	30° 16'.5N	
DR long	40° 15'.0W	
LMT Mer Pass	11:53:00	
long in time (+W) -E	2:41:00	
GMT MerPass	14:34:00	
Dec	S22° 54'.0	d 0.2
'd' corrn (+) -	0'.1	
Dec	S22° 54'.1	
SA	36° 41'.3	
IE + (-)	1'.5	
Dip (always -)	3'.7	
AA (app alt)	36° 36'.1	
corrn +	15'.0	
TA (true alt)	36° 51'.1	
ZD (90° - TA)	53° 08'.9	
Dec (same contr)	S22° 54'.1	
Lat	30° 14'.8N	

8

	sight		sight	
Date	MAY6		MAY 6	
Course/speed	106°T	6.5 KNOTS	106°T	6.5 KNOTS
DR lat	44°05'0N		°	
DR long	6°34'5W		°	
Ht of Eye	6 metres		6 metres	
Body	Sun's LL		Sun's LL	
Approx bearing	138°T		210°T	
Deck watch time	10:35:03		13:34:11	
corrn (+)-	: :12 (SLOW)		: :12 (SLOW)	
GMT	10:35:15		13:34:23	
Greenwich date	MAY 6		MAY6	
GHA	330°50'8		15°50'.9	
GHA incr	8°48'8		8°35'8	
360° + -	°		°	
GHA	339°39'6		24°26'7	
Ass long W- E+	6°39'6		5°26'7	
LHA	333°00		19°00.	
DEC	N16°27	d 0.7	N16°29'1	d 0.7
'd' corrn (+)-	+ °0'4		+ °0'4	
DEC	N16°27'4		N16°29'5	
Ass lat (same/contr)	44°00'N		44°00'N	
Hc (tabulated alt)	53°52'	d+49' Z/32°	57°42'	d+54' Z/144°
corrn for d (+)-	+ °22·		+ °27·	
Hc (calc alt)	54°14·		58°09·	
SA (sextant alt)	54°14'5		58°09·5	
IE + (-)	- °2·0		- °2·0	
DIP (always -)	4·3		4·3	
AA (app alt)	54°08'2		58°03'2	
corrn + -	+ °15'3		+ °15'4	
TA (true alt)	54°23'5		58·18'6	
Hc (calc alt)	54°14'0		58°09·0	
Intercept (T) or A	9'5 T		9·6 T	
Zn (azimuth)	132°T (Zn=z)		216·T (360°-z)	
Observed pos	Lat43°57'0N Long 05°43'0W			

A copy of the plot for question 8 is overleaf on page 120.

Plot of answer for question 8 in Final Test Piece.

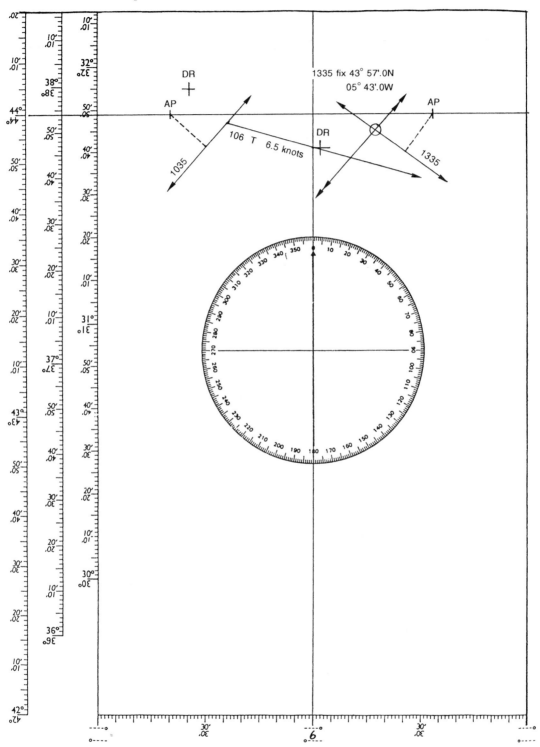

Happy sailing!

Glossary

Apparent motion	The motion of heavenly bodies as they appear to an observer on Earth.
Assumed position	A modified DR position contrived to enable convenient use of sight reduction tables.
Azimuth (Zn)	Bearing of a heavenly body.
Bearing	The direction of one object relative to another measured as an angle eastward from north through 360°.
Calculated altitude	Altitude of a heavenly body calculated without the use of a sextant (eg through the use of a set of tables).
Celestial Equator	The Earth's Equator projected outwards onto the imaginary celestial sphere (equinoctial).
Celestial sphere	A huge, imaginary sphere upon which heavenly bodies are situated. The Earth is at its centre.
Declination	Angular distance of a heavenly body north or south of the celestial equator (ie celestial latitude).
Dip (angle of)	The angle between the sensible horizon (which is on a horizontal plane through the observer's eye) and the visible horizon.
DR position	Position calculated from course steered and distance run.
Ecliptic	The path of the apparent sun on the celestial sphere.
Equinoctial	The celestial equator.
First Point of Aries	The point where the sun crosses the celestial equator in changing from south to north declination on 21 March (Vernal Equinox).
Geographical position	(GP) is a point on the Earth's surface directly beneath a heavenly body. It is denoted by co-ordinates declination and Greenwich Hour Angle.
Great Circle	A circle on a sphere the plane of which passes through the sphere's centre.
Greenwich Hour Angle	(GHA) is angular distance measured westward through 360° along a parallel of declination through the celestial meridians of Greenwich and the heavenly body.
Greenwich Mean Time	(GMT) The time at Greenwich by the mean sun. A universal time reference.
Increment	An increase.
Intercept	Difference between true and calculated altitudes.
ITP	Intercept terminal position is the point at the end of the intercept through which a line of position is plotted.

Latitude	The angular distance of a place on the Earth's surface north or south of the Equator.
Line of position (LOP)	A line somewhere on which an observer is situated.
Local Hour Angle	Angular distance measured westward through 360° along a parallel of declination between the meridians of the observer and the heavenly body.
Local Mean Time	(LMT) is mean time at any point on Earth.
Longitude	The angular measurement east or west of the Greenwich meridian.
Meridian	A great semi-circle passing through the Earth's poles.
Meridian altitude	Altitude of a heavenly body while on the observer's meridian.
Meridian passage	When a heavenly body transits (crosses) the observer's meridian.
Polar Axis	The line around which the spinning Earth rotates.
Quadrant	A quarter (90°) of a circle. The 4 compass quadrants are NE, SE, SW, NW.
Rhumb line	A line on a chart which crosses every meridian at the same angle.
Sextant altitude	Vertical angle measured by a sextant between the horizon and a heavenly body.
Sextant angle	An angle between two points as measured with a sextant.
Sidereal Hour Angle	(SHA) angular distance measured westward through 360° between the meridian at Aries and the meridian through a heavenly body.
True altitude	Sextant altitude corrected.
Universal Time (UT)	GMT.
Zenith	The point on the celestial sphere vertically overhead.
Zenith distance	The angular distance of a heavenly body from the observer's zenith.
Zone time	Mean time used at a reference meridian central to an adjacent standard area.

Conversion of Arc to Time

(Reproduced from the Nautical Almanac)

0°–59°	h m	60°–119°	h m	120°–179°	h m	180°–239°	h m	240°–299°	h m	300°–359°	h m	′	0′·00 m s	0′·25 m s	0′·50 m s	0′·75 m s
0	0 00	60	4 00	120	8 00	180	12 00	240	16 00	300	20 00	0	0 00	0 01	0 02	0 03
1	0 04	61	4 04	121	8 04	181	12 04	241	16 04	301	20 04	1	0 04	0 05	0 06	0 07
2	0 08	62	4 08	122	8 08	182	12 08	242	16 08	302	20 08	2	0 08	0 09	0 10	0 11
3	0 12	63	4 12	123	8 12	183	12 12	243	16 12	303	20 12	3	0 12	0 13	0 14	0 15
4	0 16	64	4 16	124	8 16	184	12 16	244	16 16	304	20 16	4	0 16	0 17	0 18	0 19
5	0 20	65	4 20	125	8 20	185	12 20	245	16 20	305	20 20	5	0 20	0 21	0 22	0 23
6	0 24	66	4 24	126	8 24	186	12 24	246	16 24	306	20 24	6	0 24	0 25	0 26	0 27
7	0 28	67	4 28	127	8 28	187	12 28	247	16 28	307	20 28	7	0 28	0 29	0 30	0 31
8	0 32	68	4 32	128	8 32	188	12 32	248	16 32	308	20 32	8	0 32	0 33	0 34	0 35
9	0 36	69	4 36	129	8 36	189	12 36	249	16 36	309	20 36	9	0 36	0 37	0 38	0 39
10	0 40	70	4 40	130	8 40	190	12 40	250	16 40	310	20 40	10	0 40	0 41	0 42	0 43
11	0 44	71	4 44	131	8 44	191	12 44	251	16 44	311	20 44	11	0 44	0 45	0 46	0 47
12	0 48	72	4 48	132	8 48	192	12 48	252	16 48	312	20 48	12	0 48	0 49	0 50	0 51
13	0 52	73	4 52	133	8 52	193	12 52	253	16 52	313	20 52	13	0 52	0 53	0 54	0 55
14	0 56	74	4 56	134	8 56	194	12 56	254	16 56	314	20 56	14	0 56	0 57	0 58	0 59
15	1 00	75	5 00	135	9 00	195	13 00	255	17 00	315	21 00	15	1 00	1 01	1 02	1 03
16	1 04	76	5 04	136	9 04	196	13 04	256	17 04	316	21 04	16	1 04	1 05	1 06	1 07
17	1 08	77	5 08	137	9 08	197	13 08	257	17 08	317	21 08	17	1 08	1 09	1 10	1 11
18	1 12	78	5 12	138	9 12	198	13 12	258	17 12	318	21 12	18	1 12	1 13	1 14	1 15
19	1 16	79	5 16	139	9 16	199	13 16	259	17 16	319	21 16	19	1 16	1 17	1 18	1 19
20	1 20	80	5 20	140	9 20	200	13 20	260	17 20	320	21 20	20	1 20	1 21	1 22	1 23
21	1 24	81	5 24	141	9 24	201	13 24	261	17 24	321	21 24	21	1 24	1 25	1 26	1 27
22	1 28	82	5 28	142	9 28	202	13 28	262	17 28	322	21 28	22	1 28	1 29	1 30	1 31
23	1 32	83	5 32	143	9 32	203	13 32	263	17 32	323	21 32	23	1 32	1 33	1 34	1 35
24	1 36	84	5 36	144	9 36	204	13 36	264	17 36	324	21 36	24	1 36	1 37	1 38	1 39
25	1 40	85	5 40	145	9 40	205	13 40	265	17 40	325	21 40	25	1 40	1 41	1 42	1 43
26	1 44	86	5 44	146	9 44	206	13 44	266	17 44	326	21 44	26	1 44	1 45	1 46	1 47
27	1 48	87	5 48	147	9 48	207	13 48	267	17 48	327	21 48	27	1 48	1 49	1 50	1 51
28	1 52	88	5 52	148	9 52	208	13 52	268	17 52	328	21 52	28	1 52	1 53	1 54	1 55
29	1 56	89	5 56	149	9 56	209	13 56	269	17 56	329	21 56	29	1 56	1 57	1 58	1 59
30	2 00	90	6 00	150	10 00	210	14 00	270	18 00	330	22 00	30	2 00	2 01	2 02	2 03
31	2 04	91	6 04	151	10 04	211	14 04	271	18 04	331	22 04	31	2 04	2 05	2 06	2 07
32	2 08	92	6 08	152	10 08	212	14 08	272	18 08	332	22 08	32	2 08	2 09	2 10	2 11
33	2 12	93	6 12	153	10 12	213	14 12	273	18 12	333	22 12	33	2 12	2 13	2 14	2 15
34	2 16	94	6 16	154	10 16	214	14 16	274	18 16	334	22 16	34	2 16	2 17	2 18	2 19
35	2 20	95	6 20	155	10 20	215	14 20	275	18 20	335	22 20	35	2 20	2 21	2 22	2 23
36	2 24	96	6 24	156	10 24	216	14 24	276	18 24	336	22 24	36	2 24	2 25	2 26	2 27
37	2 28	97	6 28	157	10 28	217	14 28	277	18 28	337	22 28	37	2 28	2 29	2 30	2 31
38	2 32	98	6 32	158	10 32	218	14 32	278	18 32	338	22 32	38	2 32	2 33	2 34	2 35
39	2 36	99	6 36	159	10 36	219	14 36	279	18 36	339	22 36	39	2 36	2 37	2 38	2 39
40	2 40	100	6 40	160	10 40	220	14 40	280	18 40	340	22 40	40	2 40	2 41	2 42	2 43
41	2 44	101	6 44	161	10 44	221	14 44	281	18 44	341	22 44	41	2 44	2 45	2 46	2 47
42	2 48	102	6 48	162	10 48	222	14 48	282	18 48	342	22 48	42	2 48	2 49	2 50	2 51
43	2 52	103	6 52	163	10 52	223	14 52	283	18 52	343	22 52	43	2 52	2 53	2 54	2 55
44	2 56	104	6 56	164	10 56	224	14 56	284	18 56	344	22 56	44	2 56	2 57	2 58	2 59
45	3 00	105	7 00	165	11 00	225	15 00	285	19 00	345	23 00	45	3 00	3 01	3 02	3 03
46	3 04	106	7 04	166	11 04	226	15 04	286	19 04	346	23 04	46	3 04	3 05	3 06	3 07
47	3 08	107	7 08	167	11 08	227	15 08	287	19 08	347	23 08	47	3 08	3 09	3 10	3 11
48	3 12	108	7 12	168	11 12	228	15 12	288	19 12	348	23 12	48	3 12	3 13	3 14	3 15
49	3 16	109	7 16	169	11 16	229	15 16	289	19 16	349	23 16	49	3 16	3 17	3 18	3 19
50	3 20	110	7 20	170	11 20	230	15 20	290	19 20	350	23 20	50	3 20	3 21	3 22	3 23
51	3 24	111	7 24	171	11 24	231	15 24	291	19 24	351	23 24	51	3 24	3 25	3 26	3 27
52	3 28	112	7 28	172	11 28	232	15 28	292	19 28	352	23 28	52	3 28	3 29	3 30	3 31
53	3 32	113	7 32	173	11 32	233	15 32	293	19 32	353	23 32	53	3 32	3 33	3 34	3 35
54	3 36	114	7 36	174	11 36	234	15 36	294	19 36	354	23 36	54	3 36	3 37	3 38	3 39
55	3 40	115	7 40	175	11 40	235	15 40	295	19 40	355	23 40	55	3 40	3 41	3 42	3 43
56	3 44	116	7 44	176	11 44	236	15 44	296	19 44	356	23 44	56	3 44	3 45	3 46	3 47
57	3 48	117	7 48	177	11 48	237	15 48	297	19 48	357	23 48	57	3 48	3 49	3 50	3 51
58	3 52	118	7 52	178	11 52	238	15 52	298	19 52	358	23 52	58	3 52	3 53	3 54	3 55
59	3 56	119	7 56	179	11 56	239	15 56	299	19 56	359	23 56	59	3 56	3 57	3 58	3 59

The above table is for converting expressions in arc to their equivalent in time; its main use in this Almanac is for the conversion of longitude for application to L.M.T. (*added* if *west*, *subtracted* if *east*) to give UT or vice versa, particularly in the case of sunrise, sunset, etc.

Almanac

(Reproduced from the Nautical Almanac)

MAY 4, 5, 6 (SAT., SUN., MON.)

UT (GMT) d h	ARIES G.H.A.	VENUS −4.1 G.H.A. Dec.	MARS +1.4 G.H.A. Dec.	JUPITER −2.1 G.H.A. Dec.	SATURN +0.6 G.H.A. Dec.	Name	S.H.A.	Dec.
4 00	221 23.0	137 42.7 N25 36.7	112 41.7 N24 01.1	93 29.3 N19 40.2	272 12.4 S18 54.8	Acamar	315 31.2	S40 20.3
01	236 25.5	152 42.0 36.9	127 42.6 00.9	108 31.5 40.1	287 14.8 54.8	Achernar	335 39.4	S57 16.7
02	251 27.9	167 41.3 37.1	142 43.5 00.7	123 33.7 40.1	302 17.2 54.7	Acrux	173 27.6	S63 03.4
03	266 30.4	182 40.7 ·· 37.3	157 44.5 ·· 00.5	138 35.9 ·· 40.0	317 19.6 ·· 54.7	Adhara	255 25.7	S28 57.8
04	281 32.9	197 40.0 37.5	172 45.4 00.3	153 38.1 40.0	332 22.0 54.7	Aldebaran	291 08.7	N16 29.6
05	296 35.3	212 39.3 37.7	187 46.3 24 00.1	168 40.3 39.9	347 24.4 54.7			
06	311 37.8	227 38.7 N25 37.9	202 47.3 N23 59.9	183 42.5 N19 39.8	2 26.8 S18 54.7	Alioth	166 34.5	N56 00.4
07	326 40.3	242 38.0 38.1	217 48.2 59.7	198 44.8 39.8	17 29.2 54.7	Alkaid	153 11.3	N49 21.3
S 08	341 42.7	257 37.3 38.3	232 49.1 59.5	213 47.0 39.7	32 31.6 54.7	Al Na'ir	28 04.4	S47 00.0
A 09	356 45.2	272 36.6 ·· 38.5	247 50.0 ·· 59.3	228 49.2 ·· 39.6	47 34.0 ·· 54.7	Alnilam	276 03.4	S 1 12.5
T 10	11 47.7	287 36.0 38.7	262 51.0 59.1	243 51.4 39.6	62 36.4 54.7	Alphard	218 12.3	S 8 37.4
U 11	26 50.1	302 35.3 38.9	277 51.9 58.9	258 53.6 39.5	77 38.9 54.7			
R 12	41 52.6	317 34.6 N25 39.1	292 52.8 N23 58.7	273 55.8 N19 39.4	92 41.3 S18 54.7	Alphecca	126 24.6	N26 44.4
D 13	56 55.0	332 34.0 39.3	307 53.8 58.5	288 58.0 39.4	107 43.7 54.7	Alpheratz	358 01.0	N29 02.5
A 14	71 57.5	347 33.3 39.5	322 54.7 58.3	304 00.2 39.3	122 46.1 54.6	Altair	62 24.3	N 8 50.6
Y 15	87 00.4	2 32.6 ·· 39.7	337 55.6 ·· 58.1	319 02.4 ·· 39.3	137 48.5 ·· 54.6	Ankaa	353 32.2	S42 21.0
16	102 02.4	17 32.0 39.9	352 56.5 57.9	334 04.6 39.2	152 50.9 54.6	Antares	112 46.3	S26 24.9
17	117 04.9	32 31.3 40.1	7 57.5 57.7	349 06.8 39.1	167 53.3 54.6			
18	132 07.4	47 30.6 N25 40.3	22 58.4 N23 57.5	4 09.0 N19 39.1	182 55.7 S18 54.6	Arcturus	146 10.4	N19 13.5
19	147 09.8	62 30.0 40.4	37 59.3 57.3	19 11.2 39.0	197 58.1 54.6	Atria	108 02.6	S69 00.8
20	162 12.3	77 29.3 40.6	53 00.3 57.1	34 13.4 38.9	213 00.6 54.6	Avior	234 25.0	S59 29.2
21	177 14.8	92 28.6 ·· 40.8	68 01.2 ·· 56.9	49 15.6 ·· 38.9	228 03.0 ·· 54.6	Bellatrix	278 50.0	N 6 20.5
22	192 17.2	107 27.9 41.0	83 02.1 56.6	64 17.8 38.8	243 05.4 54.6	Betelgeuse	271 19.5	N 7 24.4
23	207 19.7	122 27.3 41.2	98 03.0 56.4	79 20.0 38.7	258 07.8 54.6			
5 00	222 22.2	137 26.6 N25 41.3	113 04.0 N23 56.2	94 22.2 N19 38.7	273 10.2 S18 54.6	Canopus	264 03.8	S52 41.6
01	237 24.6	152 25.9 41.5	128 04.9 56.0	109 24.4 38.6	288 12.6 54.6	Capella	280 59.4	N45 59.5
02	252 27.1	167 25.3 41.7	143 05.8 55.8	124 26.6 38.6	303 15.0 54.6	Deneb	49 42.8	N45 14.7
03	267 29.5	182 24.6 ·· 41.9	158 06.8 ·· 55.6	139 28.8 ·· 38.5	318 17.4 ·· 54.5	Denebola	182 50.3	N14 37.1
04	282 32.0	197 23.9 42.1	173 07.7 55.4	154 31.0 38.4	333 19.9 54.5	Diphda	349 12.7	S18 02.0
05	297 34.5	212 23.3 42.2	188 08.6 55.2	169 33.2 38.4	348 22.3 54.5			
06	312 36.9	227 22.6 N25 42.4	203 09.5 N23 55.0	184 35.4 N19 38.3	3 24.7 S18 54.5	Dubhe	194 11.3	N61 48.0
07	327 39.4	242 21.9 42.6	218 10.5 54.8	199 37.6 38.2	18 27.1 54.5	Elnath	278 33.9	N28 36.1
08	342 41.9	257 21.3 42.7	233 11.4 54.6	214 39.8 38.2	33 29.5 54.5	Eltanin	90 53.4	N51 29.1
S 09	357 44.3	272 20.6 ·· 42.9	248 12.3 ·· 54.4	229 42.0 ·· 38.1	48 31.9 ·· 54.5	Enif	34 03.4	N 9 50.0
U 10	12 46.8	287 19.9 43.1	263 13.2 54.2	244 44.2 38.0	63 34.3 54.5	Fomalhaut	15 42.3	S29 40.0
N 11	27 49.3	302 19.3 43.3	278 14.2 54.0	259 46.4 38.0	78 36.7 54.5			
D 12	42 51.7	317 18.6 N25 43.4	293 15.1 N23 53.7	274 48.6 N19 37.9	93 39.2 S18 54.5	Gacrux	172 19.2	S57 04.2
A 13	57 54.2	332 17.9 43.6	308 16.0 53.5	289 50.8 37.8	108 41.6 54.5	Gienah	176 09.1	S17 29.9
Y 14	72 56.7	347 17.3 43.7	323 17.0 53.3	304 53.0 37.8	123 44.0 54.5	Hadar	149 11.0	S60 20.1
15	87 59.1	2 16.6 ·· 43.9	338 17.9 ·· 53.1	319 55.2 ·· 37.7	138 46.4 ·· 54.5	Hamal	328 19.9	N23 25.3
16	103 01.6	17 16.0 44.1	353 18.8 52.9	334 57.4 37.6	153 48.8 54.4	Kaus Aust.	84 05.5	S34 23.4
17	118 04.0	32 15.3 44.2	8 19.7 52.7	349 59.6 37.6	168 51.2 54.4			
18	133 06.5	47 14.6 N25 44.4	23 20.7 N23 52.5	5 01.8 N19 37.5	183 53.6 S18 54.4	Kochab	137 17.8	N74 11.3
19	148 09.0	62 14.0 44.5	38 21.6 52.3	20 04.0 37.4	198 56.1 54.4	Markab	13 55.0	N15 09.4
20	163 11.4	77 13.3 44.7	53 22.5 52.1	35 06.2 37.4	213 58.5 54.4	Menkar	314 32.7	N 4 03.4
21	178 13.9	92 12.6 ·· 44.9	68 23.5 ·· 51.9	50 08.4 ·· 37.3	229 00.9 ·· 54.4	Menkent	148 26.8	S36 19.9
22	193 16.4	107 12.0 45.0	83 24.4 51.6	65 10.6 37.2	244 03.3 54.4	Miaplacidus	221 43.4	S69 41.3
23	208 18.8	122 11.3 45.2	98 25.3 51.4	80 12.8 37.2	259 05.7 54.4			
6 00	223 21.3	137 10.6 N25 45.3	113 26.2 N23 51.2	95 15.0 N19 37.1	274 08.1 S18 54.4	Mirfak	309 04.7	N49 49.9
01	238 23.8	152 10.0 45.5	128 27.2 51.0	110 17.2 37.1	289 10.6 54.4	Nunki	76 18.6	S26 18.5
02	253 26.2	167 09.3 45.6	143 28.1 50.8	125 19.4 37.0	304 13.0 54.4	Peacock	53 45.0	S56 45.6
03	268 28.7	182 08.6 ·· 45.8	158 29.0 ·· 50.6	140 21.6 ·· 36.9	319 15.4 ·· 54.4	Pollux	243 48.0	N28 02.9
04	283 31.2	197 08.0 45.9	173 29.9 50.4	155 23.8 36.9	334 17.8 54.4	Procyon	245 17.2	N 5 14.8
05	298 33.6	212 07.3 46.1	188 30.9 50.2	170 26.0 36.8	349 20.2 54.4			
06	313 36.1	227 06.7 N25 46.2	203 31.8 N23 49.9	185 28.2 N19 36.7	4 22.6 S18 54.3	Rasalhague	96 21.5	N12 33.7
07	328 38.5	242 06.0 46.4	218 32.7 49.7	200 30.3 36.7	19 25.1 54.3	Regulus	208 01.0	N12 00.5
08	343 41.0	257 05.3 46.5	233 33.7 49.5	215 32.5 36.6	34 27.5 54.3	Rigel	281 28.2	S 8 12.7
M 09	358 43.5	272 04.7 ·· 46.6	248 34.6 ·· 49.3	230 34.7 ·· 36.5	49 29.9 ·· 54.3	Rigil Kent.	140 13.9	S60 48.1
O 10	13 45.9	287 04.0 46.8	263 35.6 49.1	245 36.9 36.5	64 32.3 54.3	Sabik	102 31.3	S15 43.0
N 11	28 48.4	302 03.3 46.9	278 36.4 48.9	260 39.1 36.4	79 34.7 54.3			
D 12	43 50.9	317 02.7 N25 47.1	293 37.4 N23 48.7	275 41.3 N19 36.3	94 37.1 S18 54.3	Schedar	350 00.1	N56 29.3
A 13	58 53.3	332 02.0 47.2	308 38.3 48.4	290 43.5 36.3	109 39.6 54.3	Shaula	96 44.1	S37 05.9
Y 14	73 55.8	347 01.4 47.3	323 39.2 48.2	305 45.7 36.2	124 42.0 54.3	Sirius	258 48.5	S16 42.4
15	88 58.3	2 00.7 ·· 47.5	338 40.2 ·· 48.0	320 47.9 ·· 36.1	139 44.4 ·· 54.3	Spica	158 48.4	S11 07.2
16	104 00.7	17 00.0 47.6	353 41.1 47.8	335 50.1 36.1	154 46.8 54.3	Suhail	223 04.7	S43 24.2
17	119 03.2	31 59.4 47.7	8 42.0 47.6	350 52.3 36.0	169 49.2 54.3			
18	134 05.6	46 58.7 N25 47.9	23 42.9 N23 47.4	5 54.5 N19 35.9	184 51.7 S18 54.3	Vega	80 49.9	N38 46.2
19	149 08.1	61 58.1 48.0	38 43.9 47.1	20 56.7 35.9	199 54.1 54.3	Zuben'ubi	137 23.5	S16 00.6
20	164 10.6	76 57.4 48.1	53 44.8 46.9	35 58.8 35.8	214 56.5 54.3		S.H.A.	Mer. Pass.
21	179 13.0	91 56.7 ·· 48.2	68 45.7 ·· 46.7	51 01.0 ·· 35.7	229 58.9 ·· 54.3		° '	h m
22	194 15.5	106 56.1 48.4	83 46.6 46.5	66 03.2 35.6	245 01.3 54.2	Venus	275 04.5	14 51
23	209 18.0	121 55.4 48.5	98 47.6 46.3	81 05.4 35.6	260 03.8 54.2	Mars	250 41.8	16 27
h m						Jupiter	232 00.1	17 40

MAY 4, 5, 6 (SAT., SUN., MON.)

SUN and MOON

UT (GMT) d h	SUN G.H.A.	SUN Dec.	MOON G.H.A.	v	MOON Dec.	d	H.P.
4 00	180 47.5	N15 45.3	300 33.3	11.5	S24 04.3	4.8	54.1
01	195 47.6	46.1	315 03.8	11.6	23 59.5	5.0	54.2
02	210 47.6	46.8	329 34.4	11.6	23 54.5	5.0	54.2
03	225 47.7	.. 47.5	344 05.0	11.6	23 49.5	5.1	54.2
04	240 47.8	48.3	358 35.6	11.7	23 44.4	5.3	54.2
05	255 47.8	49.0	13 06.3	11.7	23 39.1	5.4	54.2
06	270 47.9	N15 49.7	27 37.0	11.7	S23 33.7	5.4	54.2
07	285 48.0	50.5	42 07.7	11.8	23 28.3	5.6	54.2
S 08	300 48.0	51.2	56 38.5	11.9	23 22.7	5.7	54.2
A 09	315 48.1	.. 51.9	71 09.4	11.8	23 17.0	5.8	54.2
T 10	330 48.1	52.6	85 40.2	12.0	23 11.2	5.9	54.2
U 11	345 48.2	53.4	100 11.2	11.9	23 05.3	6.0	54.2
R 12	0 48.3	N15 54.1	114 42.1	12.0	S22 59.3	6.1	54.2
D 13	15 48.3	54.8	129 13.1	12.1	22 53.2	6.2	54.2
A 14	30 48.4	55.5	143 44.2	12.1	22 47.0	6.3	54.2
Y 15	45 48.4	.. 56.3	158 15.3	12.1	22 40.7	6.5	54.2
16	60 48.5	57.0	172 46.4	12.2	22 34.2	6.5	54.2
17	75 48.6	57.7	187 17.6	12.2	22 27.7	6.6	54.2
18	90 48.6	N15 58.4	201 48.8	12.3	S22 21.1	6.7	54.2
19	105 48.7	59.2	216 20.1	12.3	22 14.4	6.9	54.2
20	120 48.7	15 59.9	230 51.4	12.4	22 07.5	6.9	54.2
21	135 48.8	16 00.6	245 22.8	12.4	22 00.6	7.0	54.3
22	150 48.9	01.3	259 54.2	12.4	21 53.6	7.1	54.3
23	165 48.9	02.1	274 25.6	12.5	21 46.5	7.2	54.3
5 00	180 49.0	N16 02.8	288 57.1	12.5	S21 39.3	7.4	54.3
01	195 49.0	03.5	303 28.6	12.6	21 31.9	7.4	54.3
02	210 49.1	04.2	318 00.2	12.6	21 24.5	7.5	54.3
03	225 49.1	.. 04.9	332 31.8	12.7	21 17.0	7.6	54.3
04	240 49.2	05.7	347 03.5	12.7	21 09.4	7.7	54.3
05	255 49.3	06.4	1 35.2	12.7	21 01.7	7.8	54.3
06	270 49.3	N16 07.1	16 06.9	12.8	S20 53.9	7.9	54.3
07	285 49.4	07.8	30 38.7	12.9	20 46.0	8.0	54.4
S 08	300 49.4	08.5	45 10.6	12.8	20 38.0	8.1	54.4
U 09	315 49.5	.. 09.2	59 42.4	13.0	20 29.9	8.1	54.4
N 10	330 49.5	10.0	74 14.4	12.9	20 21.8	8.3	54.4
D 11	345 49.6	10.7	88 46.3	13.0	20 13.5	8.4	54.4
A 12	0 49.6	N16 11.4	103 18.3	13.1	S20 05.1	8.4	54.4
Y 13	15 49.7	12.1	117 50.4	13.1	19 56.7	8.5	54.4
14	30 49.7	12.8	132 22.5	13.1	19 48.2	8.7	54.4
15	45 49.8	.. 13.5	146 54.6	13.2	19 39.5	8.7	54.4
16	60 49.9	14.3	161 26.8	13.2	19 30.8	8.8	54.5
17	75 49.9	15.0	175 59.0	13.3	19 22.0	8.9	54.5
18	90 50.0	N16 15.7	190 31.3	13.3	S19 13.1	8.9	54.5
19	105 50.0	16.4	205 03.6	13.3	19 04.2	9.1	54.5
20	120 50.1	17.1	219 35.9	13.4	18 55.1	9.1	54.5
21	135 50.1	.. 17.8	234 08.3	13.4	18 46.0	9.3	54.5
22	150 50.2	18.5	248 40.7	13.4	18 36.7	9.3	54.5
23	165 50.2	19.2	263 13.1	13.5	18 27.4	9.4	54.6
6 00	180 50.3	N16 19.9	277 45.6	13.6	S18 18.0	9.5	54.6
01	195 50.3	20.7	292 18.2	13.5	18 08.5	9.5	54.6
02	210 50.4	21.4	306 50.7	13.6	17 59.0	9.7	54.6
03	225 50.4	.. 22.1	321 23.3	13.7	17 49.3	9.7	54.6
04	240 50.5	22.8	335 56.0	13.7	17 39.6	9.8	54.6
05	255 50.5	23.5	350 28.7	13.7	17 29.8	9.9	54.7
06	270 50.6	N16 24.2	5 01.4	13.7	S17 19.9	10.0	54.7
07	285 50.6	24.9	19 34.1	13.8	17 09.9	10.0	54.7
M 08	300 50.7	25.6	34 06.9	13.8	16 59.9	10.1	54.7
O 09	315 50.7	.. 26.3	48 39.7	13.9	16 49.8	10.2	54.7
N 10	330 50.8	27.0	63 12.6	13.9	16 39.6	10.3	54.7
D 11	345 50.8	27.7	77 45.5	13.9	16 29.3	10.4	54.8
A 12	0 50.9	N16 28.4	92 18.4	13.9	S16 18.9	10.4	54.8
Y 13	15 50.9	29.1	106 51.3	14.0	16 08.5	10.5	54.8
14	30 51.0	29.8	121 24.3	14.0	15 58.0	10.6	54.8
15	45 51.0	.. 30.5	135 57.3	14.1	15 47.4	10.6	54.8
16	60 51.1	31.2	150 30.4	14.1	15 36.8	10.7	54.9
17	75 51.1	32.0	165 03.5	14.1	15 26.1	10.8	54.9
18	90 51.2	N16 32.7	179 36.6	14.1	S15 15.3	10.9	54.9
19	105 51.2	33.4	194 09.7	14.2	15 04.4	10.9	54.9
20	120 51.3	34.1	208 42.9	14.2	14 53.5	11.0	54.9
21	135 51.3	.. 34.8	223 16.1	14.2	14 42.5	11.1	55.0
22	150 51.4	35.5	237 49.3	14.2	14 31.4	11.2	55.0
23	165 51.4	36.2	252 22.5	14.3	14 20.2	11.2	55.0
	S.D. 15.9	d 0.7	S.D. 14.8		14.8		14.9

Twilight, Sunrise, Moonrise

Lat.	Naut.	Civil	Sunrise	Moonrise 4	5	6	7
N 72	////	////	01 20	■	■	04 49	03 31
N 70	////	////	02 10	■	■	03 43	03 06
68	////	////	02 41	■	03 49	03 07	02 46
66	////	01 32	03 04	03 39	02 56	02 41	02 30
64	////	02 09	03 22	02 25	02 23	02 21	02 18
62	////	02 34	03 36	01 49	01 59	02 04	02 07·
60	01 22	02 54	03 49	01 23	01 40	01 50	01 57
N 58	01 55	03 09	03 59	01 03	01 24	01 39	01 49
56	02 19	03 23	04 08	00 46	01 10	01 28	01 42
54	02 37	03 34	04 17	00 31	00 58	01 19	01 35
52	02 52	03 44	04 24	00 18	00 48	01 11	01 29
50	03 05	03 53	04 30	00 07	00 39	01 03	01 24
45	03 31	04 12	04 44	24 19	00 19	00 48	01 12
N 40	03 50	04 26	04 56	24 03	00 03	00 35	01 03
35	04 06	04 38	05 06	23 49	24 24	00 24	00 55
30	04 18	04 49	05 14	23 37	24 14	00 14	00 47
20	04 38	05 06	05 29	23 17	23 57	24 35	00 35
N 10	04 54	05 20	05 42	22 59	23 42	24 24	00 24
0	05 07	05 32	05 53	22 42	23 28	24 13	00 13
S 10	05 18	05 43	06 05	22 25	23 15	24 03	00 03
20	05 28	05 54	06 17	22 07	23 00	23 51	24 43
30	05 38	06 06	06 31	21 47	22 43	23 38	24 35
35	05 43	06 13	06 39	21 35	22 32	23 31	24 30
40	05 48	06 20	06 48	21 21	22 21	23 22	24 25
45	05 53	06 28	06 59	21 04	22 07	23 12	24 18
S 50	05 58	06 37	07 12	20 43	21 51	23 00	24 11
52	06 01	06 41	07 18	20 33	21 43	22 55	24 07
54	06 03	06 46	07 24	20 22	21 34	22 48	24 03
56	06 06	06 51	07 31	20 10	21 25	22 41	23 59
58	06 09	06 56	07 40	19 55	21 13	22 33	23 54
S 60	06 12	07 03	07 49	19 37	21 00	22 24	23 49

Sunset, Twilight, Moonset

Lat.	Sunset	Civil	Naut.	Moonset 4	5	6	7
N 72	22 44	////	////	■	■	06 48	09 39
N 70	21 49	////	////	■	■	07 52	10 03
68	21 16	////	////	■	06 10	08 27	10 20
66	20 52	22 27	////	04 41	07 02	08 52	10 35
64	20 34	21 49	////	05 53	07 34	09 12	10 46
62	20 19	21 22	////	06 29	07 58	09 27	10 56
60	20 06	21 02	22 37	06 55	08 16	09 40	11 05
N 58	19 56	20 46	22 02	07 15	08 32	09 51	11 12
56	19 46	20 32	21 37	07 32	08 45	10 01	11 18
54	19 38	20 21	21 18	07 46	08 56	10 10	11 24
52	19 31	20 10	21 03	07 58	09 06	10 17	11 29
50	19 24	20 01	20 50	08 09	09 15	10 24	11 34
45	19 10	19 43	20 24	08 32	09 34	10 39	11 44
N 40	18 58	19 28	20 04	08 50	09 49	10 51	11 52
35	18 48	19 16	19 49	09 05	10 02	11 01	11 59
30	18 40	19 05	19 36	09 18	10 14	11 09	12 06
20	18 25	18 48	19 15	09 40	10 33	11 25	12 16
N 10	18 12	18 34	19 00	10 00	10 49	11 38	12 25
0	18 00	18 22	18 47	10 17	11 05	11 50	12 34
S 10	17 48	18 10	18 35	10 35	11 20	12 02	12 43
20	17 36	17 59	18 25	10 54	11 36	12 15	12 52
30	17 22	17 47	18 15	11 16	11 55	12 30	13 02
35	17 14	17 40	18 10	11 29	12 06	12 38	13 08
40	17 05	17 33	18 05	11 44	12 18	12 48	13 15
45	16 54	17 25	18 00	12 01	12 33	12 59	13 23
S 50	16 41	17 16	17 54	12 22	12 50	13 13	13 32
52	16 35	17 11	17 52	12 33	12 59	13 19	13 36
54	16 29	17 07	17 49	12 44	13 08	13 26	13 41
56	16 21	17 02	17 46	12 57	13 18	13 34	13 46
58	16 13	16 56	17 43	13 12	13 30	13 42	13 52
S 60	16 03	16 50	17 40	13 30	13 44	13 52	13 58

SUN / MOON summary

Day	SUN Eqn. of Time 00h	12h	Mer. Pass.	MOON Mer. Pass. Upper	Lower	Age	Phase
	m s	m s	h m	h m	h m	d	
4	03 10	03 13	11 57	04 06	16 30	20	
5	03 16	03 18	11 57	04 53	17 17	21	
6	03 21	03 23	11 57	05 39	18 02	22	◖

Almanac

JUNE 3, 4, 5 (MON., TUES., WED.)

UT (GMT) d h	ARIES G.H.A.	VENUS −4.2 G.H.A.	Dec.	MARS +1.6 G.H.A.	Dec.	JUPITER −1.9 G.H.A.	Dec.	SATURN +0.5 G.H.A.	Dec.	Star Name	S.H.A.	Dec.
3 00	250 57.2	131 29.0	N23 16.8	123 51.5	N20 33.7	118 59.7	N18 38.3	301 50.9	S18 59.4	Acamar	315 31.1	S40 20.1
01	265 59.6	146 28.8	16.3	138 52.4	33.4	134 01.7	38.2	316 53.4	59.5	Achernar	335 39.2	S57 16.5
02	281 02.1	161 28.5	15.7	153 53.4	33.0	149 03.8	38.1	331 56.0	59.5	Acrux	173 27.7	S63 03.5
03	296 04.6	176 28.2	·· 15.1	168 54.3	·· 32.6	164 05.8	·· 38.0	346 58.5	·· 59.5	Adhara	255 25.8	S28 57.7
04	311 07.0	191 28.0	14.6	183 55.3	32.2	179 07.9	37.9	2 01.0	59.5	Aldebaran	291 08.7	N16 29.6
05	326 09.5	206 27.7	14.0	198 56.2	31.9	194 09.9	37.7	17 03.5	59.6			
06	341 12.0	221 27.5	N23 13.5	213 57.1	N20 31.5	209 12.0	N18 37.6	32 06.1	S18 59.6	Alioth	166 34.6	N56 00.5
07	356 14.4	236 27.2	12.9	228 58.1	31.1	224 14.0	37.5	47 08.6	59.6	Alkaid	153 11.4	N49 21.4
08	11 16.9	251 27.0	12.3	243 59.0	30.8	239 16.1	37.4	62 11.1	59.6	Al Na'ir	28 04.1	S46 59.9
M 09	26 19.4	266 26.7	·· 11.8	259 00.0	·· 30.4	254 18.1	·· 37.3	77 13.7	·· 59.6	Alnilam	276 03.4	S 1 12.4
O 10	41 21.8	281 26.5	11.2	274 00.9	30.0	269 20.2	37.2	92 16.2	59.7	Alphard	218 12.4	S 8 37.4
N 11	56 24.3	296 26.2	10.6	289 01.9	29.6	284 22.2	37.1	107 18.7	59.7			
D 12	71 26.8	311 26.0	N23 10.1	304 02.8	N20 29.3	299 24.3	N18 37.0	122 21.3	S18 59.7	Alphecca	126 24.6	N26 44.5
A 13	86 29.2	326 25.8	09.5	319 03.7	28.9	314 26.4	36.9	137 23.8	59.7	Alpheratz	358 00.8	N29 02.5
Y 14	101 31.7	341 25.5	08.9	334 04.7	28.5	329 28.4	36.8	152 26.3	59.7	Altair	62 24.1	N 8 50.6
15	116 34.1	356 25.3	·· 08.4	349 05.6	·· 28.1	344 30.5	·· 36.7	167 28.9	·· 59.8	Ankaa	353 32.0	S42 20.9
16	131 36.6	11 25.0	07.8	4 06.6	27.8	359 32.5	36.6	182 31.4	59.8	Antares	112 46.1	S26 24.9
17	146 39.1	26 24.8	07.2	19 07.5	27.4	14 34.6	36.4	197 33.9	59.8			
18	161 41.5	41 24.5	N23 06.7	34 08.5	N20 27.0	29 36.6	N18 36.3	212 36.5	S18 59.8	Arcturus	146 10.5	N19 13.5
19	176 44.0	56 24.3	06.1	49 09.4	26.6	44 38.7	36.2	227 39.0	59.9	Atria	108 02.3	S69 00.9
20	191 46.5	71 24.1	05.5	64 10.3	26.2	59 40.7	36.1	242 41.5	59.9	Avior	234 25.3	S59 29.2
21	206 48.9	86 23.8	·· 05.0	79 11.3	·· 25.9	74 42.8	·· 36.0	257 44.1	·· 59.9	Bellatrix	278 50.0	N 6 20.6
22	221 51.4	101 23.6	04.4	94 12.2	25.5	89 44.8	35.9	272 46.6	59.9	Betelgeuse	271 19.5	N 7 24.4
23	236 53.9	116 23.4	03.8	109 13.2	25.1	104 46.9	35.8	287 49.2	18 59.9			
4 00	251 56.3	131 23.1	N23 03.2	124 14.1	N20 24.7	119 48.9	N18 35.7	302 51.7	S19 00.0	Canopus	264 04.0	S52 41.5
01	266 58.8	146 22.9	02.7	139 15.1	24.4	134 51.0	35.6	317 54.2	00.0	Capella	280 59.3	N45 59.5
02	282 01.2	161 22.7	02.1	154 16.0	24.0	149 53.0	35.5	332 56.8	00.0	Deneb	49 42.5	N45 14.8
03	297 03.7	176 22.4	·· 01.5	169 16.9	·· 23.6	164 55.1	·· 35.4	347 59.3	·· 00.0	Denebola	182 50.3	N14 37.1
04	312 06.2	191 22.2	00.9	184 17.9	23.2	179 57.1	35.2	3 01.8	00.1	Diphda	349 12.5	S18 01.9
05	327 08.6	206 22.0	23 00.3	199 18.8	22.8	194 59.2	35.1	18 04.4	00.1			
06	342 11.1	221 21.8	N22 59.8	214 19.8	N20 22.5	210 01.2	N18 35.0	33 06.9	S19 00.1	Dubhe	194 11.6	N61 48.0
07	357 13.6	236 21.5	59.2	229 20.7	22.1	225 03.3	34.9	48 09.4	00.1	Elnath	278 33.9	N28 36.1
T 08	12 16.0	251 21.3	58.6	244 21.7	21.7	240 05.3	34.8	63 12.0	00.2	Eltanin	90 53.3	N51 29.2
U 09	27 18.5	266 21.1	·· 58.0	259 22.6	·· 21.3	255 07.4	·· 34.7	78 14.5	·· 00.2	Enif	34 03.2	N 9 50.1
E 10	42 21.0	281 20.9	57.4	274 23.5	20.9	270 09.4	34.6	93 17.0	00.2	Fomalhaut	15 42.0	S29 39.9
S 11	57 23.4	296 20.6	56.8	289 24.5	20.6	285 11.5	34.5	108 19.6	00.2			
D 12	72 25.9	311 20.4	N22 56.3	304 25.4	N20 20.2	300 13.5	N18 34.4	123 22.1	S19 00.2	Gacrux	172 19.3	S57 04.3
A 13	87 28.4	326 20.2	55.7	319 26.4	19.8	315 15.6	34.3	138 24.7	00.3	Gienah	176 09.2	S17 29.9
Y 14	102 30.8	341 20.0	55.1	334 27.3	19.4	330 17.6	34.1	153 27.2	00.3	Hadar	149 11.1	S60 20.3
15	117 33.3	356 19.8	·· 54.5	349 28.3	·· 19.0	345 19.7	·· 34.0	168 29.7	·· 00.3	Hamal	328 19.7	N23 25.3
16	132 35.7	11 19.5	53.9	4 29.2	18.7	0 21.7	33.9	183 32.3	00.3	Kaus Aust.	84 05.3	S34 23.4
17	147 38.2	26 19.3	53.3	19 30.2	18.3	15 23.8	33.8	198 34.8	00.4			
18	162 40.7	41 19.1	N22 52.7	34 31.1	N20 17.9	30 25.8	N18 33.7	213 37.3	S19 00.4	Kochab	137 18.0	N74 11.5
19	177 43.1	56 18.9	52.1	49 32.0	17.5	45 27.9	33.6	228 39.9	00.4	Markab	13 54.8	N15 09.5
20	192 45.6	71 18.7	51.5	64 33.0	17.1	60 29.9	33.5	243 42.4	00.4	Menkar	314 32.6	N 4 03.4
21	207 48.1	86 18.5	·· 51.0	79 33.9	·· 16.7	75 32.0	·· 33.4	258 45.0	·· 00.4	Menkent	148 26.8	S36 20.0
22	222 50.5	101 18.3	50.4	94 34.9	16.4	90 34.0	33.3	273 47.5	00.5	Miaplacidus	221 43.8	S69 41.2
23	237 53.0	116 18.1	49.8	109 35.8	16.0	105 36.1	33.2	288 50.0	00.5			
5 00	252 55.5	131 17.8	N22 49.2	124 36.8	N20 15.6	120 38.1	N18 33.0	303 52.6	S19 00.5	Mirfak	309 04.6	N49 48.8
01	267 57.9	146 17.6	48.6	139 37.7	15.2	135 40.1	32.9	318 55.1	00.5	Nunki	76 18.4	S26 18.5
02	283 00.4	161 17.4	48.0	154 38.6	14.8	150 42.2	32.8	333 57.7	00.6	Peacock	53 44.6	S56 45.6
03	298 02.9	176 17.2	·· 47.4	169 39.6	·· 14.4	165 44.2	·· 32.7	349 00.2	·· 00.6	Pollux	243 48.1	N28 02.9
04	313 05.3	191 17.0	46.8	184 40.5	14.1	180 46.3	32.6	4 02.7	00.6	Procyon	245 17.2	N 5 14.8
05	328 07.8	206 16.8	46.2	199 41.5	13.7	195 48.3	32.5	19 05.3	00.6			
06	343 10.2	221 16.6	N22 45.6	214 42.4	N20 13.3	210 50.4	N18 32.4	34 07.8	S19 00.7	Rasalhague	96 21.4	N12 33.8
W 07	358 12.7	236 16.4	45.0	229 43.4	12.9	225 52.4	32.3	49 10.4	00.7	Regulus	208 01.1	N12 00.5
E 08	13 15.2	251 16.2	44.4	244 44.3	12.5	240 54.5	32.2	64 12.9	00.7	Rigel	281 28.2	S 8 12.6
D 09	28 17.6	266 16.0	·· 43.8	259 45.3	·· 12.1	255 56.5	·· 32.0	79 15.4	·· 00.7	Rigil Kent.	140 13.9	S60 48.3
N 10	43 20.1	281 15.8	43.2	274 46.2	11.8	270 58.6	31.9	94 18.0	00.8	Sabik	102 31.1	S15 43.0
E 11	58 22.6	296 15.6	42.6	289 47.2	11.4	286 00.6	31.8	109 20.5	00.8			
S 12	73 25.0	311 15.4	N22 42.0	304 48.1	N20 11.0	301 02.7	N18 31.7	124 23.1	S19 00.8	Schedar	349 59.8	N56 29.3
D 13	88 27.5	326 15.2	41.4	319 49.0	10.6	316 04.7	31.6	139 25.6	00.8	Shaula	96 43.9	S37 06.0
A 14	103 30.0	341 15.0	40.8	334 50.0	10.2	331 06.7	31.5	154 28.1	00.8	Sirius	258 48.5	S16 42.3
Y 15	118 32.4	356 14.8	·· 40.2	349 50.9	·· 09.8	346 08.8	·· 31.4	169 30.7	·· 00.9	Spica	158 48.5	S11 07.2
16	133 34.9	11 14.6	39.5	4 51.9	09.4	1 10.8	31.3	184 33.2	00.9	Suhail	223 04.9	S43 24.1
17	148 37.3	26 14.5	38.9	19 52.8	09.1	16 12.9	31.1	199 35.8	00.9			
18	163 39.8	41 14.3	N22 38.3	34 53.8	N20 08.7	31 14.9	N18 31.0	214 38.3	S19 00.9	Vega	80 49.7	N38 46.4
19	178 42.3	56 14.1	37.7	49 54.7	08.3	46 17.0	30.9	229 40.8	01.0	Zuben'ubi	137 23.4	S16 00.6
20	193 44.7	71 13.9	37.1	64 55.7	07.9	61 19.0	30.8	244 43.4	01.0		S.H.A.	Mer. Pass.
21	208 47.2	86 13.7	·· 36.5	79 56.6	·· 07.5	76 21.1	·· 30.7	259 45.9	·· 01.0	Venus	239 26.8	15 15
22	223 49.7	101 13.5	35.9	94 57.5	07.1	91 23.1	30.6	274 48.5	01.0	Mars	232 17.8	15 42
23	238 52.1	116 13.3	35.3	109 58.5	06.7	106 25.1	30.5	289 51.0	01.1	Jupiter	227 52.6	15 59
Mer. Pass. 7 11.1		v −0.2 d 0.6		v 0.9 d 0.4		v 2.0 d 0.1		v 2.5 d 0.0		Saturn	50 55.4	3 48

Almanac

JUNE 3, 4, 5 (MON., TUES., WED.)

UT (GMT)	SUN G.H.A.	SUN Dec.	MOON G.H.A.	v	Dec.	d	H.P.
d h	° ′	° ′	° ′	′	° ′	′	′
3 00	180 30.9	N22 13.4	297 01.6 14.4		S15 15.1	10.7	54.5
01	195 30.8	13.7	311 35.0 14.5		15 04.4	10.7	54.5
02	210 30.7	14.0	326 08.5 14.5		14 53.7	10.9	54.6
03	225 30.6 ..	14.4	340 42.0 14.5		14 42.8	10.9	54.6
04	240 30.5	14.7	355 15.5 14.6		14 31.9	10.9	54.6
05	255 30.4	15.0	9 49.1 14.6		14 21.0	11.1	54.6
06	270 30.3	N22 15.3	24 22.7 14.6		S14 09.9	11.1	54.6
07	285 30.2	15.6	38 56.3 14.7		13 58.8	11.1	54.6
08	300 30.1	15.9	53 30.0 14.7		13 47.7	11.2	54.7
M 09	315 30.0 ..	16.2	68 03.7 14.7		13 36.5	11.3	54.7
O 10	330 29.9	16.6	82 37.4 14.8		13 25.2	11.3	54.7
N 11	345 29.8	16.9	97 11.2 14.7		13 13.9	11.4	54.7
D 12	0 29.7	N22 17.2	111 44.9 14.8		S13 02.5	11.5	54.7
A 13	15 29.6	17.5	126 18.7 14.9		12 51.0	11.5	54.8
Y 14	30 29.5	17.8	140 52.6 14.8		12 39.5	11.6	54.8
15	45 29.4 ..	18.1	155 26.4 14.9		12 27.9	11.6	54.8
16	60 29.3	18.4	170 00.3 14.9		12 16.3	11.7	54.8
17	75 29.2	18.7	184 34.2 14.9		12 04.6	11.8	54.8
18	90 29.1	N22 19.0	199 08.1 15.0		S11 52.8	11.8	54.9
19	105 29.0	19.3	213 42.1 14.9		11 41.0	11.8	54.9
20	120 28.9	19.6	228 16.0 15.0		11 29.2	11.9	54.9
21	135 28.8 ..	20.0	242 50.0 15.0		11 17.3	12.0	54.9
22	150 28.7	20.3	257 24.0 15.0		11 05.3	12.0	54.9
23	165 28.6	20.6	271 58.0 15.1		10 53.3	12.1	55.0
4 00	180 28.5	N22 20.9	286 32.1 15.0		S10 41.2	12.1	55.0
01	195 28.4	21.2	301 06.1 15.1		10 29.1	12.2	55.0
02	210 28.3	21.5	315 40.2 15.1		10 16.9	12.2	55.0
03	225 28.2 ..	21.8	330 14.3 15.1		10 04.7	12.3	55.0
04	240 28.1	22.1	344 48.4 15.1		9 52.4	12.3	55.1
05	255 28.0	22.4	359 22.5 15.2		9 40.1	12.4	55.1
06	270 27.9	N22 22.7	13 56.7 15.1		S 9 27.7	12.4	55.1
07	285 27.8	23.0	28 30.8 15.1		9 15.3	12.5	55.1
T 08	300 27.6	23.3	43 04.9 15.2		9 02.8	12.5	55.2
U 09	315 27.5 ..	23.6	57 39.1 15.2		8 50.3	12.6	55.2
E 10	330 27.4	23.9	72 13.3 15.2		8 37.7	12.6	55.2
S 11	345 27.3	24.2	86 47.5 15.1		8 25.1	12.6	55.2
D 12	0 27.2	N22 24.4	101 21.6 15.2		S 8 12.5	12.7	55.3
A 13	15 27.1	24.7	115 55.8 15.2		7 59.8	12.7	55.3
Y 14	30 27.0	25.0	130 30.0 15.2		7 47.1	12.8	55.3
15	45 26.9 ..	25.3	145 04.2 15.2		7 34.3	12.8	55.3
16	60 26.8	25.6	159 38.4 15.2		7 21.5	12.9	55.4
17	75 26.7	25.9	174 12.6 15.2		7 08.6	12.9	55.4
18	90 26.6	N22 26.2	188 46.8 15.2		S 6 55.7	13.0	55.4
19	105 26.5	26.5	203 21.0 15.2		6 42.7	12.9	55.4
20	120 26.4	26.8	217 55.2 15.2		6 29.8	13.1	55.5
21	135 26.3 ..	27.1	232 29.4 15.2		6 16.7	13.0	55.5
22	150 26.2	27.4	247 03.6 15.2		6 03.7	13.1	55.5
23	165 26.1	27.6	261 37.8 15.2		5 50.6	13.1	55.5
5 00	180 25.9	N22 27.9	276 12.0 15.2		S 5 37.5	13.2	55.6
01	195 25.8	28.2	290 46.2 15.2		5 24.3	13.2	55.6
02	210 25.7	28.5	305 20.4 15.1		5 11.1	13.2	55.6
03	225 25.6 ..	28.8	319 54.5 15.2		4 57.9	13.3	55.7
04	240 25.5	29.1	334 28.7 15.1		4 44.6	13.3	55.7
05	255 25.4	29.4	349 02.8 15.1		4 31.3	13.4	55.7
06	270 25.3	N22 29.7	3 36.9 15.2		S 4 17.9	13.3	55.7
W 07	285 25.2	29.9	18 11.1 15.1		4 04.6	13.4	55.8
E 08	300 25.1	30.2	32 45.2 15.1		3 51.2	13.4	55.8
D 09	315 25.0 ..	30.5	47 19.3 15.0		3 37.8	13.5	55.8
N 10	330 24.9	30.8	61 53.3 15.1		3 24.3	13.5	55.9
E 11	345 24.8	31.0	76 27.4 15.0		3 10.8	13.5	55.9
S 12	0 24.6	N22 31.3	91 01.4 15.0		S 2 57.3	13.5	55.9
D 13	15 24.5	31.6	105 35.4 15.0		2 43.8	13.6	56.0
A 14	30 24.4	31.9	120 09.4 15.0		2 30.2	13.6	56.0
Y 15	45 24.3 ..	32.2	134 43.4 15.0		2 16.6	13.6	56.0
16	60 24.2	32.4	149 17.4 14.9		2 03.0	13.6	56.1
17	75 24.1	32.7	163 51.3 14.9		1 49.4	13.7	56.1
18	90 24.0	N22 33.0	178 25.2 14.9		S 1 35.7	13.7	56.1
19	105 23.9	33.3	192 59.1 14.8		1 22.0	13.7	56.1
20	120 23.8	33.5	207 32.9 14.9		1 08.3	13.7	56.2
21	135 23.7 ..	33.8	222 06.8 14.7		0 54.6	13.8	56.2
22	150 23.5	34.1	236 40.5 14.8		0 40.8	13.7	56.2
23	165 23.4	34.3	251 14.3 14.7		0 27.1	13.8	56.3
	S.D. 15.8	d 0.3	S.D. 14.9		15.1		15.2

Twilight / Sunrise / Moonrise

Lat.	Naut.	Civil	Sunrise	Moonrise 3	4	5	6
°	h m	h m	h m	h m	h m	h m	h m
N 72	□	□	□	01 58	01 16	00 46	{00 23 / 21 55}
N 70	□	□	□	01 26	00 59	00 39	00 20
68	□	□	01 01	01 02	00 46	00 33	00 20
66	////	////	01 01	00 44	00 35	00 27	00 20
64	////	////	01 52	00 29	00 26	00 23	00 20
62	////	////	02 23	00 16	00 18	00 19	00 19
60	////	01 19	02 46	00 06	00 11	00 15	00 19
N 58	////	01 56	03 04	24 05	00 05	00 12	00 19
56	////	02 21	03 20	24 00	00 00	00 10	00 19
54	01 12	02 41	03 33	23 55	24 07	00 07	00 19
52	01 46	02 57	03 44	23 50	24 05	00 05	00 19
50	02 10	03 11	03 54	23 46	24 03	00 03	00 19
45	02 51	03 39	04 15	23 38	23 58	24 19	00 19
N 40	03 19	04 00	04 32	23 30	23 55	24 18	00 18
35	03 41	04 17	04 47	23 24	23 51	24 18	00 18
30	03 59	04 32	04 59	23 18	23 49	24 18	00 18
20	04 27	04 55	05 20	23 09	23 43	24 18	00 18
N 10	04 48	05 15	05 38	23 00	23 39	24 18	00 18
0	05 06	05 32	05 55	22 52	23 35	24 18	00 18
S 10	05 22	05 48	06 11	22 44	23 31	24 18	00 18
20	05 38	06 05	06 29	22 36	23 26	24 18	00 18
30	05 53	06 23	06 49	22 26	23 21	24 17	00 17
35	06 01	06 33	07 01	22 20	23 18	24 17	00 17
40	06 10	06 44	07 14	22 14	23 15	24 17	00 17
45	06 20	06 57	07 30	22 06	23 11	24 17	00 17
S 50	06 31	07 12	07 49	21 57	23 06	24 17	00 17
52	06 35	07 19	07 59	21 53	23 04	24 17	00 17
54	06 41	07 26	08 09	21 48	23 02	24 17	00 17
56	06 46	07 35	08 21	21 43	22 59	24 17	00 17
58	06 52	07 44	08 34	21 37	22 56	24 17	00 17
S 60	06 59	07 55	08 50	21 30	22 53	24 17	00 17

Sunset / Twilight / Moonset

Lat.	Sunset	Civil	Naut.	Moonset 3	4	5	6
°	h m	h m	h m	h m	h m	h m	h m
N 72	□	□	□	07 02	09 15	11 14	13 14
N 70	□	□	□	07 33	09 29	11 19	13 10
68	□	□	□	07 55	09 40	11 23	13 07
66	22 59	////	////	08 12	09 50	11 26	13 04
64	22 06	////	////	08 26	09 57	11 29	13 02
62	21 35	////	////	08 37	10 04	11 31	13 00
60	21 12	22 40	////	08 47	10 10	11 33	12 58
N 58	20 53	22 02	////	08 56	10 15	11 35	12 57
56	20 38	21 37	////	09 03	10 19	11 36	12 55
54	20 24	21 17	22 47	09 10	10 23	11 38	12 54
52	20 13	21 00	22 12	09 16	10 27	11 39	12 53
50	20 03	20 46	21 48	09 21	10 30	11 40	12 52
45	19 41	20 18	21 06	09 33	10 37	11 43	12 50
N 40	19 24	19 57	20 38	09 42	10 43	11 45	12 48
35	19 10	19 39	20 16	09 50	10 48	11 47	12 46
30	18 58	19 25	19 58	09 57	10 52	11 48	12 45
20	18 37	19 01	19 30	10 09	10 59	11 51	12 43
N 10	18 19	18 41	19 08	10 20	11 07	11 53	12 41
0	18 02	18 24	18 50	10 30	11 13	11 55	12 39
S 10	17 45	18 08	18 34	10 40	11 19	11 57	12 37
20	17 28	17 51	18 19	10 50	11 25	12 00	12 35
30	17 07	17 33	18 03	11 02	11 33	12 02	12 32
35	16 56	17 23	17 55	11 09	11 37	12 04	12 31
40	16 42	17 12	17 46	11 17	11 42	12 05	12 29
45	16 26	17 00	17 36	11 25	11 47	12 07	12 27
S 50	16 07	16 45	17 26	11 36	11 53	12 09	12 25
52	15 57	16 38	17 21	11 41	11 56	12 10	12 24
54	15 47	16 30	17 15	11 47	12 00	12 12	12 23
56	15 35	16 21	17 10	11 53	12 03	12 13	12 22
58	15 22	16 12	17 04	11 59	12 07	12 14	12 21
S 60	15 06	16 01	16 57	12 07	12 12	12 16	12 19

SUN / MOON

Day	SUN Eqn. of Time 00ʰ	12ʰ	Mer. Pass.	MOON Mer. Pass. Upper	Lower	Age	Phase
	m s	m s	h m	h m	h m	d	
3	02 04	01 59	11 58	04 20	16 41	20	
4	01 54	01 49	11 58	05 03	17 24	21	◑
5	01 44	01 39	11 58	05 45	18 07	22	

Almanac

DECEMBER 9, 10, 11 (MON., TUES., WED.)

UT (GMT)	ARIES G.H.A.	VENUS −4.2 G.H.A.	VENUS Dec.	MARS +1.5 G.H.A.	MARS Dec.	JUPITER −2.1 G.H.A.	JUPITER Dec.	SATURN +0.7 G.H.A.	SATURN Dec.	STARS Name	S.H.A.	Dec.
d h	° ′	° ′	° ′	° ′	° ′	° ′	° ′	° ′	° ′		° ′	° ′
9 00	77 14.4	225 31.4	S10 22.2	192 01.9	S21 43.0	271 41.2	N 7 19.8	131 18.9	S19 55.8	Acamar	315 30.1	S40 20.2
01	92 16.9	240 31.0	23.2	207 02.5	43.3	286 43.5	19.8	146 21.1	55.8	Achernar	335 38.2	S57 16.8
02	107 19.4	255 30.7	24.2	222 03.1	43.6	301 45.8	19.7	161 23.3	55.7	Acrux	173 27.7	S63 03.1
03	122 21.8	270 30.4	·· 25.1	237 03.6	·· 43.9	316 48.1	·· 19.6	176 25.6	·· 55.7	Adhara	255 24.8	S28 57.6
04	137 24.3	285 30.0	26.1	252 04.2	44.3	331 50.4	19.6	191 27.8	55.6	Aldebaran	291 07.5	N16 29.7
05	152 26.8	300 29.7	27.0	267 04.7	44.6	346 52.7	19.5	206 30.0	55.6			
06	167 29.2	315 29.4	S10 28.0	282 05.3	S21 44.9	1 55.0	N 7 19.5	221 32.2	S19 55.5	Alioth	166 34.9	N55 59.9
07	182 31.7	330 29.0	28.9	297 05.9	45.2	16 57.3	19.4	236 34.5	55.4	Alkaid	153 11.8	N49 20.9
08	197 34.1	345 28.7	29.9	312 06.4	45.6	31 59.6	19.4	251 36.7	55.4	Al Na'ir	28 03.9	S47 00.2
M 09	212 36.6	0 28.4	·· 30.9	327 07.0	·· 45.9	47 01.9	·· 19.3	266 38.9	·· 55.3	Alnilam	276 02.3	S 1 12.3
O 10	227 39.1	15 28.0	31.8	342 07.6	46.2	62 04.2	19.3	281 41.1	55.3	Alphard	218 11.7	S 8 37.4
N 11	242 41.5	30 27.7	32.8	357 08.1	46.5	77 06.5	19.2	296 43.3	55.2			
D 12	257 44.0	45 27.4	S10 33.7	12 08.7	S21 46.8	92 08.8	N 7 19.2	311 45.6	S19 55.2	Alphecca	126 24.9	N26 44.4
A 13	272 46.5	60 27.0	34.7	27 09.2	47.2	107 11.1	19.1	326 47.8	55.1	Alpheratz	358 00.1	N29 03.1
Y 14	287 48.9	75 26.7	35.6	42 09.8	47.5	122 13.4	19.1	341 50.0	55.1	Altair	62 24.2	N 8 50.9
15	302 51.4	90 26.4	·· 36.6	57 10.4	·· 47.8	137 15.7	·· 19.0	356 52.2	·· 55.0	Ankaa	353 31.3	S42 21.1
16	317 53.9	105 26.0	37.5	72 10.9	48.1	152 18.0	18.9	11 54.4	55.0	Antares	112 46.4	S26 24.9
17	332 56.3	120 25.7	38.5	87 11.5	48.4	167 20.3	18.9	26 56.7	54.9			
18	347 58.8	135 25.4	S10 39.4	102 12.0	S21 48.8	182 22.6	N 7 18.8	41 58.9	S19 54.9	Arcturus	146 10.6	N19 13.3
19	3 01.3	150 25.0	40.4	117 12.6	49.1	197 25.0	18.8	57 01.1	54.8	Atria	108 03.3	S69 00.8
20	18 03.7	165 24.7	41.4	132 13.2	49.4	212 27.3	18.7	72 03.3	54.7	Avior	234 24.2	S59 28.8
21	33 06.2	180 24.3	·· 42.3	147 13.7	·· 49.7	227 29.6	·· 18.7	87 05.5	·· 54.7	Bellatrix	278 48.9	N 6 20.6
22	48 08.6	195 24.0	43.3	162 14.3	50.0	242 31.9	18.6	102 07.8	54.6	Betelgeuse	271 18.4	N 7 24.4
23	63 11.1	210 23.7	44.2	177 14.8	50.3	257 34.2	18.6	117 10.0	54.6			
10 00	78 13.6	225 23.3	S10 45.2	192 15.4	S21 50.7	272 36.5	N 7 18.5	132 12.2	S19 54.5	Canopus	264 02.7	S52 41.4
01	93 16.0	240 23.0	46.1	207 15.9	51.0	287 38.8	18.5	147 14.4	54.5	Capella	280 57.8	N45 59.5
02	108 18.5	255 22.6	47.1	222 16.5	51.3	302 41.1	18.4	162 16.6	54.4	Deneb	49 42.8	N45 15.3
03	123 21.0	270 22.3	·· 48.0	237 17.1	·· 51.6	317 43.4	·· 18.4	177 18.9	·· 54.4	Denebola	182 50.1	N14 36.9
04	138 23.4	285 22.0	49.0	252 17.6	51.9	332 45.7	18.3	192 21.1	54.3	Diphda	349 11.8	S18 01.8
05	153 25.9	300 21.6	49.9	267 18.2	52.2	347 48.0	18.3	207 23.3	54.3			
06	168 28.4	315 21.3	S10 50.9	282 18.7	S21 52.5	2 50.3	N 7 18.2	222 25.5	S19 54.2	Dubhe	194 11.1	N61 47.3
07	183 30.8	330 20.9	51.8	297 19.3	52.9	17 52.7	18.2	237 27.7	54.2	Elnath	278 32.6	N28 36.1
T 08	198 33.3	345 20.6	52.8	312 19.8	53.2	32 55.0	18.1	252 30.0	54.1	Eltanin	90 54.2	N51 29.4
U 09	213 35.8	0 20.2	·· 53.7	327 20.4	·· 53.5	47 57.3	·· 18.1	267 32.2	·· 54.0	Enif	34 03.0	N 9 50.4
E 10	228 38.2	15 19.9	54.7	342 21.0	53.8	62 59.6	18.0	282 34.4	54.0	Fomalhaut	15 41.6	S29 40.0
S 11	243 40.7	30 19.5	55.6	357 21.5	54.1	78 01.9	17.9	297 36.6	53.9			
D 12	258 43.1	45 19.2	S10 56.6	12 22.1	S21 54.4	93 04.2	N 7 17.9	312 38.8	S19 53.9	Gacrux	172 19.2	S57 03.9
A 13	273 45.6	60 18.8	57.5	27 22.6	54.7	108 06.5	17.8	327 41.0	53.8	Gienah	176 09.0	S17 29.8
Y 14	288 48.1	75 18.5	58.5	42 23.2	55.0	123 08.8	17.8	342 43.3	53.8	Hadar	149 11.4	S60 19.9
15	303 50.5	90 18.2	10 59.4	57 23.7	·· 55.4	138 11.2	·· 17.7	357 45.5	·· 53.7	Hamal	328 18.7	N23 25.7
16	318 53.0	105 17.8	11 00.4	72 24.3	55.7	153 13.5	17.7	12 47.7	53.7	Kaus Aust.	84 05.5	S34 23.4
17	333 55.5	120 17.5	01.3	87 24.8	56.0	168 15.8	17.6	27 49.9	53.6			
18	348 57.9	135 17.1	S11 02.3	102 25.4	S21 56.3	183 18.1	N 7 17.6	42 52.1	S19 53.6	Kochab	137 20.1	N74 11.0
19	4 00.4	150 16.8	03.2	117 26.0	56.6	198 20.4	17.5	57 54.3	53.5	Markab	13 54.4	N15 09.9
20	19 02.9	165 16.4	04.2	132 26.5	56.9	213 22.7	17.5	72 56.6	53.4	Menkar	314 31.6	N 4 03.6
21	34 05.3	180 16.1	·· 05.1	147 27.1	·· 57.2	228 25.0	·· 17.4	87 58.8	·· 53.4	Menkent	148 26.9	S36 19.8
22	49 07.8	195 15.7	06.0	162 27.6	57.5	243 27.3	17.4	103 01.0	53.3	Miaplacidus	221 42.7	S69 40.8
23	64 10.2	210 15.4	07.0	177 28.2	57.8	258 29.7	17.3	118 03.2	53.3			
11 00	79 12.7	225 15.0	S11 07.9	192 28.7	S21 58.1	273 32.0	N 7 17.3	133 05.4	S19 53.2	Mirfak	309 03.0	N49 50.2
01	94 15.2	240 14.7	08.9	207 29.3	58.5	288 34.3	17.2	148 07.7	53.2	Nunki	76 18.6	S26 18.5
02	109 17.6	255 14.3	09.8	222 29.8	58.8	303 36.6	17.2	163 09.9	53.1	Peacock	53 44.8	S56 45.8
03	124 20.1	270 13.9	·· 10.8	237 30.4	·· 59.1	318 38.9	·· 17.1	178 12.1	·· 53.1	Pollux	243 47.0	N28 02.7
04	139 22.6	285 13.6	11.7	252 30.9	59.4	333 41.2	17.1	193 14.3	53.0	Procyon	245 16.2	N 5 14.7
05	154 25.0	300 13.2	12.7	267 31.5	21 59.7	348 43.6	17.0	208 16.5	53.0			
06	169 27.5	315 12.9	S11 13.6	282 32.0	S22 00.0	3 45.9	N 7 17.0	223 18.7	S19 52.9	Rasalhague	96 21.7	N12 33.9
W 07	184 30.0	330 12.5	14.6	297 32.6	00.3	18 48.2	16.9	238 21.0	52.8	Regulus	208 00.5	N12 00.3
E 08	199 32.4	345 12.2	15.5	312 33.1	00.6	33 50.5	16.9	253 23.2	52.8	Rigel	281 27.2	S 8 12.6
D 09	214 34.9	0 11.8	·· 16.4	327 33.7	·· 00.9	48 52.8	·· 16.9	268 25.4	·· 52.7	Rigil Kent.	140 14.3	S60 48.0
N 10	229 37.4	15 11.5	17.4	342 34.2	01.2	63 55.1	16.8	283 27.6	52.7	Sabik	102 31.3	S15 42.9
E 11	244 39.8	30 11.1	18.3	357 34.8	01.5	78 57.5	16.8	298 29.8	52.6			
S 12	259 42.3	45 10.7	S11 19.3	12 35.3	S22 01.8	93 59.8	N 7 16.7	313 32.0	S19 52.6	Schedar	349 58.8	N56 30.0
D 13	274 44.7	60 10.4	20.2	27 35.9	02.1	109 02.1	16.7	328 34.2	52.5	Shaula	96 44.2	S37 05.9
A 14	289 47.2	75 10.0	21.2	42 36.4	02.4	124 04.4	16.6	343 36.5	52.5	Sirius	258 47.5	S16 42.2
Y 15	304 49.7	90 09.7	·· 22.1	57 37.0	·· 02.7	139 06.7	·· 16.6	358 38.7	·· 52.4	Spica	158 48.4	S11 07.2
16	319 52.1	105 09.3	23.0	72 37.5	03.0	154 09.1	16.5	13 40.9	52.4	Suhail	223 04.1	S43 23.8
17	334 54.6	120 08.9	24.0	87 38.1	03.3	169 11.4	16.5	28 43.1	52.3			
18	349 57.1	135 08.6	S11 24.9	102 38.6	S22 03.6	184 13.7	N 7 16.4	43 45.3	S19 52.2	Vega	80 50.3	N38 46.6
19	4 59.5	150 08.2	25.9	117 39.2	03.9	199 16.0	16.4	58 47.5	52.2	Zuben'ubi	137 23.5	S16 00.5
20	20 02.0	165 07.9	26.8	132 39.7	04.2	214 18.3	16.3	73 49.8	52.1			
21	35 04.5	180 07.5	·· 27.7	147 40.3	·· 04.5	229 20.7	·· 16.3	88 52.0	·· 52.1			
22	50 06.9	195 07.1	28.7	162 40.8	04.8	244 23.0	16.2	103 54.2	52.0		S.H.A.	Mer. Pass.
23	65 09.4	210 06.8	29.6	177 41.4	05.1	259 25.3	16.2	118 56.4	52.0		° ′	h m
										Venus	147 09.8	8 59
Mer. Pass. 18 44.0		v −0.3	d 0.9	v 0.6	d 0.3	v 2.3	d 0.1	v 2.2	d 0.1	Mars	114 01.5	11 11
										Jupiter	194 22.9	5 49
										Saturn	53 58.6	15 09

Almanac

DECEMBER 9, 10, 11 (MON., TUES., WED.)

UT (GMT)	SUN G.H.A.	SUN Dec.	MOON G.H.A.	v	MOON Dec.	d	H.P.
9 00	182 00.7	S22 44.7	148 22.3	12.4	S21 36.1	6.5	54.1
01	197 00.4	45.0	162 53.7	12.4	21 29.6	6.7	54.1
02	212 00.1	45.3	177 25.1	12.5	21 22.9	6.7	54.1
03	226 59.8 ..	45.5	191 56.6	12.5	21 16.2	6.8	54.1
04	241 59.5	45.8	206 28.1	12.5	21 09.4	6.9	54.1
05	256 59.3	46.0	220 59.6	12.7	21 02.5	7.0	54.1
06	271 59.0	S22 46.3	235 31.3	12.6	S20 55.5	7.0	54.1
M 07	286 58.7	46.5	250 02.9	12.8	20 48.5	7.2	54.1
O 08	301 58.4	46.8	264 34.7	12.8	20 41.3	7.3	54.1
N 09	316 58.2 ..	47.0	279 06.5	12.8	20 34.0	7.3	54.1
D 10	331 57.9	47.3	293 38.3	12.9	20 26.7	7.4	54.1
A 11	346 57.6	47.5	308 10.2	13.0	20 19.3	7.5	54.1
Y 12	1 57.3	S22 47.8	322 42.2	13.0	S20 11.8	7.7	54.1
13	16 57.0	48.0	337 14.2	13.1	20 04.1	7.6	54.0
14	31 56.8	48.3	351 46.3	13.1	19 56.5	7.8	54.0
15	46 56.5 ..	48.5	6 18.4	13.2	19 48.7	7.9	54.0
16	61 56.2	48.8	20 50.6	13.2	19 40.8	7.9	54.0
17	76 55.9	49.0	35 22.8	13.3	19 32.9	8.0	54.0
18	91 55.7	S22 49.2	49 55.1	13.3	S19 24.9	8.2	54.0
19	106 55.4	49.5	64 27.4	13.4	19 16.7	8.1	54.0
20	121 55.1	49.7	78 59.8	13.5	19 08.6	8.3	54.0
21	136 54.8 ..	50.0	93 32.3	13.5	19 00.3	8.4	54.0
22	151 54.5	50.2	108 04.8	13.5	18 51.9	8.4	54.0
23	166 54.3	50.7	122 37.3	13.7	18 43.5	8.5	54.0
10 00	181 54.0	S22 50.7	137 10.0	13.6	S18 35.0	8.6	54.0
01	196 53.7	50.9	151 42.6	13.7	18 26.4	8.6	54.0
02	211 53.4	51.2	166 15.3	13.8	18 17.8	8.8	54.0
03	226 53.1 ..	51.4	180 48.1	13.8	18 09.0	8.8	54.0
04	241 52.8	51.6	195 20.9	13.9	18 00.2	8.9	54.0
05	256 52.6	51.9	209 53.8	13.9	17 51.3	8.9	54.0
06	271 52.3	S22 52.1	224 26.7	14.0	S17 42.4	9.1	54.0
T 07	286 52.0	52.3	238 59.7	14.0	17 33.3	9.1	54.0
U 08	301 51.7	52.6	253 32.7	14.1	17 24.2	9.1	54.0
E 09	316 51.4 ..	52.8	268 05.8	14.2	17 15.1	9.3	54.0
S 10	331 51.2	53.0	282 39.0	14.1	17 05.8	9.3	54.0
D 11	346 50.9	53.3	297 12.1	14.3	16 56.5	9.4	54.0
A 12	1 50.6	S22 53.5	311 45.4	14.2	S16 47.1	9.4	54.0
Y 13	16 50.3	53.7	326 18.6	14.4	16 37.7	9.6	54.0
14	31 50.0	54.0	340 52.0	14.3	16 28.1	9.5	54.0
15	46 49.7 ..	54.2	355 25.3	14.4	16 18.6	9.7	54.1
16	61 49.5	54.4	9 58.7	14.5	16 08.9	9.7	54.1
17	76 49.2	54.6	24 32.2	14.5	15 59.2	9.8	54.1
18	91 48.9	S22 54.9	39 05.7	14.6	S15 49.4	9.9	54.1
19	106 48.6	55.1	53 39.3	14.6	15 39.5	9.9	54.1
20	121 48.3	55.3	68 12.9	14.6	15 29.6	10.0	54.1
21	136 48.0 ..	55.5	82 46.5	14.7	15 19.6	10.0	54.1
22	151 47.7	55.8	97 20.2	14.7	15 09.6	10.1	54.1
23	166 47.5	56.0	111 53.9	14.8	14 59.5	10.2	54.1
11 00	181 47.2	S22 56.2	126 27.7	14.8	S14 49.3	10.2	54.1
01	196 46.9	56.4	141 01.5	14.9	14 39.1	10.3	54.1
02	211 46.6	56.6	155 35.4	14.9	14 28.8	10.3	54.1
03	226 46.3 ..	56.9	170 09.3	14.9	14 18.5	10.4	54.1
04	241 46.0	57.1	184 43.2	15.0	14 08.1	10.5	54.1
05	256 45.8	57.3	199 17.2	15.0	13 57.6	10.5	54.1
06	271 45.5	S22 57.5	213 51.2	15.1	S13 47.1	10.6	54.1
W 07	286 45.2	57.7	228 25.3	15.1	13 36.5	10.6	54.1
E 08	301 44.9	57.9	242 59.4	15.1	13 25.9	10.7	54.1
D 09	316 44.6 ..	58.2	257 33.5	15.2	13 15.2	10.7	54.1
N 10	331 44.3	58.4	272 07.7	15.2	13 04.5	10.8	54.2
E 11	346 44.0	58.6	286 41.9	15.2	12 53.7	10.8	54.2
S 12	1 43.7	S22 58.8	301 16.1	15.3	S12 42.9	10.9	54.2
D 13	16 43.5	59.0	315 50.4	15.3	12 32.0	11.0	54.2
A 14	31 43.2	59.2	330 24.7	15.3	12 21.0	11.0	54.2
Y 15	46 42.9 ..	59.4	344 59.0	15.4	12 10.0	11.0	54.2
16	61 42.6	59.6	359 33.4	15.4	11 59.0	11.1	54.2
17	76 42.3	22 59.8	14 07.8	15.4	11 47.9	11.2	54.2
18	91 42.0	S23 00.0	28 42.2	15.5	S11 36.7	11.2	54.2
19	106 41.7	00.2	43 16.7	15.5	11 25.5	11.2	54.2
20	121 41.4	00.4	57 51.2	15.5	11 14.3	11.3	54.2
21	136 41.2 ..	00.7	72 25.7	15.5	11 03.0	11.3	54.3
22	151 40.9	00.9	87 00.2	15.6	10 51.7	11.4	54.3
23	166 40.6	01.1	101 34.8	15.6	10 40.3	11.4	54.3
	S.D. 16.3	d 0.2	S.D. 14.7		14.7		14.8

Twilight / Sunrise / Moonrise

Lat.	Naut.	Civil	Sunrise	Moonrise 9	10	11	12
N 72	08 11	10 28	▪	▪	13 42	12 51	12 21
N 70	07 52	09 36	▪	14 23	12 57	12 29	12 09
68	07 37	09 04	▪	12 53	12 27	12 12	12 00
66	07 25	08 40	10 14	12 14	12 05	11 58	11 52
64	07 15	08 22	09 37	11 46	11 47	11 46	11 45
62	07 05	08 07	09 10	11 25	11 32	11 36	11 39
60	06 57	07 54	08 50	11 08	11 20	11 28	11 34
N 58	06 50	07 42	08 33	10 54	11 09	11 20	11 29
56	06 44	07 33	08 19	10 41	10 59	11 13	11 25
54	06 38	07 24	08 07	10 30	10 51	11 07	11 21
52	06 32	07 16	07 56	10 21	10 43	11 02	11 18
50	06 27	07 09	07 47	10 12	10 37	10 57	11 15
45	06 16	06 53	07 27	09 53	10 22	10 46	11 08
N 40	06 06	06 40	07 10	09 38	10 10	10 38	11 03
35	05 57	06 29	06 57	09 26	10 00	10 30	10 58
30	05 49	06 18	06 45	09 14	09 51	10 23	10 54
20	05 33	06 00	06 24	08 55	09 35	10 12	10 46
N 10	05 17	05 43	06 06	08 38	09 21	10 01	10 40
0	05 00	05 26	05 49	08 23	09 08	09 52	10 34
S 10	04 42	05 09	05 32	08 07	08 55	09 42	10 27
20	04 20	04 49	05 13	07 50	08 41	09 32	10 21
30	03 51	04 25	04 52	07 31	08 25	09 20	10 13
35	03 33	04 10	04 39	07 19	08 16	09 13	10 09
40	03 11	03 52	04 25	07 06	08 06	09 05	10 04
45	02 41	03 30	04 07	06 51	07 53	08 56	09 58
S 50	01 58	03 01	03 45	06 32	07 38	08 44	09 51
52	01 33	02 47	03 35	06 22	07 31	08 39	09 48
54	00 54	02 30	03 23	06 12	07 23	08 34	09 44
56	////	02 09	03 09	06 01	07 14	08 27	09 41
58	////	01 42	02 53	05 47	07 03	08 20	09 36
S 60	////	01 00	02 34	05 32	06 52	08 12	09 31

Sunset / Twilight / Moonset

Lat.	Sunset	Civil	Naut.	Moonset 9	10	11	12
N 72	▪	13 17	15 34	▪	17 13	19 34	21 32
N 70	▪	14 09	15 52	14 58	17 57	19 55	21 41
68	▪	14 41	16 07	16 28	18 26	20 10	21 49
66	13 31	15 04	16 20	17 06	18 47	20 23	21 55
64	14 08	15 23	16 30	17 32	19 04	20 33	22 01
62	14 34	15 38	16 39	17 53	19 18	20 42	22 05
60	14 55	15 51	16 48	18 09	19 30	20 50	22 09
N 58	15 12	16 03	16 55	18 23	19 40	20 57	22 13
56	15 26	16 12	17 01	18 35	19 49	21 02	22 16
54	15 38	16 21	17 07	18 46	19 57	21 08	22 19
52	15 49	16 29	17 13	18 55	20 04	21 12	22 21
50	15 58	16 36	17 18	19 03	20 10	21 17	22 23
45	16 18	16 52	17 29	19 21	20 23	21 26	22 28
N 40	16 35	17 05	17 39	19 35	20 34	21 33	22 32
35	16 48	17 16	17 48	19 47	20 44	21 40	22 36
30	17 01	17 27	17 57	19 57	20 52	21 46	22 39
20	17 21	17 45	18 13	20 15	21 06	21 55	22 44
N 10	17 39	18 02	18 28	20 31	21 18	22 04	22 49
0	17 56	18 19	18 45	20 45	21 29	22 12	22 53
S 10	18 14	18 37	19 03	20 59	21 41	22 20	22 58
20	18 32	18 57	19 26	21 15	21 53	22 28	23 02
30	18 54	19 21	19 54	21 32	22 06	22 38	23 07
35	19 06	19 36	20 12	21 42	22 14	22 43	23 10
40	19 21	19 54	20 35	21 54	22 23	22 49	23 14
45	19 38	20 16	21 04	22 07	22 34	22 57	23 17
S 50	20 00	20 44	21 48	22 24	22 46	23 05	23 22
52	20 11	20 59	22 14	22 31	22 52	23 09	23 24
54	20 23	21 16	22 53	22 40	22 58	23 13	23 26
56	20 37	21 37	////	22 49	23 05	23 18	23 29
58	20 53	22 05	////	23 00	23 13	23 23	23 32
S 60	21 12	22 48	////	23 12	23 22	23 29	23 35

SUN / MOON

Day	SUN Eqn. of Time 00ʰ	12ʰ	Mer. Pass.	MOON Mer. Pass. Upper	Lower	Age	Phase
9	08 03	07 50	11 52	14 34	02 11	03	🌗
10	07 36	07 23	11 53	15 19	02 57	04	
11	07 09	06 56	11 53	16 02	03 41	05	

34ᵐ   INCREMENTS AND CORRECTIONS   **35ᵐ**

34	SUN PLANETS	ARIES	MOON	v or Corrⁿ d	v or Corrⁿ d	v or Corrⁿ d	35	SUN PLANETS	ARIES	MOON	v or Corrⁿ d	v or Corrⁿ d	v or Corrⁿ d
00	8 30·0	8 31·4	8 06·8	0·0 0·0	6·0 3·5	12·0 6·9	00	8 45·0	8 46·4	8 21·1	0·0 0·0	6·0 3·6	12·0 7·1
01	8 30·3	8 31·6	8 07·0	0·1 0·1	6·1 3·5	12·1 7·0	01	8 45·3	8 46·7	8 21·3	0·1 0·1	6·1 3·6	12·1 7·2
02	8 30·5	8 31·9	8 07·2	0·2 0·1	6·2 3·6	12·2 7·0	02	8 45·5	8 46·9	8 21·6	0·2 0·1	6·2 3·7	12·2 7·2
03	8 30·8	8 32·1	8 07·5	0·3 0·2	6·3 3·6	12·3 7·1	03	8 45·8	8 47·2	8 21·8	0·3 0·2	6·3 3·7	12·3 7·3
04	8 31·0	8 32·4	8 07·7	0·4 0·2	6·4 3·7	12·4 7·1	04	8 46·0	8 47·4	8 22·0	0·4 0·2	6·4 3·8	12·4 7·3
05	8 31·3	8 32·6	8 08·0	0·5 0·3	6·5 3·7	12·5 7·2	05	8 46·3	8 47·7	8 22·3	0·5 0·3	6·5 3·8	12·5 7·4
06	8 31·5	8 32·9	8 08·2	0·6 0·3	6·6 3·8	12·6 7·2	06	8 46·5	8 47·9	8 22·5	0·6 0·4	6·6 3·9	12·6 7·5
07	8 31·8	8 33·2	8 08·4	0·7 0·4	6·7 3·9	12·7 7·3	07	8 46·8	8 48·2	8 22·8	0·7 0·4	6·7 4·0	12·7 7·5
08	8 32·0	8 33·4	8 08·7	0·8 0·5	6·8 3·9	12·8 7·4	08	8 47·0	8 48·4	8 23·0	0·8 0·5	6·8 4·0	12·8 7·6
09	8 32·3	8 33·7	8 08·9	0·9 0·5	6·9 4·0	12·9 7·4	09	8 47·3	8 48·7	8 23·2	0·9 0·5	6·9 4·1	12·9 7·6
10	8 32·5	8 33·9	8 09·2	1·0 0·6	7·0 4·0	13·0 7·5	10	8 47·5	8 48·9	8 23·5	1·0 0·6	7·0 4·1	13·0 7·7
11	8 32·8	8 34·2	8 09·4	1·1 0·6	7·1 4·1	13·1 7·5	11	8 47·8	8 49·2	8 23·7	1·1 0·7	7·1 4·2	13·1 7·8
12	8 33·0	8 34·4	8 09·6	1·2 0·7	7·2 4·1	13·2 7·6	12	8 48·0	8 49·4	8 23·9	1·2 0·7	7·2 4·3	13·2 7·8
13	8 33·3	8 34·7	8 09·9	1·3 0·7	7·3 4·2	13·3 7·6	13	8 48·3	8 49·7	8 24·2	1·3 0·8	7·3 4·3	13·3 7·9
14	8 33·5	8 34·9	8 10·1	1·4 0·8	7·4 4·3	13·4 7·7	14	8 48·5	8 49·9	8 24·4	1·4 0·8	7·4 4·4	13·4 7·9
15	8 33·8	8 35·2	8 10·3	1·5 0·9	7·5 4·3	13·5 7·8	15	8 48·8	8 50·2	8 24·7	1·5 0·9	7·5 4·4	13·5 8·0
16	8 34·0	8 35·4	8 10·6	1·6 0·9	7·6 4·4	13·6 7·8	16	8 49·0	8 50·4	8 24·9	1·6 0·9	7·6 4·5	13·6 8·0
17	8 34·3	8 35·7	8 10·8	1·7 1·0	7·7 4·4	13·7 7·9	17	8 49·3	8 50·7	8 25·1	1·7 1·0	7·7 4·6	13·7 8·1
18	8 34·5	8 35·9	8 11·1	1·8 1·0	7·8 4·5	13·8 7·9	18	8 49·5	8 50·9	8 25·4	1·8 1·1	7·8 4·6	13·8 8·2
19	8 34·8	8 36·2	8 11·3	1·9 1·1	7·9 4·5	13·9 8·0	19	8 49·8	8 51·2	8 25·6	1·9 1·1	7·9 4·7	13·9 8·2
20	8 35·0	8 36·4	8 11·5	2·0 1·2	8·0 4·6	14·0 8·1	20	8 50·0	8 51·5	8 25·9	2·0 1·2	8·0 4·7	14·0 8·3
21	8 35·3	8 36·7	8 11·8	2·1 1·2	8·1 4·7	14·1 8·1	21	8 50·3	8 51·7	8 26·1	2·1 1·2	8·1 4·8	14·1 8·3
22	8 35·5	8 36·9	8 12·0	2·2 1·3	8·2 4·7	14·2 8·2	22	8 50·5	8 52·0	8 26·3	2·2 1·3	8·2 4·9	14·2 8·4
23	8 35·8	8 37·2	8 12·3	2·3 1·3	8·3 4·8	14·3 8·2	23	8 50·8	8 52·2	8 26·6	2·3 1·4	8·3 4·9	14·3 8·5
24	8 36·0	8 37·4	8 12·5	2·4 1·4	8·4 4·8	14·4 8·3	24	8 51·0	8 52·5	8 26·8	2·4 1·4	8·4 5·0	14·4 8·5
25	8 36·3	8 37·7	8 12·7	2·5 1·4	8·5 4·9	14·5 8·3	25	8 51·3	8 52·7	8 27·0	2·5 1·5	8·5 5·0	14·5 8·6
26	8 36·5	8 37·9	8 13·0	2·6 1·5	8·6 4·9	14·6 8·4	26	8 51·5	8 53·0	8 27·3	2·6 1·5	8·6 5·1	14·6 8·6
27	8 36·8	8 38·2	8 13·2	2·7 1·6	8·7 5·0	14·7 8·5	27	8 51·8	8 53·2	8 27·5	2·7 1·6	8·7 5·1	14·7 8·7
28	8 37·0	8 38·4	8 13·4	2·8 1·6	8·8 5·1	14·8 8·5	28	8 52·0	8 53·5	8 27·8	2·8 1·7	8·8 5·2	14·8 8·8
29	8 37·3	8 38·7	8 13·7	2·9 1·7	8·9 5·1	14·9 8·6	29	8 52·3	8 53·7	8 28·0	2·9 1·7	8·9 5·3	14·9 8·8
30	8 37·5	8 38·9	8 13·9	3·0 1·7	9·0 5·2	15·0 8·6	30	8 52·5	8 54·0	8 28·2	3·0 1·8	9·0 5·3	15·0 8·9
31	8 37·8	8 39·2	8 14·2	3·1 1·8	9·1 5·2	15·1 8·7	31	8 52·8	8 54·2	8 28·5	3·1 1·8	9·1 5·4	15·1 8·9
32	8 38·0	8 39·4	8 14·4	3·2 1·8	9·2 5·3	15·2 8·7	32	8 53·0	8 54·5	8 28·7	3·2 1·9	9·2 5·4	15·2 9·0
33	8 38·3	8 39·7	8 14·6	3·3 1·9	9·3 5·3	15·3 8·8	33	8 53·3	8 54·7	8 29·0	3·3 1·9	9·3 5·5	15·3 9·1
34	8 38·5	8 39·9	8 14·9	3·4 2·0	9·4 5·4	15·4 8·9	34	8 53·5	8 55·0	8 29·2	3·4 2·0	9·4 5·6	15·4 9·1
35	8 38·8	8 40·2	8 15·1	3·5 2·0	9·5 5·5	15·5 8·9	35	8 53·8	8 55·2	8 29·4	3·5 2·1	9·5 5·6	15·5 9·2
36	8 39·0	8 40·4	8 15·4	3·6 2·1	9·6 5·5	15·6 9·0	36	8 54·0	8 55·5	8 29·7	3·6 2·1	9·6 5·7	15·6 9·2
37	8 39·3	8 40·7	8 15·6	3·7 2·1	9·7 5·6	15·7 9·0	37	8 54·3	8 55·7	8 29·9	3·7 2·2	9·7 5·7	15·7 9·3
38	8 39·5	8 40·9	8 15·8	3·8 2·2	9·8 5·6	15·8 9·1	38	8 54·5	8 56·0	8 30·2	3·8 2·2	9·8 5·8	15·8 9·3
39	8 39·8	8 41·2	8 16·1	3·9 2·2	9·9 5·7	15·9 9·1	39	8 54·8	8 56·2	8 30·4	3·9 2·3	9·9 5·9	15·9 9·4
40	8 40·0	8 41·4	8 16·3	4·0 2·3	10·0 5·8	16·0 9·2	40	8 55·0	8 56·5	8 30·6	4·0 2·4	10·0 5·9	16·0 9·5
41	8 40·3	8 41·7	8 16·5	4·1 2·4	10·1 5·8	16·1 9·3	41	8 55·3	8 56·7	8 30·9	4·1 2·4	10·1 6·0	16·1 9·5
42	8 40·5	8 41·9	8 16·8	4·2 2·4	10·2 5·9	16·2 9·3	42	8 55·5	8 57·0	8 31·1	4·2 2·5	10·2 6·0	16·2 9·6
43	8 40·8	8 42·2	8 17·0	4·3 2·5	10·3 5·9	16·3 9·4	43	8 55·8	8 57·2	8 31·3	4·3 2·5	10·3 6·1	16·3 9·6
44	8 41·0	8 42·4	8 17·3	4·4 2·5	10·4 6·0	16·4 9·4	44	8 56·0	8 57·5	8 31·6	4·4 2·6	10·4 6·2	16·4 9·7
45	8 41·3	8 42·7	8 17·5	4·5 2·6	10·5 6·0	16·5 9·5	45	8 56·3	8 57·7	8 31·8	4·5 2·7	10·5 6·2	16·5 9·8
46	8 41·5	8 42·9	8 17·7	4·6 2·6	10·6 6·1	16·6 9·5	46	8 56·5	8 58·0	8 32·1	4·6 2·7	10·6 6·3	16·6 9·8
47	8 41·8	8 43·2	8 18·0	4·7 2·7	10·7 6·2	16·7 9·6	47	8 56·8	8 58·2	8 32·3	4·7 2·8	10·7 6·3	16·7 9·9
48	8 42·0	8 43·4	8 18·2	4·8 2·8	10·8 6·2	16·8 9·7	48	8 57·0	8 58·5	8 32·5	4·8 2·8	10·8 6·4	16·8 9·9
49	8 42·3	8 43·7	8 18·5	4·9 2·8	10·9 6·3	16·9 9·7	49	8 57·3	8 58·7	8 32·8	4·9 2·9	10·9 6·4	16·9 10·0
50	8 42·5	8 43·9	8 18·7	5·0 2·9	11·0 6·3	17·0 9·8	50	8 57·5	8 59·0	8 33·0	5·0 3·0	11·0 6·5	17·0 10·1
51	8 42·8	8 44·2	8 18·9	5·1 2·9	11·1 6·4	17·1 9·8	51	8 57·8	8 59·2	8 33·3	5·1 3·0	11·1 6·6	17·1 10·1
52	8 43·0	8 44·4	8 19·2	5·2 3·0	11·2 6·4	17·2 9·9	52	8 58·0	8 59·5	8 33·5	5·2 3·1	11·2 6·6	17·2 10·2
53	8 43·3	8 44·7	8 19·4	5·3 3·0	11·3 6·5	17·3 9·9	53	8 58·3	8 59·7	8 33·7	5·3 3·1	11·3 6·7	17·3 10·2
54	8 43·5	8 44·9	8 19·7	5·4 3·1	11·4 6·6	17·4 10·0	54	8 58·5	9 00·0	8 34·0	5·4 3·2	11·4 6·7	17·4 10·3
55	8 43·8	8 45·2	8 19·9	5·5 3·2	11·5 6·6	17·5 10·1	55	8 58·8	9 00·2	8 34·2	5·5 3·3	11·5 6·8	17·5 10·4
56	8 44·0	8 45·4	8 20·1	5·6 3·2	11·6 6·7	17·6 10·1	56	8 59·0	9 00·5	8 34·4	5·6 3·3	11·6 6·9	17·6 10·4
57	8 44·3	8 45·7	8 20·4	5·7 3·3	11·7 6·7	17·7 10·2	57	8 59·3	9 00·7	8 34·7	5·7 3·4	11·7 6·9	17·7 10·5
58	8 44·5	8 45·9	8 20·6	5·8 3·3	11·8 6·8	17·8 10·2	58	8 59·5	9 01·0	8 34·9	5·8 3·4	11·8 7·0	17·8 10·5
59	8 44·8	8 46·2	8 20·8	5·9 3·4	11·9 6·8	17·9 10·3	59	8 59·8	9 01·2	8 35·2	5·9 3·5	11·9 7·0	17·9 10·6
60	8 45·0	8 46·4	8 21·1	6·0 3·5	12·0 6·9	18·0 10·4	60	9 00·0	9 01·5	8 35·4	6·0 3·6	12·0 7·1	18·0 10·7

Altitude Correction Tables

(Reproduced from the Nautical Almanac)

A2 ALTITUDE CORRECTION TABLES 10°–90°—SUN, STARS, PLANETS

SUN

OCT.—MAR. App. Alt.	Lower Limb	Upper Limb	APR.—SEPT. App. Alt.	Lower Limb	Upper Limb
9 34	+10·8	−21·5	9 39	+10·6	−21·2
9 45	+10·9	−21·4	9 51	+10·7	−21·1
9 56	+11·0	−21·3	10 03	+10·8	−21·0
10 08	+11·1	−21·2	10 15	+10·9	−20·9
10 21	+11·2	−21·1	10 27	+11·0	−20·8
10 34	+11·3	−21·0	10 40	+11·1	−20·7
10 47	+11·4	−20·9	10 54	+11·2	−20·6
11 01	+11·5	−20·8	11 08	+11·3	−20·5
11 15	+11·6	−20·7	11 23	+11·4	−20·4
11 30	+11·7	−20·6	11 38	+11·5	−20·3
11 46	+11·8	−20·5	11 54	+11·6	−20·2
12 02	+11·9	−20·4	12 10	+11·7	−20·1
12 19	+12·0	−20·3	12 28	+11·8	−20·0
12 37	+12·1	−20·2	12 46	+11·9	−19·9
12 55	+12·2	−20·1	13 05	+12·0	−19·8
13 14	+12·3	−20·0	13 24	+12·1	−19·7
13 35	+12·4	−19·9	13 45	+12·2	−19·6
13 56	+12·5	−19·8	14 07	+12·3	−19·5
14 18	+12·6	−19·7	14 30	+12·4	−19·4
14 42	+12·7	−19·6	14 54	+12·5	−19·3
15 06	+12·8	−19·5	15 19	+12·6	−19·2
15 32	+12·9	−19·4	15 46	+12·7	−19·1
15 59	+13·0	−19·3	16 14	+12·8	−19·0
16 28	+13·1	−19·2	16 44	+12·9	−18·9
16 59	+13·2	−19·1	17 15	+13·0	−18·8
17 32	+13·3	−19·0	17 48	+13·1	−18·7
18 06	+13·4	−18·9	18 24	+13·2	−18·6
18 42	+13·5	−18·8	19 01	+13·3	−18·5
19 21	+13·6	−18·7	19 42	+13·4	−18·4
20 03	+13·7	−18·6	20 25	+13·5	−18·3
20 48	+13·8	−18·5	21 11	+13·6	−18·2
21 35	+13·9	−18·4	22 00	+13·7	−18·1
22 26	+14·0	−18·3	22 54	+13·8	−18·0
23 22	+14·1	−18·2	23 51	+13·9	−17·9
24 21	+14·2	−18·1	24 53	+14·0	−17·8
25 26	+14·3	−18·0	26 00	+14·1	−17·7
26 36	+14·4	−17·9	27 13	+14·2	−17·6
27 52	+14·5	−17·8	28 33	+14·3	−17·5
29 15	+14·6	−17·7	30 00	+14·4	−17·4
30 46	+14·7	−17·6	31 35	+14·5	−17·3
32 26	+14·8	−17·5	33 20	+14·6	−17·2
34 17	+14·9	−17·4	35 17	+14·7	−17·1
36 20	+15·0	−17·3	37 26	+14·8	−17·0
38 36	+15·1	−17·2	39 50	+14·9	−16·9
41 08	+15·2	−17·1	42 31	+15·0	−16·8
43 59	+15·3	−17·0	45 31	+15·1	−16·7
47 10	+15·4	−16·9	48 55	+15·2	−16·6
50 46	+15·5	−16·8	52 44	+15·3	−16·5
54 49	+15·6	−16·7	57 02	+15·4	−16·4
59 23	+15·7	−16·6	61 51	+15·5	−16·3
64 30	+15·8	−16·5	67 17	+15·6	−16·2
70 12	+15·9	−16·4	73 16	+15·7	−16·1
76 26	+16·0	−16·3	79 43	+15·8	−16·0
83 05	+16·1	−16·2	86 32	+15·9	−15·9
90 00			90 00		

STARS AND PLANETS

App. Alt.	Corrn		App. Alt.	Additional Corrn
9 56	−5·3			**1991**
10 08	−5·2			**VENUS**
10 20	−5·1			
10 33	−5·0			Jan. 1–May 10
10 46	−4·9			Dec. 12–Dec. 31
11 00	−4·8		°	
11 14	−4·7		0	+ 0·1
11 29	−4·6		60	
11 45	−4·5			
12 01	−4·4			May 11–June 28
12 18	−4·3			Oct. 20–Dec. 11
12 35	−4·2		°	
12 54	−4·1		0	+ 0·2
13 13	−4·0		41	+ 0·1
13 33	−3·9		76	
13 54	−3·8			
14 16	−3·7			June 29–July 21
14 40	−3·6			Sept. 26–Oct. 19
15 04	−3·5		°	
15 30	−3·4		0	+ 0·3
15 57	−3·3		34	+ 0·2
16 26	−3·2		60	+ 0·1
16 56	−3·1		80	
17 28	−3·0			
18 02	−2·9			July 22–Aug. 6
18 38	−2·8			Sept. 9–Sept. 25
19 17	−2·7		°	
19 58	−2·6		0	+ 0·4
20 42	−2·5		29	+ 0·3
21 28	−2·4		51	+ 0·2
22 19	−2·3		68	+ 0·1
23 13	−2·2		83	
24 11	−2·1			
25 14	−2·0			Aug. 7–Sept. 8
26 22	−1·9		°	
27 36	−1·8		0	+ 0·5
28 56	−1·7		26	+ 0·4
30 24	−1·6		46	+ 0·3
32 00	−1·5		60	+ 0·2
33 45	−1·4		73	+ 0·1
35 40	−1·3		84	
37 48	−1·2			
40 08	−1·1			**MARS**
42 44	−1·0			Jan. 1–Feb. 4
45 36	−0·9		°	
48 47	−0·8		0	+ 0·2
52 18	−0·7		41	+ 0·1
56 11	−0·6		76	
60 28	−0·5			Feb. 5–Dec. 31
65 08	−0·4		°	
70 11	−0·3		0	+ 0·1
75 34	−0·2		60	
81 13	−0·1			
87 03	0·0			
90 00				

DIP

Ht. of Eye (m)	Corrn	Ht. of Eye (ft)	Ht. of Eye (m)	Corrn
2·4	−2·8	8·0	1·0	− 1·8
2·6	−2·9	8·6	1·5	− 2·2
2·8		9·2	2·0	− 2·5
3·0	−3·0	9·8	2·5	− 2·8
3·2	−3·1	10·5	3·0	− 3·0
3·4	−3·2	11·2	See table	
3·6	−3·3	11·9		
3·8	−3·4	12·6	Ht. of Eye (m)	Corrn
4·0	−3·5	13·3	20	− 7·9
4·3	−3·6	14·1	22	− 8·3
4·5	−3·7	14·9	24	− 8·6
4·7	−3·8	15·7	26	− 9·0
5·0	−3·9	16·5	28	− 9·3
5·2	−4·0	17·4		
5·5	−4·1	18·3	30	− 9·6
5·8	−4·2	19·1	32	− 10·0
6·1	−4·3	20·1	34	− 10·3
6·3	−4·4	21·0	36	− 10·6
6·6	−4·5	22·0	38	− 10·8
6·9	−4·6	22·9		
7·2	−4·7	23·9	40	− 11·1
7·5	−4·8	24·9	42	− 11·4
7·9	−4·9	26·0	44	− 11·7
8·2	−5·0	27·1	46	− 11·9
8·5	−5·1	28·1	48	− 12·2
8·8	−5·2	29·2	ft.	
9·2	−5·3	30·4	2	− 1·4
9·5	−5·4	31·5	4	− 1·9
9·9	−5·5	32·7	6	− 2·4
10·3	−5·6	33·9	8	− 2·7
10·6	−5·7	35·1	10	− 3·1
11·0	−5·8	36·3	See table	
11·4	−5·9	37·6		
11·8	−6·0	38·9	ft.	
12·2	−6·1	40·1	70	− 8·1
12·6	−6·2	41·5	75	− 8·4
13·0	−6·3	42·8	80	− 8·7
13·4	−6·4	44·2	85	− 8·9
13·8	−6·5	45·5	90	− 9·2
14·2	−6·6	46·9	95	− 9·5
14·7	−6·7	48·4		
15·1	−6·8	49·8	100	− 9·7
15·5	−6·9	51·3	105	− 9·9
16·0	−7·0	52·8	110	− 10·2
16·5	−7·1	54·3	115	− 10·4
16·9	−7·2	55·8	120	− 10·6
17·4	−7·3	57·4	125	− 10·8
17·9	−7·4	58·9		
18·4	−7·5	60·5	130	− 11·1
18·8	−7·6	62·1	135	− 11·3
19·3	−7·7	63·8	140	− 11·5
19·8	−7·8	65·4	145	− 11·7
20·4	−7·9	67·1	150	− 11·9
20·9	−8·0	68·8	155	− 12·1
21·4	−8·1	70·5		

App. Alt. = Apparent altitude = Sextant altitude corrected for index error and dip.

DECLINATION (15°–29°) SAME NAME AS LATITUDE

(Reproduced from Sight Reduction Tables HO249 Vol.2)

Declination (15° 29') Same Name as Latitude

N. Lat. { LHA greater than 180°....... Zn=Z
{ LHA less than 180°....... Zn=360−Z

LHA	15° Hc d Z	16° Hc d Z	17° Hc d Z	18° Hc d Z	19° Hc d Z	20° Hc d Z	21° Hc d Z	22° Hc d Z	23° Hc d Z	24° Hc d Z	25° Hc d Z	26° Hc d Z	27° Hc d Z	28° Hc d Z	29° Hc d Z	LHA
0	75 00 +60 180	76 00 +60 180	77 00 +60 180	78 00 +60 180	79 00 +60 180	80 00 +60 180	81 00 +60 180	82 00 +60 180	83 00 +60 180	84 00 +60 180	85 00 +60 180	86 00 +60 180	87 00 +60 180	88 00 +60 180	89 00 +60 180	360
1	74 58 60 176	75 58 60 176	76 58 60 176	77 58 60 175	78 57 60 175	79 58 60 175	80 57 59 174	81 57 59 173	82 57 59 173	83 56 59 171	84 55 59 170	85 54 58 168	86 52 57 163	87 49 51 156	88 40 28 139	359
2	74 53 60 173	75 53 59 172	76 52 60 172	77 52 59 171	78 51 59 170	79 50 59 169	80 49 59 168	81 48 59 167	82 47 58 165	83 45 57 163	84 42 56 160	85 38 55 156	86 31 50 149	87 21 39 138	88 00 16 119	358
3	74 45 59 169	75 44 59 168	76 43 59 167	77 42 58 167	78 40 59 165	79 38 58 164	80 36 58 163	81 34 56 161	82 30 56 159	83 28 56 156	84 22 52 151	85 12 48 146	86 00 42 127	86 12 12 110	87 05 9 105	357
4	74 33 59 165	75 32 58 164	76 30 58 163	77 28 57 162	78 25 57 161	79 22 56 159	80 18 56 157	81 14 57 155	82 08 53 152	83 01 51 148	83 52 48 144	84 40 43 138	85 23 35 130	85 58 25 119	86 23 9 105	356
5	74 19 +57 162	75 16 +57 161	76 13 +57 160	77 10 +56 158	78 06 +56 156	79 02 +54 155	79 56 +54 152	80 50 +50 150	81 43 +47 146	82 32 +47 142	83 19 +44 137	84 03 +38 131	84 41 +31 123	85 13 +17 111	85 32 +8 102	355
6	74 01 57 159	74 58 56 157	75 54 55 156	76 49 55 154	77 44 53 152	78 37 53 150	79 30 51 148	80 21 50 145	81 11 47 141	81 58 44 137	82 42 40 132	83 23 34 126	83 56 27 118	84 23 18 109	84 41 7 99	354
7	73 41 55 155	74 36 56 154	75 31 54 152	76 25 53 150	77 18 52 148	78 10 51 146	79 01 49 143	79 50 47 140	80 37 44 137	81 21 41 132	82 03 37 127	82 38 32 121	83 14 16 106	83 34 16 106	83 50 6 98	353
8	73 18 54 152	74 12 53 151	75 05 53 149	75 58 51 147	76 49 51 145	77 40 48 142	78 28 47 139	79 15 45 135	80 00 41 133	80 41 36 128	81 18 32 122	82 38 32 121	82 22 22 111	82 44 14 98	82 58 6 96	352
9	72 52 53 149	73 45 52 148	74 37 51 146	75 28 50 144	76 18 14 143	77 06 47 139	77 53 45 136	78 38 42 133	79 20 40 129	80 00 35 125	80 35 32 120	81 07 26 115	81 33 20 109	81 53 13 102	82 06 6 95	351
10	72 24 +52 146	73 16 +51 145	74 07 +44 143	74 56 +48 141	75 44 +47 138	76 31 +45 136	77 16 +43 133	77 59 +40 129	78 39 +37 126	79 16 +34 122	79 50 +29 117	80 19 +24 112	80 43 +19 106	81 02 +13 100	81 15 +6 94	350
11	71 55 50 144	72 45 49 142	73 34 48 140	74 22 46 138	75 09 44 135	75 54 43 133	76 37 41 130	77 18 38 126	77 56 35 123	78 31 32 119	79 03 29 114	79 30 23 110	79 53 18 105	80 11 12 99	80 23 6 93	349
12	71 23 49 141	72 12 48 139	73 00 46 137	73 46 45 135	74 31 44 133	75 15 43 130	75 56 39 127	76 35 37 124	77 12 33 120	77 45 30 117	78 15 26 112	78 41 22 108	79 03 16 103	79 19 12 98	79 31 6 93	348
13	70 49 48 139	71 37 47 137	72 24 45 135	73 09 43 133	73 52 42 130	74 34 40 127	75 14 37 125	75 51 35 121	76 26 32 118	76 58 29 114	77 27 24 110	77 51 21 106	78 12 16 102	78 28 11 97	78 39 6 92	347
14	70 14 47 136	71 01 45 134	71 46 43 132	72 30 42 130	73 12 40 128	73 52 38 125	74 31 36 122	75 07 33 119	75 41 30 116	76 13 27 112	76 38 20 109	77 01 20 105	77 21 15 100	77 36 11 96	77 47 6 91	346
15	69 37 +46 134	70 23 +44 132	71 07 +42 130	71 49 +41 128	72 30 +39 126	73 09 +37 123	73 46 +35 120	74 21 +32 117	74 53 +29 114	75 22 +26 111	75 48 +23 107	76 11 +19 103	76 30 +14 99	76 44 +5 95	76 55 +6 91	345
16	68 59 45 132	69 44 42 130	70 28 42 128	71 08 39 126	71 47 38 124	72 25 36 121	73 01 33 118	73 34 31 115	74 05 28 112	74 32 24 108	74 58 22 106	75 20 18 102	75 38 15 98	75 53 10 94	76 03 6 90	344
17	68 20 45 130	69 03 42 128	69 45 40 126	70 25 39 124	71 04 37 122	71 40 35 119	72 15 32 117	72 47 30 114	73 17 27 111	73 44 24 108	74 08 21 104	74 29 18 101	74 47 14 97	75 01 10 94	75 11 7 90	343
18	67 40 42 128	68 22 41 126	69 03 39 124	69 42 37 122	70 19 35 120	70 54 34 117	71 28 31 115	72 00 28 112	72 28 26 109	72 54 24 106	73 17 20 103	73 38 17 100	73 55 14 96	74 09 10 93	74 19 7 89	342
19	66 59 41 127	67 40 39 125	68 19 38 123	68 57 36 121	69 33 35 118	70 08 32 116	70 40 31 113	71 11 28 111	71 39 25 108	72 04 23 105	72 27 20 102	72 47 16 99	73 03 14 96	73 17 10 93	73 27 7 89	341
20	66 16 +40 125	66 56 +39 123	67 35 +37 121	68 12 +35 119	68 47 +34 117	69 21 +31 114	69 52 +30 112	70 22 +27 109	70 49 +25 107	71 14 +22 104	71 36 +19 101	71 55 +17 98	72 12 +13 95	72 25 +10 92	72 35 +7 88	340
21	65 33 39 123	66 12 38 121	66 50 36 119	67 26 35 117	68 01 32 115	68 33 31 113	69 04 29 111	69 33 26 108	69 59 24 105	70 23 22 103	70 45 19 100	71 02 15 97	71 19 13 94	71 33 10 91	71 43 7 88	339
22	64 50 38 122	65 28 36 120	66 04 36 118	66 40 33 116	67 13 32 114	67 45 30 112	68 15 28 109	68 43 26 107	69 09 23 104	69 32 22 102	69 54 18 99	70 12 16 96	70 28 13 93	70 41 10 91	70 51 8 88	338
23	64 05 37 120	64 42 36 119	65 18 35 117	65 53 33 115	66 26 31 113	66 57 29 110	67 26 27 108	67 53 25 106	68 18 23 103	68 41 20 101	69 02 18 98	69 20 16 96	69 36 13 93	69 49 10 90	69 59 8 87	337
24	63 20 36 119	63 56 35 117	64 32 33 115	65 06 32 113	65 37 31 111	66 08 28 109	66 36 26 107	67 03 25 105	67 28 22 102	67 50 20 100	68 11 18 98	68 28 15 95	68 44 13 92	68 57 11 90	69 08 7 87	336
25	62 34 +36 118	63 10 +34 116	63 44 +33 114	64 17 +32 112	64 49 +29 110	65 18 +29 108	65 47 +26 106	66 13 +24 104	66 37 +22 101	66 59 +20 99	67 19 +18 97	67 37 +15 94	67 52 +13 92	68 05 +11 89	68 16 +8 86	335
26	61 48 35 116	62 23 34 115	62 57 32 113	63 29 31 111	64 00 29 109	64 29 27 107	64 56 26 105	65 22 24 103	65 46 22 100	66 08 19 98	66 27 18 96	66 45 15 94	67 00 13 91	67 13 11 89	67 24 8 86	334
27	61 01 34 116	61 35 34 114	62 09 32 112	62 40 30 110	63 10 29 108	63 39 27 106	64 06 25 104	64 31 24 102	64 55 21 100	65 16 20 98	65 35 18 95	65 53 15 93	66 08 13 91	66 21 11 88	66 32 8 85	333
28	60 14 34 114	60 48 32 112	61 20 31 111	61 51 30 109	62 21 28 107	62 49 27 105	63 16 24 103	63 40 24 101	64 04 21 99	64 25 18 96	64 44 17 95	65 01 15 92	65 16 13 90	65 29 10 88	65 40 9 85	332
29	59 26 33 113	59 59 31 111	60 31 31 110	61 02 28 108	61 31 28 106	61 59 26 104	62 25 24 102	62 49 23 100	63 12 21 98	63 33 19 96	63 52 17 94	64 09 15 92	64 24 14 90	64 38 10 87	64 48 8 85	331
30	58 38 +33 112	59 11 +31 110	59 42 +30 108	60 12 +29 107	60 41 +27 105	61 08 +26 103	61 34 +24 101	61 58 +23 99	62 21 +20 98	62 41 +19 95	63 00 +17 93	63 15 +13 91	63 32 +14 89	63 46 +11 87	63 57 +9 85	330
31	57 50 32 111	58 22 31 109	58 53 29 107	59 22 29 106	59 51 27 104	60 18 25 102	60 43 24 101	61 07 22 99	61 30 20 97	61 50 18 95	62 08 17 93	62 23 14 91	62 41 13 89	62 54 11 87	63 05 9 84	329
32	57 01 32 110	57 33 30 108	58 03 29 107	58 32 28 105	59 00 26 103	59 26 25 101	59 52 23 100	60 15 21 98	60 37 20 96	60 58 19 94	61 15 16 93	61 33 14 91	61 48 12 89	62 01 10 87	62 12 9 84	328
33	56 12 32 109	56 43 30 107	57 13 29 106	57 42 28 104	58 10 25 103	58 36 25 101	59 01 22 99	59 24 22 97	59 46 20 96	60 06 18 94	60 23 16 92	60 41 16 90	60 56 12 88	61 10 12 86	61 21 9 84	327
34	55 23 31 108	55 54 29 107	56 23 29 105	56 52 27 103	57 19 26 102	57 45 24 100	58 09 23 99	58 33 22 97	58 54 20 95	59 14 19 93	59 33 17 92	59 50 15 90	60 05 13 88	60 18 12 86	60 30 10 84	326
35	54 33 +31 107	55 04 +29 106	55 33 +28 104	56 01 +27 103	56 28 +26 101	56 54 +24 99	57 18 +23 98	57 41 +21 96	58 02 +20 94	58 22 +19 92	58 41 +17 91	58 57 +14 89	59 13 +13 87	59 26 +12 85	59 38 +11 83	325
36	53 43 30 106	54 13 29 105	54 42 28 103	55 09 26 102	55 37 25 100	56 02 24 99	56 26 23 97	56 49 21 95	57 10 20 94	57 30 19 92	57 49 17 91	58 06 15 89	58 21 14 87	58 35 12 85	58 47 10 83	324
37	52 53 30 106	53 23 29 104	53 52 27 103	54 19 27 101	54 46 25 100	55 11 24 98	55 35 22 97	55 57 21 95	56 18 20 93	56 38 18 92	56 57 17 90	57 14 15 88	57 29 13 86	57 43 12 84	57 55 11 82	323
38	52 03 30 105	52 33 28 103	53 01 27 102	53 28 26 100	53 54 25 99	54 19 24 97	54 43 22 96	55 05 21 94	55 26 20 93	55 46 18 91	56 05 16 90	56 22 15 88	56 37 14 86	56 51 12 84	57 04 10 82	322
39	51 13 29 104	51 42 28 103	52 10 27 101	52 37 26 100	53 03 25 98	53 28 23 97	53 51 22 95	54 14 21 94	54 35 19 92	54 54 19 91	55 13 16 89	55 30 14 88	55 46 14 86	56 00 12 84	56 12 12 82	321
40	50 22 +29 103	50 51 +28 102	51 19 +27 100	51 46 +25 99	52 11 +25 98	52 36 +23 96	52 59 +23 95	53 22 +21 93	53 43 +19 92	54 02 +19 90	54 21 +17 89	54 38 +16 88	54 54 +14 85	55 08 +13 83	55 21 +12 81	320
41	49 32 28 103	50 00 28 101	50 28 26 100	50 54 26 98	51 19 24 97	51 44 24 95	52 08 22 94	52 30 21 92	52 51 19 91	53 10 19 90	53 29 17 89	53 46 16 86	54 02 15 84	54 17 13 83	54 30 11 81	319
42	48 41 28 102	49 09 28 100	49 37 26 99	50 03 25 98	50 28 25 96	50 53 23 95	51 16 22 94	51 39 21 92	51 59 20 91	52 19 18 89	52 37 17 88	52 54 16 86	53 10 15 84	53 25 13 82	53 38 12 80	318
43	47 50 28 101	48 18 27 100	48 45 26 98	49 11 26 97	49 37 24 96	50 01 23 94	50 24 22 93	50 47 20 92	51 07 20 90	51 27 18 89	51 45 18 87	52 03 16 86	52 19 15 84	52 34 13 82	52 47 12 80	317
44	46 59 27 100	47 27 27 99	47 54 26 98	48 20 25 96	48 45 24 95	49 09 24 94	49 32 22 92	49 54 21 91	50 15 20 89	50 35 18 88	50 53 18 86	51 11 16 85	51 27 15 83	51 42 14 82	51 56 12 80	316
45	46 08 +28 100	46 36 +26 99	47 02 +26 97	47 29 +24 96	47 53 +24 95	48 17 +23 93	48 40 +22 92	49 02 +20 90	49 23 +20 89	49 43 +18 87	50 01 +18 86	50 19 +16 84	50 35 +16 83	50 51 +14 81	51 05 +12 80	315
46	45 17 27 99	45 44 26 98	46 11 26 97	46 36 25 96	47 01 24 94	47 25 23 93	47 48 21 92	48 10 21 90	48 31 20 89	48 51 17 87	49 10 17 86	49 27 17 84	49 44 14 82	49 58 15 81	50 13 12 79	314
47	44 25 28 99	44 53 26 97	45 19 26 96	45 45 24 95	46 09 24 94	46 33 23 92	46 56 22 91	47 18 20 90	47 39 20 88	47 59 18 87	48 17 16 85	48 34 16 84	48 52 16 82	49 08 15 81	49 23 13 79	313
48	43 34 27 98	44 01 26 97	44 27 26 96	44 53 24 94	45 17 24 93	45 41 22 92	46 03 22 91	46 26 20 89	46 47 20 88	47 07 17 86	47 24 17 85	47 41 16 83	47 58 16 82	48 17 14 80	48 31 14 79	312
49	42 42 27 97	43 09 27 96	43 36 25 95	44 01 24 94	44 26 23 92	44 49 23 91	45 12 21 90	45 34 21 89	45 55 20 87	46 14 18 86	46 33 17 85	46 51 15 83	47 07 14 81	47 23 14 80	47 41 13 79	311
50	41 51 +27 97	42 18 +26 95	42 44 +25 94	43 09 +24 93	43 34 +23 92	43 57 +23 91	44 20 +21 90	44 42 +21 88	45 03 +20 87	45 23 +18 85	45 43 +18 84	46 01 +17 83	46 18 +16 81	46 34 +16 80	46 50 +14 78	310
51	40 59 27 96	41 26 26 95	41 52 25 94	42 17 25 93	42 42 23 91	43 05 23 90	43 28 21 89	43 50 21 87	44 11 21 86	44 30 18 85	44 51 18 84	45 09 18 82	45 27 16 81	45 43 16 79	45 59 14 78	309
52	40 07 27 96	40 34 26 94	41 00 25 93	41 25 23 92	41 50 24 91	42 13 22 89	42 36 22 88	42 58 21 87	43 20 20 86	43 40 18 84	44 00 18 83	44 18 18 82	44 36 16 81	44 52 16 79	45 08 15 78	308
53	39 16 26 95	39 42 26 94	40 08 25 93	40 33 24 91	40 58 23 90	41 21 23 89	41 44 21 88	42 06 21 86	42 28 20 85	42 48 18 84	43 08 18 83	43 26 17 81	43 44 16 80	44 01 16 79	44 17 15 77	307
54	38 24 26 94	38 50 26 94	39 16 25 92	39 41 24 91	40 06 23 90	40 29 23 89	40 52 22 87	41 15 21 86	41 36 21 85	41 57 19 84	42 16 18 82	42 35 18 81	42 53 17 80	43 10 17 78	43 27 15 77	306
55	37 32 +27 94	37 59 +25 93	38 24 +25 92	38 50 +24 91	39 14 +24 89	39 38 +23 88	40 01 +22 87	40 23 +21 86	40 44 +21 84	41 05 +20 83	41 25 +19 82	41 44 +18 81	42 02 +17 79	42 19 +17 78	42 36 +16 77	305
56	36 40 27 93	37 07 25 92	37 32 25 92	37 58 24 90	38 22 23 89	38 46 23 88	39 09 22 87	39 31 22 85	39 53 20 84	40 13 20 83	40 33 19 82	40 52 19 80	41 10 18 79	41 28 17 78	41 45 16 76	304
57	35 48 27 93	36 15 25 92	36 40 26 91	37 06 24 90	37 30 24 88	37 54 22 87	38 17 22 86	38 39 22 85	39 01 21 84	39 21 20 83	39 42 19 81	40 01 18 80	40 19 18 79	40 38 17 77	40 55 16 76	303
58	34 56 27 92	35 23 25 91	35 48 26 91	36 14 24 89	36 38 24 88	37 02 23 87	37 25 22 86	37 48 21 84	38 09 21 83	38 30 20 82	38 50 19 81	39 10 18 80	39 29 18 78	39 47 17 77	40 05 16 76	302
59	34 04 27 92	34 31 26 91	34 57 25 90	35 22 24 89	35 46 24 88	36 10 23 87	36 33 22 86	36 56 22 84	37 18 21 83	37 39 20 82	37 59 19 81	38 18 19 79	38 37 17 77	38 57 17 77	39 14 15 76	301
60	33 12 +27 91	33 39 +26 90	34 05 +25 89	34 30 +24 89	34 54 +24 87	35 18 +24 86	35 42 +22 85	36 04 +22 84	36 26 +22 82	36 48 +20 81	37 08 +20 79	37 28 +19 79	37 48 +18 78	38 06 +19 76	38 24 +17 75	300
61	32 20 27 91	32 47 26 90	33 13 25 89	33 38 25 88	34 02 24 87	34 26 24 86	34 50 22 85	35 13 22 83	35 35 21 82	35 56 21 81	36 17 20 80	36 37 20 78	36 57 19 77	37 16 18 76	37 34 17 75	299
62	31 29 26 90	31 55 26 89	32 21 25 89	32 46 25 88	33 11 24 87	33 34 23 85	33 58 22 84	34 21 22 83	34 44 21 82	35 05 21 80	35 26 20 79	35 47 19 78	36 06 19 77	36 25 19 75	36 44 17 75	298
63	30 37 26 90	31 03 26 89	31 29 25 88	31 54 25 87	32 19 24 86	32 43 23 85	33 07 23 84	33 30 22 83	33 52 22 81	34 14 20 80	34 35 20 79	34 56 19 78	35 15 19 76	35 35 19 75	35 54 16 74	297
64	29 45 27 89	30 12 26 89	30 37 25 87	31 02 25 86	31 27 24 86	31 51 24 85	32 15 23 84	32 38 23 82	33 01 21 81	33 22 21 80	33 44 21 79	34 05 20 77	34 25 20 76	34 45 18 75	35 04 18 74	296
65	28 53 +26 89	29 19 +26 88	29 45 +25 87	30 10 +25 86	30 35 +24 85	30 59 +24 84	31 23 +23 83	31 47 +23 81	32 10 +22 80	32 32 +21 80	32 53 +21 78	33 14 +21 77	33 35 +19 76	33 55 +19 75	34 14 +18 73	295
66	28 01 26 88	28 27 26 87	28 53 26 86	29 18 24 86	29 43 24 85	30 08 24 84	30 32 23 83	30 55 23 81	31 18 23 80	31 41 22 79	32 02 20 78	32 24 21 77	32 45 20 76	33 05 19 74	33 24 19 73	294
67	27 09 26 88	27 35 26 87	28 01 25 86	28 27 25 85	28 52 25 84	29 16 25 84	29 41 23 83	30 04 23 81	30 27 23 80	30 50 22 79	31 12 21 78	31 33 21 77	31 54 21 75	32 14 20 74	32 34 19 73	293
68	26 17 26 87	26 43 26 87	27 09 26 86	27 35 25 85	28 00 25 84	28 25 24 83	28 49 24 82	29 13 23 81	29 36 23 80	29 59 22 79	30 21 22 78	30 43 21 76	31 04 21 75	31 25 20 74	31 45 19 73	292
69	25 25 27 87	25 52 26 86	26 18 25 85	26 43 25 84	27 08 25 84	27 33 25 83	27 58 24 82	28 22 23 80	28 45 23 79	29 09 22 78	29 31 22 77	29 53 21 76	30 15 21 75	30 35 20 73	30 55 20 72	291

15°	16°	17°	18°	19°	20°	21°	22°	23°	24°	25°	26°	27°	28°	29°

S. Lat. { LHA greater than 180°....... Zn=180−Z
{ LHA less than 180°....... Zn=180+Z

LAT 30°

DECLINATION (15°–29°) SAME NAME AS LATITUDE

LAT 30°

APPENDIX E cont Declination (15° 29′) Same Name as Latitude

(Reproduced from Sight Reduction Tables HO249 Vol.3)

LAT 44°

DECLINATION (15°-29°) SAME NAME AS LATITUDE

N. Lat. {LHA greater than 180°……Zn=Z; LHA less than 180°……Zn=360−Z}

LHA	15° Hc	d	Z	16° Hc	d	Z	17° Hc	d	Z	18° Hc	d	Z	19° Hc	d	Z
	° ′	′	°	° ′	′	°	° ′	′	°	° ′	′	°	° ′	′	°
0	61 00	+60	180	62 00	+60	180	63 00	+60	180	64 00	+60	180	65 00	+60	180
1	60 59	60	178	61 59	60	178	62 59	60	178	63 59	60	178	64 59	60	178
2	60 57	60	176	61 57	60	176	62 57	60	176	63 57	60	176	64 57	60	176
3	60 53	60	174	61 53	60	174	62 53	60	174	63 53	59	174	64 52	60	173
4	60 48	60	172	61 48	59	172	62 47	60	172	63 47	60	171	64 47	59	171
5	60 41	+60	170	61 41	+59	170	62 40	+60	170	63 40	+59	169	64 39	+59	169
6	60 33	60	168	61 33	59	168	62 32	59	168	63 31	59	167	64 30	59	167
7	60 24	59	166	61 23	59	166	62 22	59	165	63 21	58	165	64 19	59	165
8	60 13	58	164	61 11	59	164	62 10	59	163	63 09	58	163	64 07	58	163
9	60 00	59	162	60 59	58	162	61 57	58	162	62 55	58	161	63 53	58	160
10	59 47	+58	161	60 45	+58	160	61 43	+57	160	62 40	+58	159	63 38	+58	158
11	59 32	57	159	60 29	58	158	61 27	57	158	62 24	57	157	63 21	57	156
12	59 15	58	157	60 13	57	156	61 10	57	156	62 07	56	155	63 03	57	154
13	58 58	57	155	59 55	56	155	60 51	57	154	61 48	56	153	62 44	56	152
14	58 39	56	153	59 35	57	153	60 32	56	152	61 28	55	151	62 23	56	150
15	58 19	+56	152	59 15	+56	151	60 11	+55	150	61 06	+55	149	62 01	+55	149
16	57 58	55	150	58 53	56	149	59 49	55	148	60 44	54	148	61 38	55	147
17	57 36	55	148	58 31	54	147	59 25	55	147	60 20	54	146	61 14	54	145
18	57 12	55	147	58 07	54	146	59 01	54	145	59 55	54	144	60 49	53	143
19	56 48	54	145	57 42	54	144	58 36	53	143	59 29	53	142	60 22	53	142
20	56 23	+53	143	57 16	+54	143	58 10	+53	142	59 03	+52	141	59 55	+52	140
21	55 57	53	142	56 50	52	141	57 42	53	140	58 35	52	139	59 27	51	138
22	55 29	53	140	56 22	52	139	57 14	52	139	58 06	51	138	58 57	51	137
23	55 01	53	139	55 54	51	138	56 45	52	137	57 37	50	136	58 27	51	135
24	54 33	51	137	55 24	51	137	56 15	51	136	57 06	51	135	57 57	49	134
25	54 03	+51	136	54 54	+51	135	55 45	+50	134	56 35	+50	133	57 25	+49	132
26	53 33	50	135	54 23	50	134	55 13	50	133	56 03	50	132	56 53	48	131
27	53 01	51	133	53 52	49	132	54 41	50	131	55 31	48	130	56 19	49	129
28	52 30	49	132	53 19	50	131	54 09	48	130	54 57	49	129	55 46	47	128
29	51 57	49	131	52 46	49	130	53 35	49	129	54 24	47	128	55 11	48	127
30	51 24	+49	129	52 13	+48	128	53 01	+48	127	53 49	+47	126	54 36	+47	125
31	50 50	49	128	51 39	48	127	52 27	47	126	53 14	47	125	54 01	46	124
32	50 16	48	127	51 04	48	126	51 52	46	125	52 38	47	124	53 25	46	123
33	49 41	48	126	50 29	47	125	51 16	46	124	52 02	46	123	52 48	46	122
34	49 06	47	124	49 53	47	124	50 40	46	123	51 26	45	122	52 11	45	120
35	48 30	+47	123	49 17	+46	122	50 03	+46	121	50 49	+45	120	51 34	+44	119
36	47 54	46	122	48 40	46	121	49 26	45	120	50 11	45	119	50 56	44	118
37	47 17	46	121	48 03	45	120	48 48	45	119	49 33	45	118	50 18	44	117
38	46 40	45	120	47 25	46	119	48 11	44	118	48 55	44	117	49 39	44	116
39	46 02	45	119	46 47	45	118	47 32	44	117	48 16	44	116	49 00	43	115
40	45 24	+45	118	46 09	+45	117	46 54	+43	116	47 37	+44	115	48 21	+43	114
41	44 46	44	117	45 30	45	116	46 15	43	115	46 58	43	114	47 41	43	113
42	44 07	44	116	44 51	44	115	45 35	44	114	46 19	42	113	47 01	43	112
43	43 28	44	115	44 12	44	114	44 56	43	113	45 39	42	112	46 21	42	111
44	42 49	44	114	43 33	43	113	44 16	42	112	44 58	43	111	45 41	41	110
45	42 09	+44	113	42 53	+43	112	43 36	+42	111	44 18	+42	110	45 00	+41	109
46	41 29	43	112	42 12	43	111	42 55	42	110	43 37	42	109	44 19	41	108
47	40 49	43	111	41 32	43	110	42 15	41	109	42 56	42	108	43 38	41	107
48	40 09	42	110	40 51	43	109	41 34	41	108	42 15	42	107	42 57	40	106
49	39 28	43	109	40 11	42	108	40 53	41	107	41 34	41	106	42 15	41	105
50	38 47	+42	108	39 29	+42	107	40 11	+42	107	40 53	+40	106	41 33	+41	105
51	38 06	42	108	38 48	42	107	39 30	41	106	40 11	41	105	40 52	40	104
52	37 25	42	107	38 07	41	106	38 48	41	105	39 29	41	104	40 10	40	103
53	36 43	42	106	37 25	41	105	38 06	41	104	38 47	40	103	39 27	40	102
54	36 02	41	105	36 43	41	104	37 24	41	103	38 05	40	102	38 45	40	101
55	35 20	+41	104	36 01	+41	103	36 42	+41	102	37 23	+40	101	38 03	+39	100
56	34 38	41	103	35 19	41	102	36 00	40	102	36 40	40	101	37 20	40	100
57	33 56	41	103	34 37	41	102	35 18	40	101	35 58	40	100	36 38	39	99
58	33 14	41	102	33 55	40	101	34 35	40	100	35 15	40	99	35 55	39	98
59	32 31	41	101	33 12	41	100	33 53	40	99	34 33	39	98	35 12	39	97
60	31 49	+41	100	32 30	+40	99	33 10	+40	98	33 50	+39	98	34 29	+39	97
61	31 07	40	99	31 47	40	99	32 27	40	98	33 07	39	97	33 46	39	96
62	30 24	40	99	31 04	40	98	31 44	40	97	32 24	39	96	33 03	39	95
63	29 41	41	98	30 22	40	97	31 02	39	96	31 41	39	95	32 20	39	94
64	28 58	41	97	29 39	40	96	30 19	39	95	30 58	39	95	31 37	39	94
65	28 16	+40	96	28 56	+40	96	29 36	+39	95	30 15	+39	94	30 54	+39	93
66	27 33	40	96	28 13	40	95	28 53	39	94	29 32	39	93	30 11	39	92
67	26 50	40	95	27 30	39	94	28 09	40	93	28 49	39	92	29 28	39	92
68	26 07	40	94	26 47	39	93	27 26	40	93	28 06	39	92	28 45	39	91
69	25 24	40	93	26 04	39	93	26 43	40	92	27 23	39	91	28 02	39	90

LHA	20° Hc	d	Z	21° Hc	d	Z	22° Hc	d	Z	23° Hc	d	Z	24° Hc	d	Z
	° ′	′	°	° ′	′	°	° ′	′	°	° ′	′	°	° ′	′	°
0	66 00	+60	180	67 00	+60	180	68 00	+60	180	69 00	+60	180	70 00	+60	180
1	65 59	60	178	66 59	60	178	67 59	60	178	68 59	60	177	69 59	60	177
2	65 57	59	175	66 56	60	175	67 56	60	175	68 56	60	175	69 56	60	175
3	65 52	60	173	66 52	60	173	67 52	59	173	68 51	60	172	69 51	60	172
4	65 46	60	171	66 46	59	171	67 45	60	170	68 45	59	170	69 44	59	169
5	65 38	+60	169	66 38	+59	168	67 37	+59	168	68 36	+59	167	69 35	+59	167
6	65 29	59	166	66 28	59	166	67 27	59	165	68 26	58	165	69 24	59	164
7	65 18	59	164	66 17	58	164	67 15	59	163	68 14	58	162	69 12	58	162
8	65 05	59	162	66 04	58	161	67 02	58	161	68 00	57	160	68 57	58	159
9	64 51	58	160	65 49	58	159	66 47	57	158	67 44	57	158	68 41	57	157
10	64 36	+57	158	65 33	+57	157	66 30	+57	156	67 27	+56	155	68 23	+57	155
11	64 18	57	156	65 15	57	155	66 12	56	154	67 08	56	153	68 04	56	152
12	64 00	56	154	64 56	56	153	65 52	56	152	66 48	55	151	67 43	55	150
13	63 40	56	152	64 36	55	151	65 31	55	150	66 26	55	149	67 21	54	148
14	63 19	55	150	64 14	55	149	65 09	54	148	66 03	54	147	66 57	54	146
15	62 56	+55	148	63 51	+54	147	64 45	+54	146	65 39	+53	145	66 32	+53	144
16	62 33	54	146	63 27	53	145	64 20	53	144	65 13	53	143	66 06	52	142
17	62 08	53	144	63 01	53	143	63 54	53	142	64 47	52	141	65 39	51	140
18	61 42	53	142	62 35	52	141	63 27	52	140	64 19	51	139	65 10	51	138
19	61 15	52	141	62 07	52	140	62 59	51	138	63 50	51	137	64 41	49	136
20	60 47	+52	139	61 39	+51	138	62 30	+50	137	63 20	+50	135	64 10	+49	134
21	60 18	51	137	61 09	51	136	62 00	49	135	62 49	50	134	63 39	48	133
22	59 48	51	136	60 39	50	135	61 29	49	133	62 18	48	132	63 06	48	131
23	59 18	50	134	60 08	49	133	60 57	48	132	61 45	48	131	62 33	48	129
24	58 46	50	133	59 36	48	131	60 24	48	130	61 12	48	129	62 00	46	128
25	58 14	+49	131	59 03	+48	130	59 51	+47	129	60 38	+47	128	61 25	+46	126
26	57 41	48	130	58 29	48	129	59 17	47	127	60 04	46	126	60 50	45	125
27	57 08	47	128	57 55	47	127	58 42	47	126	59 29	45	125	60 14	45	123
28	56 33	48	127	57 21	46	126	58 07	46	125	58 53	45	123	59 38	44	122
29	55 59	46	126	56 45	46	124	57 31	45	123	58 16	45	122	59 01	44	121
30	55 23	+46	124	56 09	+46	123	56 55	+45	122	57 40	+44	121	58 24	+43	119
31	54 47	46	123	55 33	45	122	56 18	44	121	57 02	44	119	57 46	42	118
32	54 11	45	122	54 56	44	121	55 40	44	119	56 24	43	118	57 07	43	117
33	53 34	45	121	54 19	44	119	55 03	43	118	55 46	43	117	56 29	42	116
34	52 56	45	119	53 41	43	118	54 24	43	117	55 07	43	116	55 50	41	115
35	52 18	+44	118	53 02	+44	117	53 46	+42	116	54 28	+42	115	55 10	+41	113
36	51 40	44	117	52 24	43	116	53 07	42	115	53 49	41	114	54 30	41	112
37	51 02	43	116	51 45	42	115	52 27	42	114	53 09	41	113	53 50	41	111
38	50 23	42	115	51 05	43	114	51 48	41	113	52 29	41	112	53 10	40	110
39	49 43	43	114	50 26	42	113	51 08	41	112	51 49	40	110	52 29	40	109
40	49 04	+42	113	49 46	+41	112	50 27	+41	111	51 08	+41	109	51 49	+39	108
41	48 24	42	112	49 06	41	111	49 47	41	110	50 28	39	109	51 07	40	107
42	47 44	41	111	48 25	41	110	49 06	40	109	49 46	40	108	50 26	39	106
43	47 03	41	110	47 44	41	109	48 25	40	108	49 05	40	107	49 45	38	105
44	46 22	41	109	47 03	41	108	47 44	40	107	48 24	39	106	49 03	38	105
45	45 41	+41	108	46 22	+40	107	47 02	+40	106	47 42	+39	105	48 21	+38	104
46	45 00	41	107	45 41	40	106	46 21	39	105	47 00	39	104	47 39	38	103
47	44 19	40	106	44 59	40	105	45 39	39	104	46 18	39	103	46 57	38	102
48	43 37	41	105	44 18	39	104	44 57	39	103	45 36	39	102	46 15	37	101
49	42 56	40	104	43 36	39	103	44 15	39	102	44 54	38	101	45 32	38	100
50	42 14	+40	104	42 54	+39	103	43 33	+38	102	44 11	+39	100	44 50	+37	99
51	41 32	39	103	42 11	39	102	42 50	39	101	43 29	38	100	44 07	37	99
52	40 50	39	102	41 29	39	101	42 08	38	100	42 46	38	99	43 24	37	98
53	40 07	40	101	40 47	38	100	41 25	39	99	42 04	37	98	42 41	38	97
54	39 25	39	100	40 04	39	99	40 43	38	98	41 21	38	97	41 59	37	96
55	38 42	+39	100	39 21	+39	99	40 00	+38	98	40 38	+38	97	41 16	+37	96
56	38 00	39	99	38 39	38	98	39 17	38	97	39 55	38	96	40 33	37	95
57	37 17	39	98	37 56	38	97	38 34	38	96	39 12	38	95	39 50	36	94
58	36 34	39	97	37 13	38	96	37 51	38	95	38 29	38	94	39 07	36	93
59	35 51	39	96	36 30	38	95	37 08	38	95	37 46	37	94	38 23	37	93
60	35 08	+39	96	35 47	+38	95	36 25	+38	94	37 03	+37	93	37 40	+37	92
61	34 25	39	95	35 04	38	94	35 42	38	93	36 20	37	92	36 57	37	91
62	33 42	39	94	34 21	38	93	34 59	38	92	35 37	37	91	36 14	37	90
63	32 59	39	93	33 38	38	93	34 16	38	92	34 54	37	91	35 31	37	90
64	32 16	39	93	32 55	38	92	33 33	37	91	34 10	38	90	34 48	36	89
65	31 33	+39	92	32 12	+38	91	32 50	+37	90	33 27	+38	89	34 05	+36	88
66	30 50	38	91	31 28	38	90	32 06	38	90	32 44	37	89	33 21	37	88
67	30 07	38	91	30 45	38	90	31 23	38	89	32 01	37	88	32 38	37	87
68	29 24	38	90	30 02	38	89	30 40	38	88	31 18	37	87	31 55	37	86
69	28 41	38	89	29 19	38	88	29 57	38	87	30 35	37	87	31 12	37	86

25° Hc	d	Z	26° Hc	d	Z	27° Hc	d	Z	28° Hc	d	Z	29° Hc	d	Z	LHA
° ′	′	°	° ′	′	°	° ′	′	°	° ′	′	°	° ′	′	°	
71 00	+60	180	72 00	+60	180	73 00	+60	180	74 00	+60	180	75 00	+60	180	360
70 59	60	177	71 59	60	177	72 59	60	177	73 59	60	177	74 59	60	177	359
70 56	60	174	71 56	59	174	72 55	60	174	73 55	60	174	74 55	60	173	358
70 51	59	172	71 50	60	171	72 50	59	171	73 49	60	171	74 49	59	170	357
70 43	60	169	71 43	59	169	72 42	59	168	73 41	59	167	74 40	59	167	356
70 34	+59	166	71 33	+59	166	72 32	+58	165	73 30	+59	164	74 29	+58	163	355
70 23	58	164	71 21	59	163	72 20	58	162	73 18	57	161	74 15	58	160	354
70 10	58	161	71 08	57	160	72 05	58	159	73 03	57	158	74 00	56	157	353
69 55	57	159	70 52	57	158	71 49	57	157	72 46	56	156	73 42	56	154	352
69 38	57	156	70 35	56	155	71 31	56	154	72 27	55	153	73 22	55	151	351
69 20	+56	154	70 16	+55	153	71 11	+55	151	72 06	+55	150	73 01	+54	149	350
69 00	55	151	69 55	55	150	70 50	54	149	71 44	54	148	72 38	52	146	349
68 38	55	149	69 33	54	148	70 27	53	146	71 20	53	145	72 13	51	144	348
68 15	54	147	69 09	53	145	70 02	52	144	70 54	52	143	71 46	51	141	347
67 51	53	145	68 44	52	143	69 36	52	142	70 28	50	140	71 18	50	139	346
67 25	+52	142	68 17	+52	141	69 09	+50	140	69 59	+50	138	70 49	+49	136	345
66 58	51	140	67 49	51	139	68 40	50	138	69 30	49	136	70 19	48	134	344
66 30	50	138	67 20	50	137	68 10	49	136	68 59	48	134	69 47	48	132	343
66 01	49	137	66 50	50	135	67 40	48	134	68 28	47	132	69 15	46	130	342
65 30	50	135	66 20	48	133	67 08	47	132	67 55	47	130	68 42	45	128	341
64 59	+49	133	65 48	+47	131	66 35	+47	130	67 22	+45	128	68 07	+45	127	340
64 27	48	131	65 15	47	130	66 02	46	128	66 48	44	127	67 32	44	125	339
63 54	47	130	64 41	46	128	65 27	46	127	66 13	44	125	66 57	43	123	338
63 21	46	128	64 07	45	126	64 52	45	125	65 37	43	123	66 20	42	122	337
62 46	46	126	63 32	45	125	64 17	43	123	65 00	43	122	65 43	42	120	336
62 11	+45	125	62 56	+44	123	63 40	+43	122	64 23	+43	120	65 06	+40	119	335
61 35	45	123	62 20	43	122	63 03	43	121	63 46	41	119	64 27	41	117	334
60 59	44	122	61 43	43	121	62 26	42	119	63 08	41	118	63 49	40	116	333
60 22	43	121	61 05	43	119	61 48	41	118	62 29	41	116	63 10	39	115	332
59 45	43	119	60 28	41	118	61 09	41	116	61 50	40	115	62 30	39	113	331
59 07	+42	118	59 49	+42	117	60 31	+40	115	61 11	+39	114	61 50	+39	112	330
58 28	42	117	59 10	41	115	59 51	40	114	60 31	39	113	61 10	38	111	329
57 50	41	116	58 31	41	114	59 12	39	113	59 51	39	111	60 30	37	110	328
57 11	41	114	57 52	40	113	58 32	39	112	59 11	38	110	59 49	37	109	327
56 31	41	113	57 12	40	112	57 52	38	111	58 30	38	109	59 08	37	108	326
55 51	+41	112	56 32	+39	111	57 11	+38	109	57 49	+38	108	58 27	+36	107	325
55 11	40	111	55 51	39	110	56 30	38	108	57 08	37	107	57 45	36	106	324
54 31	39	110	55 10	39	109	55 49	38	107	56 27	37	106	57 04	35	105	323
53 50	39	109	54 29	39	108	55 08	37	106	55 45	37	105	56 22	35	104	322
53 09	39	108	53 48	38	107	54 26	37	105	55 03	37	104	55 40	35	103	321
52 28	+39	107	53 07	+38	106	53 45	+36	104	54 21	+37	103	54 58	+35	102	320
51 47	38	106	52 25	38	105	53 03	36	104	53 39	36	102	54 15	35	101	319
51 05	38	105	51 43	38	104	52 21	36	103	52 57	36	101	53 33	34	100	318
50 23	38	104	51 01	37	103	51 38	37	102	52 15	35	100	52 50	35	99	317
49 41	38	103	50 19	37	102	50 56	36	101	51 32	36	100	52 08	34	98	316
48 59	+38	102	49 37	+37	101	50 14	+36	100	50 50	+35	99	51 25	+34	97	315
48 17	37	102	48 54	37	100	49 31	36	99	50 07	35	98	50 42	34	97	314
47 35	37	101	48 12	36	100	48 48	36	98	49 24	35	97	49 59	34	96	313
46 52	37	100	47 29	37	99	48 06	35	98	48 41	35	96	49 16	34	95	312
46 10	37	99	46 47	36	98	47 23	35	97	47 58	35	96	48 33	34	94	311
45 27	+37	98	46 04	+36	97	46 40	+35	96	47 15	+35	95	47 50	+34	94	310
44 44	37	98	45 21	36	96	45 57	35	95	46 32	35	94	47 07	34	93	309
44 01	37	97	44 38	36	96	45 14	35	94	45 49	35	93	46 24	34	92	308
43 19	36	96	43 55	36	95	44 31	35	94	45 06	35	93	45 41	33	91	307
42 36	36	95	43 12	36	94	43 48	35	93	44 23	34	92	44 57	34	91	306
41 53	+36	94	42 29	+36	93	43 05	+35	92	43 40	+34	91	44 14	+34	90	305
41 10	36	94	41 46	36	93	42 22	35	92	42 57	34	90	43 31	34	89	304
40 26	37	93	41 03	35	92	41 38	36	91	42 14	34	90	42 48	34	89	303
39 43	37	92	40 20	35	91	40 55	35	90	41 30	35	89	42 05	34	88	302
39 00	36	92	39 36	36	91	40 12	35	89	40 47	35	88	41 22	34	87	301
38 17	+36	91	38 53	+36	90	39 29	+35	89	40 04	+35	88	40 39	+34	87	300
37 34	36	90	38 10	36	89	38 46	35	88	39 21	35	87	39 56	34	86	299
36 51	36	89	37 27	36	88	38 03	35	87	38 38	35	86	39 13	34	85	298
36 08	36	89	36 44	36	88	37 20	35	87	37 55	35	86	38 30	34	85	297
35 24	37	88	36 01	36	87	36 37	35	86	37 12	35	85	37 47	34	84	296
34 41	+37	87	35 18	+35	86	35 53	+36	85	36 29	+35	84	37 04	+34	83	295
33 58	37	87	34 35	35	86	35 10	36	85	35 46	35	84	36 21	34	83	294
33 15	37	86	33 52	36	85	34 28	35	84	35 03	35	83	35 38	35	82	293
32 32	37	85	33 09	36	84	33 45	35	84	34 20	35	83	34 55	35	82	292
31 49	37	85	32 26	36	84	33 02	35	83	33 37	36	82	34 13	34	81	291

S. Lat. {LHA greater than 180°……Zn=180−Z; LHA less than 180°……Zn=180+Z}

DECLINATION (15°-29°) SAME NAME AS LATITUDE

LAT 44°

APPENDIX E cont **Declination (15° 29′) Contrary Name as Latitude**

(Reproduced from Sight Reduction Tables HO249 Vol.3)

LAT 44°

DECLINATION (15°-29°) CONTRARY NAME TO LATITUDE

N. Lat. {LHA greater than 180°……. Zn=Z; LHA less than 180°………. Zn=360−Z}

LHA	15° Hc	d	Z	16° Hc	d	Z	17° Hc	d	Z	18° Hc	d	Z	19° Hc	d	Z
	° ′	′	°	° ′	′	°	° ′	′	°	° ′	′	°	° ′	′	°
69	03 58	44	115	03 14	45	116	02 29	44	117	01 45	45	117	01 00	44	118
68	04 37	45	116	03 52	44	117	03 08	45	117	02 23	45	118	01 38	44	119
67	05 16	45	117	04 31	45	117	03 46	45	118	03 01	45	119	02 16	45	119
66	05 54	45	118	05 09	45	118	04 24	45	119	03 39	45	119	02 54	46	120
65	06 32	−45	118	05 47	−45	119	05 02	−46	120	04 16	−45	120	03 31	−46	121
64	07 10	45	119	06 25	46	120	05 39	46	120	04 53	45	121	04 08	46	122
63	07 48	46	120	07 02	46	120	06 16	46	121	05 30	46	122	04 44	46	122
62	08 25	46	120	07 39	46	121	06 53	46	122	06 07	46	122	05 21	47	123
61	09 02	46	121	08 16	46	122	07 30	47	123	06 43	46	123	05 57	47	124
60	09 39	−47	122	08 52	−46	123	08 06	−47	123	07 19	−46	124	06 33	−47	125
59	10 16	47	123	09 29	47	123	08 42	47	124	07 55	47	125	07 08	47	125
58	10 52	47	124	10 05	48	124	09 17	47	125	08 30	47	125	07 43	47	126
57	11 27	47	124	10 40	47	125	09 53	48	126	09 05	47	126	08 18	48	127
56	12 03	48	125	11 15	47	126	10 28	48	126	09 40	48	127	08 52	48	128
55	12 38	−48	126	11 50	−48	126	11 02	−48	127	10 14	−48	128	09 26	−48	128
54	13 13	48	127	12 25	48	127	11 37	49	128	10 48	48	128	10 00	48	129
53	13 47	48	127	12 59	48	128	12 11	49	129	11 22	49	129	10 33	48	130
52	14 22	49	128	13 33	49	129	12 44	49	129	11 55	49	130	11 06	49	131
51	14 55	49	129	14 06	49	130	13 17	49	130	12 28	49	131	11 39	49	131
50	15 29	−50	130	14 39	−49	130	13 50	−49	131	13 01	−50	132	12 11	−50	132
49	16 02	50	131	15 12	50	131	14 22	49	132	13 33	50	132	12 43	50	133
48	16 34	50	132	15 44	50	132	14 54	50	133	14 04	50	133	13 14	50	134
47	17 06	50	132	16 16	50	133	15 26	50	134	14 36	51	134	13 45	50	135
46	17 38	51	133	16 47	50	134	15 57	51	134	15 06	50	135	14 16	51	135
45	18 09	−51	134	17 18	−50	135	16 28	−51	135	15 37	−51	136	14 46	−51	136
44	18 40	51	135	17 49	51	136	16 58	51	136	16 07	52	137	15 15	51	137
43	19 10	51	136	18 19	51	136	17 28	52	137	16 36	52	137	15 44	51	138
42	19 40	51	137	18 49	52	137	17 57	52	138	17 05	52	138	16 13	52	139
41	20 10	52	138	19 18	52	138	18 26	53	139	17 33	52	139	16 41	52	140
40	20 38	−52	138	19 46	−52	139	18 54	−53	140	18 01	−52	140	17 09	−53	141
39	21 07	53	139	20 14	52	140	19 22	53	140	18 29	53	141	17 36	53	141
38	21 35	53	140	20 42	53	141	19 49	53	141	18 56	53	142	18 03	53	142
37	22 02	53	141	21 09	53	142	20 16	54	142	19 22	53	143	18 29	53	143
36	22 29	54	142	21 35	53	143	20 42	54	143	19 48	53	144	18 55	54	144
35	22 55	−54	143	22 01	−53	144	21 08	−54	144	20 14	−54	145	19 20	−54	145
34	23 21	54	144	22 27	54	144	21 33	54	145	20 39	55	145	19 44	54	146
33	23 46	54	145	22 52	55	145	21 57	54	146	21 03	55	146	20 08	54	147
32	24 10	54	146	23 16	55	146	22 21	55	147	21 26	54	147	20 32	55	148
31	24 34	55	147	23 39	55	147	22 44	55	148	21 49	55	148	20 54	55	149
30	24 58	−56	148	24 02	−55	148	23 07	−55	149	22 12	−55	149	21 17	−56	150
29	25 20	55	149	24 25	56	149	23 29	55	150	22 34	56	150	21 38	55	151
28	25 42	55	150	24 47	56	150	23 51	56	151	22 55	56	151	21 59	56	151
27	26 04	56	151	25 08	56	151	24 12	56	152	23 16	56	152	22 20	57	152
26	26 24	56	152	25 28	56	152	24 32	56	153	23 36	57	153	22 39	56	153
25	26 44	−56	153	25 48	−57	153	24 51	−56	154	23 55	−57	154	22 58	−56	154
24	27 04	57	154	26 07	57	154	25 10	56	155	24 14	57	155	23 17	57	155
23	27 23	57	155	26 26	57	155	25 29	57	156	24 32	58	156	23 34	57	156
22	27 41	58	156	26 43	57	156	25 46	57	157	24 49	57	157	23 52	58	157
21	27 58	58	157	27 00	57	157	26 03	58	158	25 05	57	158	24 08	58	158
20	28 14	−57	158	27 17	−58	158	26 19	−58	159	25 21	−57	159	24 24	−58	159
19	28 30	58	159	27 32	58	159	26 34	58	160	25 36	57	160	24 39	58	160
18	28 45	58	160	27 47	58	160	26 49	58	161	25 51	58	161	24 53	58	161
17	29 00	59	161	28 01	58	161	27 03	58	162	26 05	59	162	25 06	58	162
16	29 13	58	162	28 15	59	163	27 16	58	163	26 18	59	163	25 19	58	163
15	29 26	−59	163	28 27	−58	164	27 29	−59	164	26 30	−59	164	25 31	−59	164
14	29 38	59	164	28 39	59	165	27 40	59	165	26 41	58	165	25 43	59	165
13	29 49	59	166	28 50	59	166	27 51	59	166	26 52	59	166	25 53	59	166
12	29 59	59	167	29 00	59	167	28 01	59	167	27 02	59	167	26 03	59	167
11	30 09	59	168	29 10	59	168	28 11	60	168	27 11	59	168	26 12	59	168
10	30 18	−60	169	29 18	−59	169	28 19	−59	169	27 20	−60	169	26 20	−59	169
9	30 26	60	170	29 26	59	170	28 27	60	170	27 27	59	170	26 28	60	171
8	30 33	60	171	29 33	59	171	28 34	60	171	27 34	59	171	26 35	60	172
7	30 39	59	172	29 40	60	172	28 40	60	172	27 40	59	173	26 41	60	173
6	30 45	60	173	29 45	60	173	28 45	60	174	27 45	59	174	26 46	60	174
5	30 49	−59	174	29 50	−60	175	28 50	−60	175	27 50	−60	175	26 50	−60	175
4	30 53	60	176	29 53	60	176	28 53	59	176	27 54	60	176	26 54	60	176
3	30 56	60	177	29 56	60	177	28 56	60	177	27 56	60	177	26 56	59	177
2	30 58	60	178	29 58	60	178	28 58	60	178	27 58	60	178	26 58	60	178
1	31 00	60	179	30 00	60	179	29 00	60	179	28 00	60	179	27 00	60	179
0	31 00	−60	180	30 00	−60	180	29 00	−60	180	28 00	−60	180	27 00	−60	180

LHA	20° Hc	d	Z	21° Hc	d	Z	22° Hc	d	Z	23° Hc	d	Z	24° Hc	d	Z
	° ′	′	°	° ′	′	°	° ′	′	°	° ′	′	°	° ′	′	°
69	00 16	44	119	−0 28	45	119	−1 13	44	120	−1 57	45	121	−2 42	44	121
68	00 54	45	119	00 09	45	120	−0 36	44	121	−1 20	45	121	−2 05	45	122
67	01 31	45	120	00 46	45	121	00 01	45	121	−0 44	45	122	−1 29	45	123
66	02 08	45	121	01 23	45	121	00 38	45	122	−0 07	45	123	−0 52	46	123
65	02 45	−45	122	02 00	−46	122	01 14	−45	123	00 29	−46	123	−0 17	−45	124
64	03 22	46	122	02 36	45	123	01 51	46	124	01 05	46	124	00 19	46	125
63	03 58	46	123	03 12	46	124	02 26	46	124	01 40	46	125	00 54	46	126
62	04 34	46	124	03 48	46	124	03 02	46	125	02 16	47	126	01 29	46	126
61	05 10	46	124	04 24	47	125	03 37	46	126	02 51	47	126	02 04	47	127
60	05 46	−47	125	04 59	−47	126	04 12	−47	126	03 25	−47	127	02 38	−47	128
59	06 21	47	126	05 34	47	127	04 47	48	127	03 59	47	128	03 12	47	128
58	06 56	48	127	06 08	47	127	05 21	48	128	04 33	47	128	03 46	47	129
57	07 30	47	127	06 43	48	128	05 55	48	129	05 07	48	129	04 19	47	130
56	08 04	48	128	07 16	48	129	06 28	48	129	05 40	48	130	04 52	48	131
55	08 38	−48	129	07 50	−48	130	07 02	−49	130	06 13	−48	131	05 25	−48	131
54	09 12	49	130	08 23	49	130	07 34	48	131	06 46	49	131	05 57	48	132
53	09 45	49	130	08 56	49	131	08 07	49	132	07 18	49	132	06 29	49	133
52	10 17	49	131	09 28	49	132	08 39	49	132	07 50	49	133	07 01	50	134
51	10 50	50	132	10 00	49	133	09 11	50	133	08 21	49	134	07 32	50	134
50	11 21	−49	133	10 32	−50	133	09 42	−50	134	08 52	−50	135	08 02	−49	135
49	11 53	50	134	11 03	50	134	10 13	50	135	09 23	50	135	08 33	50	136
48	12 24	50	134	11 34	51	135	10 43	50	136	09 53	50	136	09 03	51	137
47	12 55	51	135	12 04	51	136	11 13	50	136	10 23	51	137	09 32	51	137
46	13 25	51	136	12 34	51	137	11 43	51	137	10 52	51	138	10 01	51	138
45	13 55	−52	137	13 03	−51	137	12 12	−51	138	11 21	−51	138	10 30	−52	139
44	14 24	52	138	13 32	51	138	12 41	52	139	11 49	51	139	10 58	52	140
43	14 53	52	139	14 01	52	139	13 09	52	140	12 17	52	140	11 25	51	141
42	15 21	52	139	14 29	52	140	13 37	52	140	12 45	52	141	11 53	53	141
41	15 49	52	140	14 57	53	141	14 04	52	141	13 12	53	142	12 19	52	142
40	16 16	−52	141	15 24	−53	142	14 31	−53	142	13 38	−52	143	12 46	−53	143
39	16 43	53	142	15 50	53	142	14 57	53	143	14 04	53	143	13 11	53	144
38	17 10	53	143	16 17	54	143	15 23	53	144	14 30	53	144	13 37	54	145
37	17 36	54	144	16 42	53	144	15 49	54	145	14 55	54	145	14 01	53	146
36	18 01	54	145	17 07	54	145	16 13	54	145	15 19	53	146	14 26	54	146
35	18 26	−54	145	17 32	−54	146	16 38	−55	146	15 43	−54	147	14 49	−54	147
34	18 50	54	146	17 56	55	147	17 01	54	147	16 07	55	148	15 12	54	148
33	19 14	55	147	18 19	55	148	17 24	54	148	16 30	55	149	15 35	55	149
32	19 37	55	148	18 42	55	149	17 47	55	149	16 52	55	149	15 57	55	150
31	19 59	55	149	19 04	55	149	18 09	55	150	17 14	56	150	16 18	55	151
30	20 21	−55	150	19 26	−56	150	18 30	−55	151	17 35	−56	151	16 39	−55	152
29	20 43	56	151	19 47	56	151	18 51	56	152	17 55	56	152	16 59	55	152
28	21 03	56	152	20 07	56	152	19 11	56	153	18 15	56	153	17 19	56	153
27	21 23	56	153	20 27	56	153	19 31	56	154	18 35	57	154	17 38	56	154
26	21 43	57	154	20 46	56	154	19 50	57	154	18 53	56	155	17 57	57	155
25	22 02	−57	155	21 05	−57	155	20 08	−57	155	19 11	−56	156	18 15	−57	156
24	22 20	57	156	21 23	57	156	20 26	57	156	19 29	57	157	18 32	57	157
23	22 37	57	157	21 40	57	157	20 43	57	157	19 46	58	158	18 48	57	158
22	22 54	57	158	21 57	58	158	20 59	57	158	20 02	58	159	19 04	57	159
21	23 10	57	159	22 13	58	159	21 15	58	159	20 17	57	159	19 20	58	160
20	23 26	−58	160	22 28	−58	160	21 30	−58	160	20 32	−58	160	19 34	−58	161
19	23 41	58	161	22 43	59	161	21 44	58	161	20 46	58	161	19 48	58	162
18	23 55	59	162	22 56	58	162	21 58	58	162	21 00	58	162	20 02	59	163
17	24 08	58	163	23 10	59	163	22 11	58	163	21 13	59	163	20 14	58	164
16	24 21	59	164	23 22	59	164	22 23	58	164	21 25	59	164	20 26	58	164
15	24 32	−58	165	23 34	−59	165	22 35	−59	165	21 36	−59	165	20 37	−58	165
14	24 44	59	166	23 45	59	166	22 46	59	166	21 47	59	166	20 48	59	166
13	24 54	59	167	23 55	59	167	22 56	59	167	21 57	59	167	20 58	59	167
12	25 04	59	168	24 05	60	168	23 05	59	168	22 06	59	168	21 07	59	168
11	25 13	60	169	24 13	59	169	23 14	59	169	22 15	60	169	21 15	59	169
10	25 21	−60	170	24 21	−59	170	23 22	−59	170	22 23	−60	170	21 23	−59	170
9	25 28	59	171	24 29	60	171	23 29	59	171	22 30	60	171	21 30	59	171
8	25 35	60	172	24 35	59	172	23 36	60	172	22 36	60	172	21 36	59	172
7	25 41	60	173	24 41	60	173	23 41	59	173	22 42	60	173	21 42	60	173
6	25 46	60	174	24 46	60	174	23 46	59	174	22 47	60	174	21 47	60	174
5	25 50	−60	175	24 50	−59	175	23 51	−60	175	22 51	−60	175	21 51	−60	175
4	25 54	60	176	24 54	60	176	23 54	60	176	22 54	60	176	21 54	60	176
3	25 57	60	177	24 57	60	177	23 57	60	177	22 57	60	177	21 57	60	177
2	25 58	60	178	24 58	59	178	23 59	60	178	22 59	60	178	21 59	60	178
1	26 00	60	179	25 00	60	179	24 00	60	179	23 00	60	179	22 00	60	179
0	26 00	−60	180	25 00	−60	180	24 00	−60	180	23 00	−60	180	22 00	−60	180

LHA	25° Hc	d	Z	26° Hc	d	Z	27° Hc	d	Z	28° Hc	d	Z	29° Hc	d	Z	LHA
	° ′	′	°	° ′	′	°	° ′	′	°	° ′	′	°	° ′	′	°	
69	−3 26	45	122	−4 11	44	123	−4 55	44	123	−5 39	45	124				291
68	−2 50	44	123	−3 34	45	123	−4 19	45	124	−5 04	44	125	−5 48	45	125	292
67	−2 14	44	123	−2 58	45	124	−3 43	45	125	−4 28	45	125	−5 13	45	126	293
66	−1 38	45	124	−2 23	45	125	−3 08	45	125	−3 53	45	126	−4 38	45	127	294
65	−1 02	−46	125	−1 48	−45	125	−2 33	−45	126	−3 18	−46	127	−4 04	−45	127	295
64	−0 27	46	125	−1 13	45	126	−1 58	46	127	−2 44	46	127	−3 30	45	128	296
63	00 08	46	126	−0 38	46	127	−1 24	46	127	−2 10	46	128	−2 56	46	129	297
62	00 43	46	127	−0 03	47	127	−0 50	46	128	−1 36	46	129	−2 22	47	129	298
61	01 17	46	128	00 31	47	128	−0 16	47	129	−1 03	46	129	−1 49	47	130	299
60	01 51	−47	128	01 04	−46	129	00 18	−47	129	−0 29	−47	130	−1 16	−47	131	300
59	02 25	47	129	01 38	47	130	00 51	48	130	00 03	47	131	−0 44	47	131	301
58	02 59	48	130	02 11	48	130	01 23	47	131	00 36	48	132	−0 12	47	132	302
57	03 32	48	130	02 44	48	131	01 56	48	132	01 08	48	132	00 20	48	133	303
56	04 04	48	131	03 16	48	132	02 28	48	132	01 40	48	133	00 52	48	134	304
55	04 37	−49	132	03 48	−48	132	03 00	−49	133	02 11	−48	134	01 23	−49	134	305
54	05 09	49	133	04 20	49	133	03 31	49	134	02 42	48	134	01 54	49	135	306
53	05 40	49	133	04 51	49	134	04 02	49	134	03 13	49	135	02 24	49	136	307
52	06 11	49	134	05 22	49	135	04 33	50	135	03 43	49	136	02 54	50	136	308
51	06 42	49	135	05 53	50	135	05 03	50	136	04 13	50	137	03 23	49	137	309
50	07 13	−50	136	06 23	−50	136	05 33	−50	137	04 43	−50	137	03 53	−50	138	310
49	07 43	51	136	06 52	50	137	06 02	50	138	05 12	51	138	04 21	50	139	311
48	08 12	50	137	07 22	51	138	06 31	51	138	05 40	50	139	04 50	51	139	312
47	08 41	51	138	07 50	50	138	07 00	51	139	06 09	51	140	05 18	51	140	313
46	09 10	51	139	08 19	51	139	07 28	51	140	06 37	52	140	05 45	51	141	314
45	09 38	−51	140	08 47	−52	140	07 55	−51	141	07 04	−52	141	06 12	−51	142	315
44	10 06	52	140	09 14	51	141	08 23	52	141	07 31	52	142	06 39	52	142	316
43	10 34	53	141	09 41	52	142	08 49	52	142	07 57	52	143	07 05	52	143	317
42	11 00	52	142	10 08	52	142	09 16	53	143	08 23	52	143	07 31	53	144	318
41	11 27	53	143	10 34	52	143	09 42	53	144	08 49	53	144	07 56	53	145	319
40	11 53	−53	144	11 00	−53	144	10 07	−53	144	09 14	−53	145	08 21	−53	145	320
39	12 18	53	144	11 25	53	145	10 32	53	145	09 39	54	146	08 45	53	146	321
38	12 43	53	145	11 50	54	146	10 56	53	146	10 03	54	147	09 09	54	147	322
37	13 08	54	146	12 14	54	146	11 20	54	147	10 26	54	147	09 32	54	148	323
36	13 32	55	147	12 37	54	147	11 43	54	148	10 49	54	148	09 55	54	149	324
35	13 55	−54	148	13 01	−55	148	12 06	−54	149	11 12	−55	149	10 17	−54	149	325
34	14 18	55	149	13 23	55	149	12 28	54	149	11 34	55	150	10 39	55	150	326
33	14 40	55	149	13 45	55	150	12 50	55	150	11 55	55	151	11 00	55	151	327
32	15 02	55	150	14 07	56	151	13 11	55	151	12 16	55	151	11 21	55	152	328
31	15 23	55	151	14 28	56	151	13 32	55	152	12 37	56	152	11 41	55	153	329
30	15 44	−56	152	14 48	−56	152	13 52	−56	153	12 56	−55	153	12 01	−56	153	330
29	16 04	56	153	15 08	56	153	14 12	56	154	13 16	56	154	12 20	56	154	331
28	16 23	56	154	15 27	56	154	14 31	57	154	13 34	56	155	12 38	56	155	332
27	16 42	57	155	15 45	56	155	14 49	56	155	13 53	57	156	12 56	57	156	333
26	17 00	57	156	16 03	56	156	15 07	57	156	14 10	57	157	13 13	57	157	334
25	17 18	−57	156	16 21	−57	157	15 24	−57	157	14 27	−57	157	13 30	−57	158	335
24	17 35	57	157	16 38	58	158	15 40	57	158	14 43	57	158	13 46	57	159	336
23	17 51	57	158	16 54	58	159	15 56	57	159	14 59	57	159	14 02	58	159	337
22	18 07	58	159	17 09	57	159	16 12	58	160	15 14	58	160	14 16	57	160	338
21	18 22	58	160	17 24	58	160	16 26	57	161	15 29	58	161	14 31	58	161	339
20	18 36	−58	161	17 38	−58	161	16 40	−58	162	15 42	−58	162	14 44	−58	162	340
19	18 50	58	162	17 52	58	162	16 54	58	162	15 56	59	163	14 57	58	163	341
18	19 03	58	163	18 05	58	163	17 07	59	163	16 08	58	164	15 10	59	164	342
17	19 16	59	164	18 17	58	164	17 19	59	164	16 20	58	164	15 22	59	165	343
16	19 28	59	165	18 29	59	165	17 30	59	165	16 31	58	165	15 33	59	166	344
15	19 39	−59	166	18 40	−59	166	17 41	−59	166	16 42	−59	166	15 43	−59	166	345
14	19 49	59	167	18 50	59	167	17 51	59	167	16 52	59	167	15 53	59	167	346
13	19 59	59	168	19 00	60	168	18 00	59	168	17 01	59	168	16 02	59	168	347
12	20 08	59	168	19 09	60	169	18 09	59	169	17 10	59	169	16 11	60	169	348
11	20 16	59	169	19 17	60	170	18 17	59	170	17 18	59	170	16 19	60	170	349
10	20 24	−60	170	19 24	−59	171	18 25	−60	171	17 25	−59	171	16 26	−60	171	350
9	20 31	60	171	19 31	60	171	18 31	59	172	17 32	60	172	16 32	59	172	351
8	20 37	60	172	19 37	60	172	18 37	59	173	17 38	60	173	16 38	60	173	352
7	20 42	60	173	19 42	59	173	18 43	60	173	17 43	60	174	16 43	60	174	353
6	20 47	60	174	19 47	60	174	18 47	60	174	17 47	59	174	16 48	60	175	354
5	20 51	−60	175	19 51	−60	175	18 51	−60	175	17 51	−60	175	16 51	−59	175	355
4	20 54	60	176	19 54	60	176	18 54	60	176	17 54	59	176	16 55	60	176	356
3	20 57	60	177	19 57	60	177	18 57	60	177	17 57	60	177	16 57	60	177	357
2	20 59	60	178	19 59	60	178	18 59	60	178	17 59	60	178	16 59	60	178	358
1	21 00	60	179	20 00	60	179	19 00	60	179	18 00	60	179	17 00	60	179	359
0	21 00	−60	180	20 00	−60	180	19 00	−60	180	18 00	−60	180	17 00	−60	180	360

S. Lat. {LHA greater than 180°……. Zn=180−Z; LHA less than 180°………. Zn=180+Z}

DECLINATION (15°-29°) CONTRARY NAME TO LATITUDE

LAT 44°

Table 5 – Correction to Tabulated Attitude for Minutes of Declination

(Extract from Sight Reduction Tables HO249 Vols 2 and 3)

TABLE 5.—Correction to Tabulated Altitude for Minutes of Declination

Sextant Error and Adjustment

Errors which are introduced through misalignment of the mirrors can be reduced. However, any serious distortion of the instrument due to damage should be repaired by an experienced sextant adjuster.

ERROR OF PERPENDICULARITY

This is caused through incorrect alignment of the index mirror. To check it out, swing the index bar to about 60°, move the shades out of view, and hold the instrument horizontally so that you can see the real and reflected arc. (You may have to remove or set back the telescope in order to get a clear view.) If there is a step in the view there is error which will have to be taken out by adjusting the screw at the rear of the index mirror. (See Fig A.)

Fig A

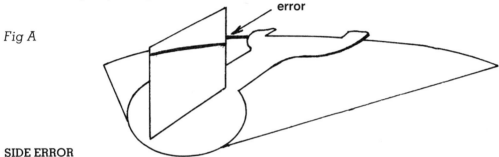

error

SIDE ERROR

This is due to misalignment of the horizon mirror. You can ascertain this error by setting the index bar to zero and holding the instrument horizontally. View the horizon and if it is distorted (ie the real and reflected horizons are not continuous) there is error. (See Fig B.) Correct by adjusting the horizon mirror.

Fig B

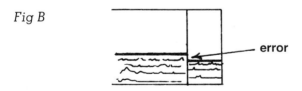

error

INDEX ERROR

After corrections have been made to the sextant for error of perpendicularity and side error there will remain a residual error which, as you know, is called index error. You should develop a habit of checking out the IE frequently. It takes very little time and you will always keep check of any distortions which may be caused through usage. You have already been instructed regarding the measurement of IE (page 61, Fig 7:5).

Above are adjustments using the horizon. There are others, and these may be found in such publications as the manufacturer's manual.

Sextant Error and Adjustment

REFRACTION, PARALLAX AND SEMI-DIAMETER

Corrections for refraction, parallax and semi-diameter are combined as a total correction contained in the Altitude Correction Tables published in the Almanac.

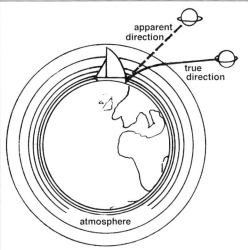

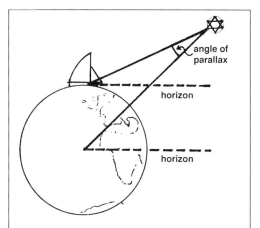

REFRACTION occurs when a ray of light from a heavenly body bends as it passes through the atmosphere. The altitude appears greater.

Refraction is greatest at low altitudes. Correction for refraction is contained in the Altitude Correction Tables in the Almanac. Further small corrections have to be made where abnormal atmospheric conditions prevail (ie altitude less than 10°). In this case refer to Table A4 in the Almanac.

PARALLAX occurs because the navigator measures altitude on the Earth's surface and not its centre.

There is no parallax when the heavenly body is at the observer's zenith.

There is maximum parallax when the body is on the horizon.

Parallax is greater if the heavenly body is nearer (eg the moon).

Parallax therefore varies with altitude and distance.

Corrections for parallax are contained in the 'Altitude Correction Tables' in the Almanac.

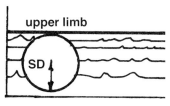

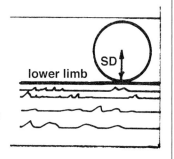

SEMI-DIAMETER must be taken into account when correcting altitude readings. We can easily guess the centre of stars and planets but, because of the size of the sun and moon, semi-diameter has to be read from the tables.

Plotting Sheet (for practice only)

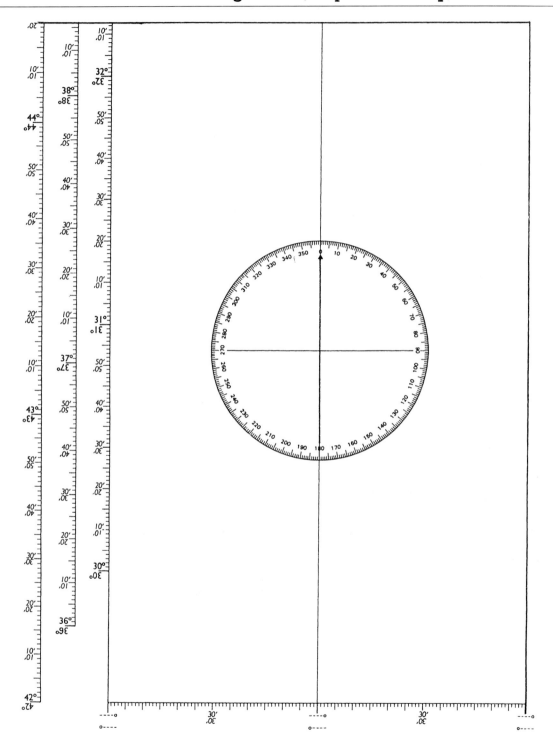

Index